Europe's Nuclear Umbrella

Since the mid 2010s, the collapse of key arms control treaties between great powers has unravelled the post-Cold War security architecture in Europe, heightening nuclear risks to Europe. At the same time, a fresh movement has emerged, calling for the total abolition of nuclear weapons, due to their catastrophic humanitarian consequences. European policymakers have found themselves between a rock and a hard place – between the global strategic conundrum calling for growing attention to nuclear deterrence, and domestic audiences demanding just the opposite. *Europe's Nuclear Umbrella* is about how they have navigated this balance. Building on combined insights from public administration, comparative politics, foreign policy analysis, and international relations, Michal Onderco offers a novel theory which reflects the complexity of democratic foreign policy-making in the twenty-first century.

MICHAL ONDERCO is Professor of International Relations at Erasmus University Rotterdam and an affiliate at Charles University, Prague. His research focuses on the domestic roots of foreign policy and the politics of nuclear weapons in Europe and globally. He is the author of *Networked Nonproliferation* (2021) and *Iran's Nuclear Programme and the Global South* (2015).

This book offers a timely and compelling account of how domestic politics shapes nuclear weapons policies and policies on nuclear sharing. Focusing on a diverse set of European cases, Onderco makes a distinctive theoretical contribution and backs it with careful, wide-ranging empirical analysis. He reveals how domestic political debates, institutions, and identities are deeply intertwined with international security commitments and alliance politics. The result is a work of lasting value for scholars and students of international relations, foreign policy, and European politics.

>   Gary Marks, University of North Carolina at Chapel Hill
>   and European University Institute, Florence

In a moment when the debate about nuclear weapons in Europe is intensifying again, Onderco delivers the much needed candid and compelling analysis of the forces that shape both support and opposition across the continent. It is a highly recommended essential reading for policymakers and scholars alike.

>   Claudia Major, German Marshall Fund

A valuable study of that tackles an enduring question in nuclear security: how do European governments balance global pressures to enhance nuclear deterrence by hosting nuclear weapons on their territory with domestic pressures to leave the nuclear age behind? Onderco provides a thorough and nuanced answer, bringing a wealth of original data to bear on an old question that has taken on renewed urgency in contemporary geopolitics. A must-read for those interested in security policy in Europe.

>   Elizabeth N. Saunders, Columbia University

In this incredibly timely book, Onderco explores European support for one of the pillars of US extended deterrence to NATO: nuclear sharing. With a wealth of new data, from public opinion surveys to rich archival work to dozens of interviews with senior officials, Onderco shows how the policy of nuclear sharing has largely endured over time despite public misgivings, or outright opposition in some cases. As the European security environment deteriorates, Onderco's superb and original book shows that policy elites should be able to persist with nuclear sharing, mitigating public opinion and, if necessary, shielding the policy due to national security imperatives. This has important implications for the future of extended nuclear deterrence in NATO

>   Vipin Narang, Massachusetts Institute of Technology

Michal Onderco is renowned for his superb empirical work on nuclear matters and his scholarly skills to put order in the confusing complexity of this field. His book is an essential must-read contribution to a burning issue of European security, the future of nuclear deterrence and nuclear sharing.

>   Harald Müller, Leibniz Peace Research Institute Frankfurt

Europe's Nuclear Umbrella
Contesting Nuclear Sharing Since 2010

MICHAL ONDERCO
Erasmus University Rotterdam

CAMBRIDGE
UNIVERSITY PRESS

Shaftesbury Road, Cambridge CB2 8EA, United Kingdom

One Liberty Plaza, 20th Floor, New York, NY 10006, USA

477 Williamstown Road, Port Melbourne, VIC 3207, Australia

314–321, 3rd Floor, Plot 3, Splendor Forum, Jasola District Centre, New Delhi – 110025, India

103 Penang Road, #05–06/07, Visioncrest Commercial, Singapore 238467

Cambridge University Press is part of Cambridge University Press & Assessment, a department of the University of Cambridge.

We share the University's mission to contribute to society through the pursuit of education, learning and research at the highest international levels of excellence.

www.cambridge.org
Information on this title: www.cambridge.org/9781009698689

DOI: 10.1017/9781009698665

© Michal Onderco 2026

This publication is in copyright. Subject to statutory exception and to the provisions of relevant collective licensing agreements, no reproduction of any part may take place without the written permission of Cambridge University Press & Assessment.

When citing this work, please include a reference to the DOI 10.1017/9781009698665

First published 2026

A catalogue record for this publication is available from the British Library

A Cataloging-in-Publication data record for this book is available from the Library of Congress

ISBN 978-1-009-69867-2 Hardback
ISBN 978-1-009-69868-9 Paperback

Cambridge University Press & Assessment has no responsibility for the persistence or accuracy of URLs for external or third-party internet websites referred to in this publication and does not guarantee that any content on such websites is, or will remain, accurate or appropriate.

For EU product safety concerns, contact us at Calle de José Abascal, 56, 1°, 28003 Madrid, Spain, or email eugpsr@cambridge.org

Contents

List of Figures	*page* vi	
List of Tables	vii	
Acknowledgements	viii	
List of Abbreviations	xi	
	Introduction	1
1	A (Very) Brief History of Nuclear Sharing	16
2	Technocratic Responsiveness and Nuclear Sharing	31
3	Public Opinion	48
4	Political Parties	72
5	Civil Society	101
6	Allies	129
7	Elites	146
	Conclusion	169
	Bibliography	184
	Index	225

Figures

1.1	Number of US nuclear weapons in Europe.	page 20
2.1	Conceptual model.	45
3.1	Trust in government to do the right thing.	52
3.2	Public knowledge about nuclear weapons.	54
3.3	Coefficient plot: foreign policy attitudes.	64
3.4	Coefficient plot: populism.	65
3.5	Coefficient plot: technocracy.	65
3.6	War in Ukraine, nuclear posture, and its adjustment.	69
4.1	Distribution of mentions of nuclear weapons in party manifestos over time.	79
4.2	Parliamentary votes in host nations.	98
5.1	Reynold Klooker, an anti-nuclear activist.	102
5.2	ICAN partners by country.	118
5.3	Location of cities that signed the ICAN Cities Appeal.	123
5.4	Left–right ideology and support for the ICAN Cities Appeal.	125

Tables

3.1	Public views of deterrent function of nuclear weapons	*page* 56
3.2	Public views of nuclear weapons use	57
3.3	Public views of nuclear weapons withdrawal	59
5.1	ICAN partners across regions	117
5.2	Population of cities that signed the ICAN Cities Appeal	124

Acknowledgements

This book almost never happened. Two grant applications for the necessary research were rejected, one of them due to the low relevance of nuclear weapons for European security (due to confidentiality requirements, I am sadly not allowed to cite from the rejection letter or disclose the funder). But here it is. Even though it is single authored, writing it was not a lonely endeavour.

Over the years, I have benefitted enormously from discussions on all things nuclear with a number of outstanding academics whom I am proud to call friends today. At some point, Tobias Bunde, Rebecca Davis Gibbons, Stephen Herzog, Liviu Horovitz, Jeff Knopf, Jiyoung Ko, Ulrich Kühn, and Michal Smetana all read various portions of this book and provided insightful comments, ultimately enhancing its quality. Heather Williams and Scott Sagan provided immensely helpful feedback in the early stages of the project, and Scott also offered excellent advice on my book proposal, helping me to make it tighter. Although not an expert on nuclear weapons, Gary Marks was the first person to read the full manuscript and provided excellent comments that helped me make it accessible for more general academic audience.

I wrote the book itself largely during my sabbatical, which I was privileged to spend at the Robert Schuman Center for Advanced Studies at the European University Institute in Florence. This would never have been possible without Stephanie Hoffman's willingness to host me and Monika Baár's enormous generosity in sharing her office in Villa Schifanoia. Stephanie also generously suggested organising a book workshop for the manuscript, which provided a focusing point for my stay in Florence. At this workshop in June 2024, Stephanie, Michael Bauer, Fabrizio Coticchia, Trine Flockhart, Nina Hall, Henriette Mueller, and Valerio Vignoli provided constructive feedback, significantly improving the book. Mia Saugmann was essential in helping me with the workshop organisation and logistics.

I am also indebted to the participants of other workshops where I presented portions of this work. Chapter 2 partially builds on a heated exchange at a workshop in Hamburg in February 2023. It forced me to put my theoretical argument on paper for the first time, initially in the chapter for the edited volume that was a result of the workshop and then redeveloped in my inaugural lecture at Erasmus University Rotterdam in December 2023. On both occasions, I received helpful feedback (or at least reactions) from the audience. Different drafts of various chapters were presented at the 2023 workshop 'European Security Architectures and Their Implications' at the European University Institute in Florence, the International Studies Association Annual Convention in San Francisco in 2024, the European Initiative for Security Studies' 2024 Conference in Prague, the University of Genova, and the University of Edinburgh. Participants and discussants at these events could not have been more generous with their feedback and wisdom.

My colleagues in Rotterdam have been willing victims of my rambling about nuclear weapons but kept reading my drafts and provided comments whenever I called on their theoretical and methodological expertise. I am incredibly thankful to Clara Egger, Markus Haverland, Geske Dijkstra, Wil Hout, Saliha Metinsoy, and Pieter Tuytens for being excellent colleagues over the years. I am also grateful to Kim Wever, Marinke Moeliker, and our faculty's finance team for being a project support dream team.

Once you dive into the book, you will notice that an enormous amount of data collection work went into it. It would have been unfeasible for me to collect and process that data alone, often because I simply lacked the skill (linguistic or otherwise). Therefore, the thanks go to all my research assistants who helped me at any point. In particular, I wish to thank Tom Etienne, Mahmoud Javadi, Kathy Nguyen, and Emma Prebreza for excellent assistance in the final stretch of the project. Ioannis Aivatidis, Feike Coppens, Ruth

IJbema, Berfu Söbe, Femke Verburg, and Anna Urbani contributed to the earlier data collection stage. I am also grateful to Jordan Becker and Hans Kristensen (and the Federation of American Scientists) for sharing their as yet unpublished data with me. Tasha Bigelow edited the book with much care.

None of this would be possible without those willing to invest serious capital into this project. I am grateful to Charles University project UNCE 24/SSH/018 (Peace Research Center Prague II). The main gratitude goes to the Stanton Foundation, which in 2022 decided to fund my project 'Nuclear Politics in Europe' and gave me the time, and the resources, to complete it. In particular, I want to thank Erica Carere for being the best possible grant administrator.

Academia has always been, for me, about the great people whom I have met along the way and who make me realise, every day, that this is the best job I could have ever wanted. Nicolas Blarel, Sandra Destradi, Francesco Giumelli, Irena Kalhousová, Filip Kostelka, Hana Kubátová, Falk Ostermann, Clara Portela, Bertjan Verbeek, Reinout van der Veer, Dagmar Vorlíček, and Wolfgang Wagner make my academic life better by being excellent comrades in arms.

But most importantly, I am eternally grateful to Martina. She was the one with whom I could always share my ups and downs and who provided me with unwavering support and endless back scratches. Though this book may not bring us the riches she once optimistically envisioned, I am sure that she will forgive me as she has forgiven me the frequent travels and long working hours. Ďakujem za všetko.

Abbreviations

AfD	Alternative for Germany
CD&V	Christian Democratic and Flemish
CDA	Christian Democratic Appeal
CDU	Christian Democratic Union
CHES	Chapel Hill Expert Survey
CI	Cooperative internationalism
CMP	Comparative Manifesto Project
CSIS	Center for Strategic and International Studies
CSNO	Conventional Support for Nuclear Operations
CU	Christian Union
DCA	Dual-capable aircraft
DDPR	Deterrence and Defence Posture Review
ECFR	European Council on Foreign Relations
ECPR	European Consortium for Political Research
FDP	Free Democratic Party
FIIA	Finnish Institute for International Affairs
FMCT	Fissile Material Cut-Off Treaty
GDP	Gross domestic product
GL	GroenLinks
HLG	High-Level Group
ICAN	International Campaign to Abolish Nuclear
IKV	Inter-Church Peace Council
ILPI	International Law and Policy Institute
INF	Intermediate nuclear forces
IPNDV	International Partnership for Nuclear Disarmament Verification
IPPNW	International Physicians for Prevention of Nuclear War
ISG	International Steering Group
JSF	Joint Strike Fighter

MFA	Ministry of Foreign Affairs
MI	Militant internationalism
MSP	Meeting of States Parties
NAC	North Atlantic Council
NAIL	Norwegian Academy of International Law
NPDI	Non-Proliferation and Disarmament Initiative
NPG	Nuclear Planning Group
NPR	Nuclear Posture Review
NPIHP	Nuclear Proliferation International History Review
NPT	Nonproliferation Treaty, also known as the Treaty on the Nonproliferation of Nuclear Weapons
OEWG	Open-Ended Working Group
PVDA	Labour Party (The Netherlands)
PvdD	Animal Rights Party (The Netherlands)
PVV	Freedom Party (The Netherlands)
SACEUR	Supreme Commander in Europe
SHAPE	Supreme Headquarters Allied Powers Europe
SP	Socialist Party
SPD	Social Democratic Party (Germany)
TPNW	Treaty on Prohibition of Nuclear Weapons
VVD	Party for Freedom and Democracy (The Netherlands)
WEOG	Western European and Others Group
WILPF	Women's International League for Peace and Freedom

Introduction

What do a coup, an arrested Member of Parliament, and a pink shovel have in common? The attempted coup in Turkey in 2016 prominently involved the Incirlik base; the Belgian Green Member of Parliament Zoé Genot was arrested at Kleine-Brogel during a security breach in 2018; and anti-nuclear activists at the Volkel airbase in 2023 invited participants to dig under the fence with pink shovels. These are three of the six airbases where the United States still stores nuclear weapons in Europe. Down from over 7,000 at the height of the Cold War to just above 100, these weapons are still stationed in five European countries.

For some of you, this information might be surprising. But for the North Atlantic Alliance, nuclear deterrence has been at the core of its business almost since its inception. However, politically, nuclear weapons have disappeared from the radar after the end of the Cold War. As Vipin Narang, a senior US government official and an MIT professor on leave, said in one of his final speeches while in government, after the end of the Cold War was a period of 'nuclear intermission'. The first nuclear act took place in the Cold War. The second act has started recently.[1] During this nuclear intermission, many called on European countries to radically rethink their reliance on nuclear deterrence and perhaps step away from hosting them in Europe in the first place.

This second act started partially through what *Time Magazine* called the 'collapse of global arms control'.[2] Since the mid-2010s, numerous arms control treaties between great powers, which structured and secured European security since the end of the Cold War, have collapsed, following the violations and/or withdrawal by

[1] Center for Strategic and International Studies (2024)
[2] Hammer (2020)

Russia, as a sign of the deteriorating relations between Russia, the United States, and European countries. At the same time, a fresh movement has sprung up in Europe, aiming to once and for all do away with nuclear weapons, banning them because of their unacceptable humanitarian damage. Obviously, it would be hard to ban them in Russia and China, and therefore the movement has set its eyes on a somewhat less ambitious goal – to have them removed from Western Europe.

European policymakers found themselves between a rock and a hard place – between the global strategic conundrum calling for growing attention to nuclear deterrence and domestic audiences demanding just the opposite (doing less). This book is about how they navigated this balance.

For most European countries, nuclear deterrence is provided by the North Atlantic Treaty Organization (NATO) nuclear umbrella, which is meant to protect European countries against external adversaries.[3] As a part of this umbrella, the United States stations nuclear weapons in Belgium, Germany, Italy, the Netherlands, and Turkey.[4] The countries hosting the weapons have a role in their deployment and delivery. This important physical connection gives the United States a direct material stake in European security. This practice is called 'nuclear sharing', a name rooted in the 1950s idea, which actually foresaw sharing US weapons with European allies, though in the course of 1960s, the scale of 'sharing' was tapered down.[5]

As I explain in Chapter 1 of this book, nuclear sharing serves a number of political, strategic, and military goals. It is meant to deter adversaries, assure allies, and avoid division of the alliance. The policy intimately involves allies in the nuclear policy of the alliance, which proudly calls itself a 'nuclear' one.[6] However, it has been

---

[3] Fuhrmann and Sechser (2014b); Sechser (2016)
[4] Kristensen et al. (2023)
[5] Trachtenberg (1999)
[6] NATO (2010)

heavily contested by the public opinion, civil society, and political parties in Europe ever since its beginnings.

The main research question this book asks is why nuclear sharing continues despite being an unpopular and contested policy. Addressing it requires answering three related research questions: where does the domestic contestation come from? How do the allies view nuclear sharing? How do elites make sense of these contradicting preferences?

To answer these questions, I look into the domestic contestation of nuclear sharing in the European host nations since 2010.[7] I choose 2010 because it is the start of the new period in the history of NATO. In 2009, US President Barack Obama, in his speech at Prague Castle, offered a vision of a world without nuclear weapons, for which he received the Nobel Peace Prize in the same year. One year later, the foreign ministers of Belgium, Germany, Luxembourg, the Netherlands, and Norway wrote to the secretary general with a request to re-evaluate stationing nuclear weapons in Europe.[8] Instead, NATO doubled down on its mission by underscoring that it is a 'nuclear alliance' in its Strategic Concept.[9] Since 2010, European countries had to deal with not only growing instability after deteriorating relations with Russia but also a renewed push for nuclear disarmament. Activities of civil society, under the umbrella of the International Campaign to Abolish Nuclear Weapons (ICAN), led to the adoption of the 2017 Treaty on the Prohibition of Nuclear Weapons (TPNW). While none of the NATO governments signed or ratified the treaty, it created enough attention to spur the alliance to denounce it on the day when it was open for ratification.[10]

In this book, I offer a novel theory, building on combined insights from public administration, comparative politics, foreign policy

---

[7] The research for this book was completed in June 2024. The developments during the early months of the second Trump administration are covered only in the conclusion.
[8] Borger (2010b)
[9] NATO (2010)
[10] NATO (2017)

analysis, and international relations, which reflects the complexity of democratic foreign policy-making in the twenty-first century.

I do not opine on whether US nuclear weapons should remain or be withdrawn and why. While I do have a view on this issue, a reader will hopefully *not* find it in this book. Rather, this is a book about a policy puzzle, and I want to offer an answer based on a rigorous approach using social science theory and method. Therefore, I hope that this book can elucidate the roots of contestation of nuclear weapons in Europe, the reaction which this contestation creates, and perhaps a more nuanced take on nuclear politics in Europe in the twenty-first century.

THE BOOK'S ARGUMENT IN SHORT

In Chapter 3, I develop the theoretical argument of this book in full, but presenting its capsule version now might be helpful to a reader to understand the book's key contribution.

If the question is why nuclear weapons are hosted even if large swathes of the public dislike them and many parties oppose them, the answer is that nuclear sharing is a policy which ends up being controlled by policy elites, primarily bureaucrats (and technocrats) in various ministries. Despite attracting high levels of opposition, it is a low-salience policy, like most other foreign policy issues.

As the late political science titan Peter Mair argued, two sources of control exist for policy-making: responsiveness and responsibility.[11] Responsiveness is a sympathetic response 'to the short-term demands of voters, public opinion, interest groups, and the media'.[12] Responsibility is the 'necessity ... to take into account (a) the long-term needs of their people and countries, which ... underlie and go beyond the short-term demands of those same people; (and) (b) the claims of audiences other than the national electoral audience, including ... the international commitments and organizations that

---

[11] Mair (2009)
[12] Bardi et al. (2014, p. 237)

are the root of their international credibility'.[13] Mair argued that one implication of responsibility as a form of control in democratic polities is that leaders' hands are sometimes tied.[14]

The academic proponents of nuclear disarmament often suggest that continuing deterrence policies in the face of the lack of public support is undemocratic (I outline this argument in greater depth in Chapter 3). However, using Mair's logic, doing so is not necessarily undemocratic per se, and it also is relatively common to remove certain policies from democratic control. Citizens, for instance, have only a limited impact on central bank interest rates, and central banks are sometimes (especially in the Westminster system) completely insulated from democratic politics.[15] Withdrawing certain policies from democratic politics means leaving them to policy elites, including bureaucrats and technocrats, which is a core of democratic policy-making. Those who oppose it are usually interested in centralising power with the executive. In the United States, this is known as a 'unitary executive' theory.[16] Others, however, see such centrality as a core of growing authoritarianism.[17]

For these policy elites, who often derive their views from their expertise and knowledge, following public opinion would be seen as antithetical to their mission. However, as the theories of technocratic responsiveness developed in the study of public administration underscore,[18] they cannot be completely ignorant of them, certainly not when the backlash against expertise is so high. Therefore, policy elites resort to symbolic adjustment steps – such as attending the TPNW Meetings of State Parties (MSPs) as observers.

My new theory borrows from comparative politics, the study of lobbying, public opinion, and international relations to explain

---

[13] Bardi et al. (2014, p. 237)
[14] Mair (2013)
[15] Lijphart (1999)
[16] Savage (2007)
[17] Driesen (2020)
[18] van der Veer (2020)

how these individual pressures emerge and then uses theories of technocratic responsiveness to explain how elites react to these popular pressures.[19]

CONTRIBUTION TO THE STUDY OF NUCLEAR POLITICS

The simplest reason for writing this book is that no other book systematically studies the domestic contestation of nuclear sharing and how policy elites engage with it in all five host nations.

A more elaborate answer obviously needs to acknowledge that scholars have already paid extensive attention to nuclear sharing and extended nuclear deterrence. However, they have either focused on strategic questions or based their methodology on single-country case studies.

The study of strategic questions has centred on strategic causes, specific effects of nuclear sharing, or extended deterrence in general. While I review this work in more detail in Chapter 2, it has focused on the origins and rationale of nuclear sharing for European security. Some of the most foundational work by historians studies the origins of this practice and how it was crafted early on by European leaders.[20] The traditional strategic literature has highlighted that nuclear weapons strengthen the link between Europe and the United States and thus contribute to Europe's defence. For instance, in a recent edited collection, international relations scholars Stéfanie von Hlatky and Andreas Wenger led a team of scholars who explored the role of extended deterrence in the interactions between NATO and its adversaries.[21] Focusing on nuclear sharing, US international relations professors Matthew Fuhrmann and Tom Sechser argued that these deployments do not have *additional* deterrent power, compared to formal alliance commitments.[22] In another paper, they doubted whether these dissuade allies from pursuing nuclear weapons, an

---

[19] Caramani (2020); van der Veer (2020, 2021)
[20] See, for example, Trachtenberg (1999); Gavin (2012)
[21] von Hlatky and Wenger (2015)
[22] Fuhrmann and Sechser (2014b)

oft-stated argument in favour of nuclear sharing.[23] Similarly, historians have conducted case studies to study the effect of nuclear sharing on national non-proliferation policy.[24] In more recent years, scholars have studied strategic dynamics and how nuclear sharing might fit into a broader pattern of nuclear deterrence.[25]

The scholarship on domestic politics and its link to nuclear sharing has thus focused strongly on single case studies. While this work is abundant and has a long tradition, scholars have focused on explaining the patterns of contestation within individual countries rather than across countries. Many of the contributions to this scholarship could be found in the 2014 special issue of *European Security* edited by Stéfanie von Hlatky. In the wake of the war in Ukraine, more attention has been paid to these factors, but this emerging work is again fundamentally based on country case studies.[26] With the growing attention to using surveys to study public opinion, some comparative work has started to emerge comparing findings from multiple countries, but it is very limited.[27]

The scholarship on the domestic politics of nuclear sharing has offered a multitude of arguments for national foreign policies. Some scholars pinned the cause of domestic discord on the tension between principles and interests.[28] Others found its roots in diplomatic culture.[29] Some, especially diplomatic historians and political scientists focusing on Italy, have looked for reasons in the bilateral relationship with the United States.[30] Earlier studies focused on the socialisation of individuals and their coming of age.[31] Some case studies, such as early work from the 1980s on Germany, examined

---

[23] Fuhrmann and Sechser (2014a)
[24] Melissen (1994); Lutsch (2020); Gerzhoy (2015)
[25] Frühling and O'Neil (2017)
[26] For example, Bunde and Onderco (2023); Kühn (2024b)
[27] See, for instance, the work on Germany and the Netherlands (Onderco et al. 2022, 2023); and Germany and Czechia (Sorg and Wucherpfennig 2023)
[28] Davis and Jasper (2014)
[29] Sauer (2014)
[30] Foradori (2012, 2014); Nuti (2016)
[31] Müller and Risse-Kappen (1987)

the role of bureaucracies in the host states.[32] Scholars have also provided illuminating historical case studies,[33] descriptions of party platforms,[34] and analyses of the role of civil society, especially in the national setting.[35] Some even explored links to the national strategic culture.[36]

As much as this scholarship provides relevant insights into the political dynamics related to nuclear sharing in individual countries, its value has been more restricted when it comes to delivering more systematic insights into domestic political dynamics. The very limited comparative work in the nuclear field in Europe almost exclusively focuses on the countries actually possessing or pursuing nuclear weapons and tends to be more historical rather than contemporary.[37] If the attitudes were studied comparatively, they privileged the technocratic elites and their perspectives.[38]

This book aims at overcoming these limitations in two ways. Firstly, it offers a systematic comparative study of the domestic politics in the five host countries. For all the elements which the book will touch on – public opinion, parties, civil society, or elites – all five countries were studied using the same methodology, with the same theory used to interpret the findings. This strengthens our knowledge base about the contestation of nuclear sharing and allows us to draw comparative conclusions. The focus on all five countries also corrects the limitations due to unequal attention that the individual host nations have received in the literature. Secondly, it offers a new, fresh, and compelling theory to explain both the bottom-up pressure and how elites engage with it. As I explain in the next section, and then throughout the book, this theory offers us a more modern understanding of democratic policy-making than has been

[32] Risse-Kappen (1988)
[33] Portela (2014); van Dijk (2012)
[34] van der Zeijden (2014)
[35] Everts (1984); Brinkel (1982); ter Veer (1988).
[36] Suchy and Thayer (2014); Oppenheimer (2010); Udum (2020)
[37] See, for example, Born et al. (2011); Fraise (2023).
[38] Rapnouil et al. (2018)

commonly assumed among nuclear theorists and allows us to understand both grassroots contestation and how it affects policy.

CONTRIBUTION TO THE BROADER FIELD

While this book deals primarily with a question aimed at understanding the domestic challenges to nuclear sharing, it carries broader implications for diverse strands of scholarship.

Most directly, it speaks to scholars of nuclear weapons. While this work has paid some attention to domestic political considerations, doing so in depth and systematically has been uncommon in this field.[39] As this book underscores, using the tools of comparative politics and foreign policy analysis offers us new insights into how preferences around nuclear weapons come about and also how they interact with other views. For instance, the link between anti-capitalism and anti-nuclear views, which is clearly exploited by civil society in the Cities Appeal and which I discuss in Chapter 6, is something that would be otherwise difficult to discover. More importantly, however, as the perceived importance of nuclear sharing increases, it is imperative to understand what domestic political conditions this practice intersects with. Importantly, this book brings much more nuance and colour to understanding how European publics, parties, civil society, and also policy leaders engage with nuclear weapons and what reactions nuclear weapons stir in them.

More broadly, the book speaks to scholars of US alliances, who have often paid only limited attention to the domestic dimension. To be sure, numerous works have explored how NATO politics has intersected with domestic debates in Europe – for instance, related to the Euromissiles crisis or the military interventions in the Balkans.[40] However, numerous works on NATO overlook the importance of domestic politics, which further feeds into the perception

---

[39] For a recent overview of the work on domestic politics and nuclear weapons, see Saunders (2019).

[40] On the Euromissiles crisis, see Colbourn (2022); on the interventions in the Balkans, see Rathbun (2004).

that democracy and domestic politics somehow do not matter for the alliance.[41] By contrast, my work underscores that policy elites in NATO countries have to act often under very complex domestic political constraints. They balance the demands stemming from responsiveness and responsibility and therefore often end up producing outcomes which might be difficult to comprehend from the outside, such as attending the TPNW MSPs.

For the scholars of European security, my book offers a few lessons on how domestic politics influences an issue which they have often overlooked – nuclear weapons. The book underscores that, contrary to the many perceptions, nuclear weapons are front and centre in the debates about European security, and many domestic political dynamics, known from the study of European security, apply equally well to these debates. As my work demonstrates, many of the forces known all too well to the scholars of European security – including executive dominance and low issue salience – are replicated in the study of nuclear weapons. Parties – a well-known subject in the study of European security and foreign policy – matter for nuclear weapons too. Realising this connection has consequences for seeing both European security and nuclear weapons in a broader political and theoretical context.

For students of executive action, particularly from the fields of public administration and public policy, my book offers a lesson on how elites respond to various audiences. For public policy scholars, the insight that policy elites work under the twin pressures of responsiveness and responsibility is not revolutionary. However, only very limited scholarship still actually realises how elites make sense of various audiences. That they prefer the responsibility induced by international commitments is an important insight from this work. My book further elucidates this connection in the understudied area of foreign policy. By studying policy adjustments under responsiveness demands, I contribute to the scholarship on policy changes.

[41] Most recently by Rynning (2024)

Last but certainly not least, my work offers insights for the scholars of civil society, public opinion, and political parties, as it provides empirical material for engagement of many of their theories in an issue area which has been traditionally overlooked by these scholars. By using their methods and theories, this book offers a novel test for them and a new field where these theories could be further refined and developed.

HOW THE BOOK WAS RESEARCHED

This book offers a methodology which combines three elements of study: domestic contestation, alliance audiences, and the consequences of their heterogeneous interaction. This requires splitting the exploration into individual chunks, each of which was researched independently, but with the goal of combining them in the end.

In the three chapters on contestation by domestic audiences, I rely on the state-of-the-art social science concepts, theories, and methods in each of the separate issue areas to explain the patterns of contestation. Therefore, in the chapter on public opinion (Chapter 3), I rely on the scholarship on public opinion and public attitudes in foreign policy. In the chapter on parties and parliaments (Chapter 4), I engage with the relevant work. In the chapter on civil society (Chapter 5), I engage with the theories and tools used in the study of civil society. In the chapter focused on the responses from the allied audience (Chapter 6), I use the tools from the study of foreign policy preferences. And then, to bring it all together, I rely on the tools from the study of elite decision-making. Throughout this research, I have purposefully tried to keep focus on all five countries in which the nuclear sharing mission is being executed – Belgium, Germany, Italy, the Netherlands, and Turkey.

The individual methodology for each chapter is explained in detail in the relevant chapter. In the three chapters on domestic audiences, I use a mix of pre-existing data and freshly collected data on public opinion, party positions, and civil society mobilising. In the chapter on allied perceptions, I study strategic documents, primarily from the immense corpus collected by the research team led by political scientist Jordan Becker at West Point.[42]

The chapter on elites (Chapter 7) relies on, and the remainder of the book benefits from, interviews conducted specifically for this book and those for another project on civil society and nuclear risk. All the interviewees were selected from policy elites, experts, and senior members of parliament in the host countries. Both projects for which the interviews were intended were in line with the ethics approval received from the Ethics Board of the Department of Public Administration & Sociology at Erasmus University Rotterdam. However, the two projects and their ethics approval differ slightly. The project on civil society and nuclear risk was primarily an oral history interviews, focused on prominent respondents, and therefore operated under the assumption that the interviewees would be identified by name. All of them agreed to this, so they are all also identified by name in this book. The interviews conducted specifically for this book were done separately under a different ethics approval that gave the respondents an opportunity to choose how they wish to be identified – some wanted to be identified by name and others by their professional identity, and yet others wished to remain completely anonymous. I have respected those wishes.

Taken together, this book offers a comparative study of five countries, using a mix of quantitative and qualitative methods in an integrated framework that allows me to study the research questions linked to this book in a systematic, coherent, and conceptually sound manner.

STRUCTURE OF THE BOOK

It is best to understand this book as a jigsaw, which comes in four big blocks. The first block is the history and theory, providing historical and conceptual basis. The second is the domestic demands related to nuclear sharing, looking at public opinion, parties, and civil society.

---

[42] Becker et al. (2024)

STRUCTURE OF THE BOOK 13

The third is the contrasting demands regarding nuclear sharing made by allies. And the fourth emerges by studying how elites interact and make sense of these conflicting demands. In practice, this jigsaw structures the book into nine chapters, including the introduction.

Some readers might not be familiar with the details and history of nuclear sharing in Europe, so Chapter 1 provides an introduction that presents the historical origins, political and strategic rationale, major debates during the late Cold War (the so-called Euromissiles crisis), and debates in the post-Cold War period up until 2010, when the last major proposal to remove the weapons from Europe was withdrawn. It also introduces more recent debates about nuclear sharing, particularly with the focus on the challenges introduced by the humanitarian disarmament movement and the Russian invasion in Ukraine.

Chapter 2 introduces the reader to the theoretical argument. Outlining the theory of technocratic responsiveness requires some preliminary steps, however. Firstly, the chapter outlines the critique of nuclear sharing as an undemocratic practice, which has been advanced by scholars both in the past and more recently. It then provides the concept of responsiveness and responsibility as two forms of control in democratic policy-making, along the lines of work introduced by Peter Mair. The chapter explains how nuclear sharing is an archetypal technocratic policy, which means that the critics who posit that it is undemocratic mistake its main feature for a bug. Lastly, the chapter outlines how the theory of technocratic responsiveness actually works: that is, how different societal stakeholders – such as voters, parties, and civil society – influence technocrats and also that these technocrats are responsive to not only a domestic audience but also a foreign one – their allies.

In Chapter 3, I look at the public opinion on nuclear weapons in Europe. This chapter has three portions. In the first, I provide an extensive overview of public opinion research in Europe on issues related to nuclear weapons. Next, I present results of a unique, unpublished survey of public opinion in all five host nations, mapping and explaining views on the deterrent effect of nuclear weapons, their use, and possible disarmament. I explain these views with a reference to fundamental foreign policy attitudes, such as militarism or cooperativeness, but also technocratic attitudes and populism, which are more aligned with the theory of technocratic responsiveness. Finally, I outline which lessons the public seem to draw from the war in Ukraine for the future of nuclear sharing, based on the same unpublished data.

Chapter 4 introduces the reader to the positioning of European political parties on nuclear sharing in the five host nations. After outlining the theoretical and conceptual reasons why parties matter for studying foreign and security policy, I compare the views among European far-left, centre-left, centre-right, and far-right parties on the basis of their party manifestos from the Comparative Manifesto Project's Manifesto Corpus. In the second half of the chapter, I investigate the parliamentary activity in four out of five countries (Turkey has none), looking at voting patterns on various parliamentary motions critical of nuclear sharing, using novel data on all parliamentary votes on nuclear weapons in these countries.

In Chapter 5, I look primarily at the influence of civil society. The chapter examines contemporary civil society activities in four of the five countries (except for Turkey, which seems to have no active civil society on the issue). The analysis is primarily based on the activities of ICAN and more specifically through the lenses of support for the ICAN's flagship Cities Appeal, an initiative to gain support for the TPNW from city councils. I investigate how successful (or not) the Cities Appeal is in the host nations and what explains the patterns of varying success.

As the theory of technocratic responsiveness holds, technocrats care about external audiences too. In this book, that external audience is composed of the allies. Chapter 6 addresses the allies of the host nations – the alliance, the United States as the patron, and other European countries. Using the insights from the strategic documents, I examine how the allies talk about nuclear sharing and extended deterrence.

Chapter 7 looks at technocratic elites and how they respond to all these pressures. I base this chapter on interviews conducted with them and report how they think about the purpose of hosting nuclear weapons and the legitimacy of various audiences and explain their views on interaction with diverse stakeholders. This section also provides an overview of national strategic documents and government communications in the host nations to the public, parliament, and civil society on issues related to nuclear sharing. This chapter furthermore discusses how elites react and defend nuclear sharing abroad, in an increasingly hostile international environment.

The Conclusion summarises and answers the main question of the book. However, it also provides three other arguments. Firstly, it looks at the ongoing debates in the aftermath of the Russian invasion of Ukraine, from the enlargement of nuclear sharing to supplementing it with other types of nuclear equipment in Europe, and discusses the likely reception in the host nations. Secondly, it studies the growing international backlash against nuclear sharing and how it is likely to develop further. Finally, it offers suggestions for how technocrats could be even more responsive and how the public legitimacy of nuclear sharing could be enhanced.

I   A (Very) Brief History of Nuclear Sharing

'Why would we have American nukes in Europe?' is a great question to ask students in an essay. On the surface, it is a question about a few dozen warheads stationed at half a dozen airbases in Europe. More deeply, however, it reveals a lot about European security, the dynamic of the transatlantic relationship, the US role in that security, and even about European countries' perceptions of each other.

The purpose of this chapter is not to write a detailed history of NATO's nuclear sharing. Instead, I aim to provide a brief overview of how it came about and what purposes it fulfils, according to the scholarship. Last but not least, I provide a summary of the most recent political changes and challenges to nuclear sharing. This chapter offers a springboard for the remainder of the book, preparing readers for the rest and giving them the basic information needed to understand nuclear sharing and its transformation over time.

I should make a very brief terminological detour to discuss where the notion of 'nuclear sharing' comes from. Initially, the idea was that the US would indeed 'share' the weapons with Europeans, which means that the latter could actually use them independently.[1] Unsurprisingly, this thought terrified American congressional leaders. Later, an idea emerged that nuclear weapons within NATO could be manned by multinational forces. This option was not only hard to execute politically and logistically but also unacceptable to Russia in the context of the Treaty on Nonproliferation of Nuclear Weapons (NPT) negotiation. As a result, the US maintained a strong level of control. Therefore, the current form of sharing is not truly sharing. It entails stationing the weapons on

---

[1] Trachtenberg (1999)

allied territory, for eventual delivery by allied aircraft.[2] While, in this book, I speak of 'host nations' as the countries hosting nuclear weapons, one also sometimes hears of 'DCA countries', which are those that host dual-capable aircraft (DCA) to deliver them. This is the only surviving form of nuclear sharing.[3] While the list of DCA countries is classified, it is widely assumed to include the five host nations, the US, and Greece.[4]

THE EMERGENCE OF NUCLEAR SHARING

When I try to explain to my students how nuclear sharing emerged, I ask them to think about the security predicament of the Western European countries a few short years after the end of World War II. They were concerned about a possible Soviet invasion that would overrun Western Europe. The primary source of this worry was European division, not European weakness. As the nuclear historian Marc Trachtenberg recalled, US General Dwight Eisenhower stated in March 1951 that the Western European countries 'could tell Russia to go to hell if only they would get together, raise enough men, and produce enough equipment'.[5] Yet this unification was not forthcoming. Attempts to push them towards more security cooperation, in the form of the European Defence Community, failed. It was encouraged by both the US and UK, but after the conclusion of the Treaty of Paris in 1952, it remained unratified in France and soon unravelled.[6] Europe had too much concern about German power, and the end of nation states was nowhere near.[7] That division among European allies led to the massive conventional superiority of the Soviet Union over Western European countries. Therefore,

---

[2] Alberque (2017). While the list of countries which host nuclear weapons, I rely on widely circulated lists, for example in Kristensen et al (2023).
[3] The current form of nuclear sharing presents but a small part of the many forms of nuclear deployments in Europe that once existed. See Sorg (2023).
[4] Kristensen et al. (2023)
[5] Trachtenberg (1999, pp. 147–148)
[6] For a detailed historical study of this, see Fursdon (1980).
[7] Trachtenberg discusses this issue at length in his book. See the chapter 'Eisenhower and nuclear sharing' in Trachtenberg (1999).

a nuclear deterrent was meant to provide further protection to the allies.[8] This led to a strategy that aimed at concentrating nuclear power in US hands, while encouraging Europeans to develop conventional defence capabilities.[9]

For Europeans, the main source of fear was not the threat of a Russian nuclear attack against the West. It was 'a Soviet strategic threat or a limited ground attack on one or more of the European members of the alliance'.[10] The Soviets might not be deterred by the US nuclear threat, and conventionally weak Europeans would not be able to prevent such an attack. Therefore, the European allies of the US faced a set of options: invest in massive amounts of conventional armaments; seek nuclear weapons themselves; or seek nuclear weapons assurances from the US. The first option was politically unpalatable in countries that were still focused on propping up economies devastated by World War II.[11] The second was difficult because the US was not particularly keen on having its allies develop their own nuclear weapons,[12] and the allies themselves were often divided about whether doing so was a wise idea.[13] And the third option was difficult because once the Soviets were able to deploy intercontinental missiles, the US promise of defending Western Europe with a strategic nuclear deterrent was no longer credible.[14]

A 'solution' to this problem was found in stationing nuclear weapons in Europe, on the allies' territory.[15] Their deployment started in 1953, following 'the widely shared perception that the

---

[8] This history of nuclear sharing and NATO nuclear strategy is, of course, very simplified. For more insight, see Heuser (1995); Lieber and Press (2020); Fuhrmann and Sechser (2014a); Sechser (2016); Freedman and Michaels (2019); Sayle (2019).
[9] Trachtenberg (1999)
[10] Knorr (1959, pp. 6–7)
[11] See, for instance, the in-depth case study of the Netherlands in van der Harst (1997).
[12] Much of the work focuses on Germany, which faced arguably the most significant political pressures. See Heuser (1995); Kelleher (1975). However, Gheorge debates this policy in general; see Gheorghe (2022).
[13] Deutsch (1966)
[14] Heuser and Stoddart (2017)
[15] Colbourn (2022); Hunt (2022)

Lisbon goals of 1952 designating conventional force levels would not be met'.[16] In December 1954, NATO adopted MC 58, a strategic document 'built on the assumption that there was one, and only, way in which the Soviets could be prevented from overrunning Europe in the event of war, and that was through the very rapid and massive use of nuclear weapons, both tactically and strategically'.[17] Nuclear weapons, deployed in Europe, were implemented in the plans developed by the Supreme Headquarters Allied Powers Europe (SHAPE).[18] In this vein, during the 1950s and 1960s, the US started to deploy its nuclear weapons in Europe, first in the UK in 1954, and then in West Germany after it had joined NATO in 1955. While the deployment was based on NATO strategic documents, the related political aspects were not necessarily broadly developed. As the nuclear historian Eliza Gheorghe recalls, the Americans were not too keen on consulting extensively with their allies on the nuclear question.[19] The key reason behind this hesitation was the reluctance to make the alliance potentially captive to a single member veto.[20] Eisenhower, as both the Supreme Allied Commander and eventual US president, had no doubt that any US military confrontation with Soviets would turn nuclear. While, politically, the allies were supposed to have the right of 'final decision', in practice, the US was unwilling to commit to that single veto power.[21]

The US position was not welcomed by the allies, to say the least. Using terminology from the realist theory of international politics, they were afraid both of being entrapped in a nuclear war and of abandoned in their hour of need.[22] One reason was the quickly growing number of nuclear weapons in Europe. A little more than a decade after the first

---

[16] Buteux (1983, p. 1)
[17] Trachtenberg (1999, p. 158)
[18] Buteux (1983)
[19] Gheorghe (2022)
[20] See also Knorr (1959).
[21] Trachtenberg (1999, pp. 166–168); see also Gheorghe (2022).
[22] On entrapment and abandonment, see Snyder (1984). For a more contemporary debate and application to NATO's nuclear history, see Nuti (2021). See also Bunde (2024).

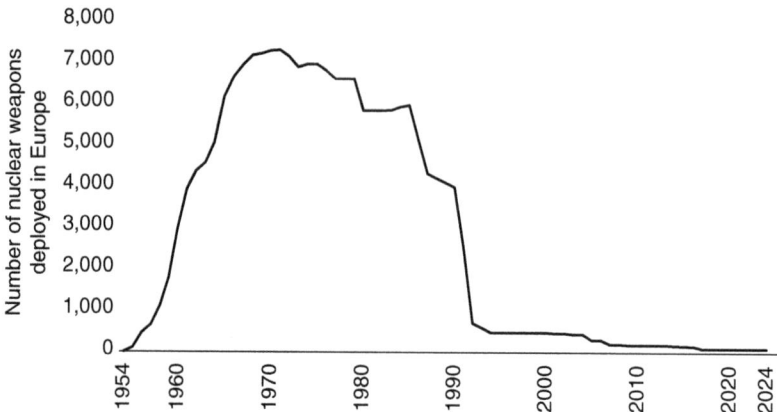

FIGURE 1.1 Number of US nuclear weapons in Europe.
Source: Hans Kristensen, Federation of American Scientists.

deployment, around 7,000 warheads were stationed on delivery vehicles in eight countries – the UK, West Germany, Italy, France, Turkey, the Netherlands, Greece, and Belgium (see also Figure 1.1).[23] Canadian Prime Minister Lester Pearson, in the mid 1950s, coined the phrase 'no annihilation without representation'.[24] While the US developed a set of bilateral consultations with allies (which became rather robust over a longer time), consultation within the alliance was lacking. As the nuclear historian Jeffrey Michaels wrote, the US had not defined the procedures for nuclear use within NATO, even as it was deploying these weapons in Europe. It was not clear what the roles of the North Atlantic Council, the secretary general, or the Supreme Commander in Europe (SACEUR) were.[25] At the alliance level, therefore, there was a severe lack of clarity, underscored by the growing US reluctance to discuss nuclear issues with allies.

There was another reason to consider. By the mid 1960s, the US was in serious discussions at the United Nations, and separately with Soviets, about establishing what became ultimately the NPT.[26]

---

[23] Norris and Kristensen (2004); Norris et al. (1999)
[24] For the quote and its background, see Michaels (2022).
[25] Michaels (2022).
[26] On the history of the NPT negotiations, see Hunt (2022).

For the US, the challenge was twofold – to make sure that the treaty effectively prevented the spread of nuclear weapons, even among its allies (and chiefly among them West Germany), and that the allies would buy into it. That meant assuring them that the NATO nuclear umbrella would remain in place. That created political problems, as the European allies, for reasons described earlier, were no longer willing to blindly trust the US. This was especially true for West Germany, whose nuclearisation the NPT was supposed to prevent. For Americans and Soviets alike, preventing the acquisition of a nuclear weapon by West Germany was an important goal.[27] One possible solution floated was a multilateral nuclear force, which would see US nuclear missiles stationed on various platforms, operated by multinational crews. However, this failed, not least because it was unacceptable to the Soviets in the context of the NPT negotiations.[28]

Therefore, the only possible solution – the one also reflected in the bilateral exchanges between Americans and Soviets at the time of the conclusion of NPT – was that the nuclear weapons in Europe would remain under US control. However, to supplement this, a whole system of consultation was developed,[29] with the change of US bureaucratic personnel, particularly the growing role of US Secretary of Defence Robert McNamara. As historian Timothy Sayle makes clear, McNamara's persuasion became that the alliance – and the US – had more to gain than lose from sharing information with the allies.[30] To discuss nuclear policy issues, NATO established the Nuclear Planning Group (NPG), which met for the first time in 1968. Its model was influenced by the US–German bilateral consultation meetings but aimed at broader, alliance-wide participation.

NPG continues to meet and is the primary spot for debating nuclear policy issues for the alliance. During the Cold War, it met biannually on the ministerial level and more frequently at the

---

[27] On Germany and the NPT, see Lutsch (2016, 2019); Khalessi (2015).
[28] Alberque (2017).
[29] Khalessi (2015).
[30] Sayle (2020).

ambassadorial level. Since then, the frequency of the meetings has declined, but the NPG Staff Group – a working-level meeting of diplomats with the nuclear portfolio of all NATO members – meets weekly and is supported by the NATO International Staff. NPG's work is supplemented by senior national strategic experts, the High-Level Group (HLG). Although the US would decide about the ultimate use of nuclear weapons, NPG would play a role as well.[31]

The remaining Cold War history of nuclear weapons stationed in Europe is dominated by two keywords – 'Euromissiles' and 'dual track'. The two are strongly interconnected. In 1976, the Soviet Union developed missile SS-20, which could have hit Western Europe from Soviet territory. It was seen as a game-changer, as it was not capable of reaching the US (and hence could not threaten US security directly) but could target European allies. In practice, this meant that European and US security could be 'decoupled' in a war, which was antithetical to everything that Europeans had strived for since the start of the alliance. Hence, they demanded a response that would be more modern than the battlefield nuclear weapons available in Europe at that time. However, this proved immensely contentious with domestic publics and politicians.[32] The protests associated with the Euromissile crisis were some of the largest in Europe's post-World War II history. This is why the second keyword was 'dual track'. That choice, made by NATO in 1979, opened two tracks – on one hand, it offered the Warsaw Pact countries a possibility to open arms control discussions, particularly related to the SS-20; on the other hand, it stipulated that NATO would deploy medium-range missiles on its own, which started in 1983. However, in 1985, arms control discussions between the Soviets and US picked up again, which culminated in

---

[31] This paragraph draws on the work of Simon Lunn, one of the very few open sources that describes contemporary arrangements within NPG and HLG; see Lunn (2018). For more information about the decision-making within the NPG, see Chapter 6.

[32] For instance, on Germany, see Risse-Kappen (1983); Müller and Risse-Kappen (1987); on the Netherlands, see Everts (1985a, 1985b).

the Intermediate Nuclear Forces (INF) Treaty in 1987. This treaty banned intermediate-range missiles and brought about a much needed period of stability in Europe.[33]

Following the end of the Cold War, the number of nuclear weapons in Europe drastically declined. Thousands were removed as a part of the Presidential Nuclear Initiatives, a set of unilateral steps coordinated between the US and Soviet Union (later Russia) in the early 1990s.[34] In 1995, about 520 were left, stationed in seven countries.[35] This further decreased when the US withdrew nuclear weapons from the Araxos base in Greece in 2001 and the Lakenheath base in 2007.[36] Furthermore, in all host countries except for Italy, nuclear weapons were consolidated to one base per country. Their number declined to approximately 230 in 2019 and is about 100 at the time of writing in May 2024.[37] As nuclear scholar Jeffrey Larsen wrote in the mid 2010s, the importance of nuclear weapons also declined bureaucratically within the alliance – the nuclear policy director, for instance, was demoted within the organigram of the alliance.[38]

In 2010, the nuclear sharing mission went through a near-death experience. Spurred by the vision of President Obama of a world without nuclear weapons, and encouraged by NATO just beginning its broad Defence and Deterrence Posture Review, German Foreign Minister Guido Westerwelle advanced the idea of withdrawing US nuclear weapons from Europe. For Westerwelle, it was clear that these weapons were not necessary and should be withdrawn.[39] There was a clear view that the threat from Russia had diminished and Europe had no need for these weapons. Although Obama advocated the idea of a world without nuclear weapons, relations with

---

[33] This historical overview is heavily simplified, of course. Readers interested in more detail should most certainly read Colbourn (2022).
[34] Koch (2012)
[35] Kristensen (1995)
[36] Kristensen et al. (2023)
[37] Kristensen et al. (2023)
[38] Larsen (2015, p. 51)
[39] Sonne (2018)

Russia were not ideal – after all, after entering office, Obama initiated a 'reset' of those relations.[40]

Even if countries felt that more needed to be done on nuclear disarmament, they did not necessarily share Germany's view. For instance, while the Netherlands saw itself as 'forward leaning' on disarmament, it viewed that strictly within the context of the arms control discussions between the US and Russia.[41] Nevertheless, in March 2010, five allied governments – Germany, the Netherlands, Norway, Luxembourg, and Belgium – sent a letter to the NATO secretary general with a request to place this item on the agenda of the Tallinn ministerial in April 2010.[42] As the official evaluation conducted by the Dutch Ministry of Foreign Affairs discussed, the main opposition to any unilateral steps came from France and some Eastern European capitals. According to Paris, 'NATO ... was above all a military alliance, not a disarmament club.'[43] The US tried to mediate this debate, including by organising the Daalder Group, named after US Ambassador to NATO Ivo Daalder. The group, composed of the US, Norway, the Netherlands, Italy, Germany, Luxembourg, Belgium, France, and Estonia (though the composition varied, as Daalder apparently did not always invite all participants), was a primarily informal forum meant to be a place to overcome difficulties across various members.[44] Ultimately, however, the alliance response was to double down on nuclear deterrence and formalise its status as a 'nuclear alliance'.[45] It seemed like the issue died.

Yet forward-deployed nuclear weapons in Europe were kept on the agenda for two reasons. The first was the US commitment under the Obama administration to upgrade and modernise the B61,

---

[40] On the reset and its aftermath, see Pifer (2015).
[41] See the official evaluation published by the Dutch Foreign Ministry's Inspection for Development Cooperation and Policy Evaluation, Ministerie van Buitenlandse Zaken (2012).
[42] Ministerie van Buitenlandse Zaken (2012)
[43] Ministerie van Buitenlandse Zaken (2012, pp. 94–95)
[44] Ministerie van Buitenlandse Zaken (2012, pp. 95–96)
[45] NATO (2010)

the nuclear warhead deployed by the US in Europe. This decision was partially driven by the desired consolidation of a family of warheads into a single one, with improved capabilities and variable yield, hence providing significantly upgraded military capabilities.[46] The deployment of the modernised B61-12 warhead in Europe was expedited after Russia's invasion of Ukraine in December 2022 and was completed by April 2025.[47] Importantly, the US is not the only or even the first to invest in nuclear modernisation – all nuclear powers have been undertaking significant modernisation.[48]

The second reason is that the then-current carriers of the forward-deployed nuclear weapons in Europe, the F-16 and Tornado fighter jets, were nearing the end of their lives. Therefore, in most host nations, in the last fifteen years, a major debate was held on whether and how the fighter jets should be replaced. Yet as NATO decided that the F-35 II fighter jet, also known as the Joint Strike Fighter (JSF), would become a preferred replacement, the debate shifted (at least in some countries) to whether the replacement aircraft should be "dual capable". While aircraft modernisation was relevant for all five countries, the responses to this challenge were far from unified. In the Netherlands, a major debate was whether JSF should be purchased with a dual-capable kit.[49] In Germany, the debate was whether the aircraft even needed to be purchased at all. In Italy, the debate focused on the cost but not the nuclear mission.[50] Turkey would have liked to purchase it but was removed from the programme due to its purchase of a Russian air defence system.[51]

These two issues assured that attention to nuclear sharing remained. However, the last ten years have also seen growing debates about nuclear disarmament. I discuss these in depth in

---

[46] For details on modernization, see Kristensen (2015).
[47] On deployment, see Bender et al. (2022). On completion, see NATO (2025, p. 14).
[48] Kristensen and Korda (2023b)
[49] Onderco (2021)
[50] Coticchia (2016)
[51] Garamone (2019)

Chapter 5 when debating the role of civil society; suffice it to say that growing attention to the humanitarian consequences has given increasing impetus to civil society in Europe to create awareness of the continuing participation in nuclear sharing among European publics and political leaders. Of particular importance is the role of ICAN, which has spearheaded efforts that, in cooperation with a few friendly countries, led to TPNW. NATO has rejected the treaty repeatedly and views it as incompatible with the alliance commitments,[52] but many civil society actors continue to push for it. While no NATO country has yet joined TPNW, the necessity of making new decisions (such as whether to go ahead with a purchase of new, expensive fighter jets) and the anti-nuclear salience created by the attention to the humanitarian costs of nuclear weapons has assured that they have remained high on the policy agenda.

POLITICAL AND MILITARY REASONS FOR NUCLEAR SHARING

Proponents of nuclear sharing offer both military and political reasons in support of it. This has to do with the military and political functions the weapons were meant to play, as discussed in the following brief history.

Militarily, nuclear deterrence theorists have argued that nuclear sharing, and particularly in Europe, is supposed to deter both nuclear and nonnuclear attacks on European allies.[53] As Trachtenberg recalls, in the early days of the Cold War, the decision to use nuclear weapons was in the hands of the local commanders. This was supposed to deter Soviets from attacking Western Europe.[54] Because of their conventional superiority, it was not expected that Soviets would have to rely on nuclear escalation. By contrast, because of the division discussed earlier, NATO feared that a conventional attack could lead to a defeat and catastrophic consequences. For nuclear theorists Kier

---

[52] NATO (2017, 2020b)
[53] Freedman and Michaels (2019, pp. 361–364).
[54] Trachtenberg (1999) See also Biddle and Feaver (1989).

Lieber and Daryl Press, these are the key reasons for NATO's adoption of an escalatory posture.[55] It also made nuclear weapons 'a key element of the containment strategy' during the Cold War, as they literally were meant to keep the Soviets away.[56] In doing so, proponents' argument goes, the forward basing provided additional security for US allies.[57] By having comparatively lower yield than the US strategic nuclear arsenal, the weapons in Europe are meant to provide more options in the escalation ladder in a conflict in Europe.[58] This is why some proponents still see them as an indispensable contribution to European security and a key element of the NATO nuclear deterrence strategy.[59] In his recent paper, Belgian strategist Alexander Mattelaer argues that nuclear weapons are, within the alliance, the basic tool to prevent war.[60] Canadian scholars Stéphanie von Hlatky and Émile Lambert-Deslandes similarly confirm that nuclear sharing has *continually* contributed to NATO's deterrence mission, even more so after Russia's invasion of Ukraine.[61]

For critics, the military deterrent promise of nuclear sharing is ephemeral at best. One problem with the argument rests on its credibility. For any nuclear deterrence strategy (or nuclear coercive strategy), credibility is key. Yet rendering threats credible is problematic. There are many reasons for this, and scholars and policymakers recognised this difficulty early on.[62] After all, the famous question that French President De Gaulle asked US President Kennedy, 'whether [the US] would be ready to trade New York for Paris', goes to the heart of this credibility question.[63] Over time, this problem has become bigger, not smaller. As argued in a paper with my co-authors

---

[55] Lieber and Press (2020)
[56] Gavin (2015, p. 31)
[57] Larsen (2015)
[58] Schwartz (1983)
[59] Yost (2011); Pilat (2016); Mattelaer (2021)
[60] Mattelaer (2024)
[61] von Hlatky and Lambert-Deslandes (2024)
[62] Schelling (1960); Schelling (1966)
[63] For the quote, see PRESIDENT'S VISIT, Paris, 31 May–2 June 1961. Memorandum of Conversation (1961).

Anna Clara Arndt and Liviu Horovitz, 'the main challenge is rendering nuclear threats credible within the current international order in which nuclear use would involve both stark strategic and moral costs'.[64] Especially in a world where the nuclear taboo still carries a significant normative value, albeit primarily among elites, rendering nuclear threats credible is very difficult.[65] Such credibility is also recognised by policymakers – former US officials Steven Fetter and Jon Wolfsthal, for instance, argued that extended nuclear deterrence against Russia and China is particularly difficult.[66] Hans Kristensen even goes as far as to argue that this makes nuclear sharing a form of 'fake reassurance' and 'the least credible form of reassurance because it is the least likely to be used under any foreseeable condition'.[67]

The second problem is the technical capability to execute nuclear missions. Amy Woolf, who spent decades analysing the US nuclear policy at the Congressional Research Service, questioned the actual utility of the weapons stationed in Europe for achieving any military goals.[68] Experts Karl-Heinz Kemp and Robertus Remkes labelled the idea of a successful execution of a nuclear strike using nuclear weapons stationed in Europe 'essentially a mission of "seven consecutive miracles"':

> (1) surviving a first attack by an adversary; (2) receiving the authority from the President of the United States to arm the weapons and conduct such a mission; (3) takeoff and proceeding to the target; (4) rejoining with a tanker and getting enough fuel to make it to the target; (5) surviving air and surface defences along the way; (6) locating and correctly identifying the target; and (7) dropping the weapon and it works as designed.[69]

---

[64] Arndt et al. (2023, p. 170).
[65] On the nuclear taboo and its evolution over time, see Tannenwald (2002). See also Smetana and Wunderlich (2021).
[66] Fetter and Wolfsthal (2018).
[67] Kristensen (2015, p. 146).
[68] Woolf (2021).
[69] Kamp and Remkes (2011, p. 82).

Some of these issues – especially the ability to defeat Russian air defences and deliver the weapon – will be ameliorated as JSF becomes more broadly deployed and certified for the nuclear mission.[70] However, the broader concern about the credibility of the nuclear sharing mission is unlikely to go away with some simple technical fixes, as it is deeply political at its core.

Politically, the main goal of nuclear weapons deployment is seen in being a physical demonstration of the ties between the US and Europe. Thomas Schelling in the 1960s argued that because the US is on the other side of the ocean, its commitment to European security lacks fundamental credibility, because it could easily "sit one out", should a war in Europe happen.[71] Stationing the weapons in Europe is a material manifestation of the US commitment to European security, which helps to address the alliance security dilemma at a relatively low cost.[72] It is seen as a credible signal (as compared to, for instance, the offshore deterrence model more common in Asia). It therefore makes nuclear weapons symbols of transatlantic connection.[73] Seen from this angle, as the former US official Elaine Bunn wrote, nuclear weapons in the alliance are like wedding bands. If you never wore one, nobody would ask why you did not have one. But if you used to wear one, people would ask why you stopped.[74] As experts and historians argued, this view was prevalent during the Cold War in Germany and is now common in Central and Eastern Europe.[75]

A related but separate view holds that nuclear sharing allows the alliance to demonstrate political and military unity. As the British scholar Paul Schulte wrote, 'the essential purpose of these weapons is improved deterrence through demonstrable politico-military cohesion, through widespread allied military participation

---

[70] Kuhn (2023)
[71] Schelling (1966)
[72] On alliance security dilemma, see Snyder (1984). On nuclear weapons and alliance security, see Haftendorn (1996).
[73] Rudolf (2020)
[74] Bunn (2009)
[75] On Germany, see Nuti (2010). On Central and Eastern Europe, see Horovitz (2014).

to conduct or assist the nuclear mission, rather than optimal nuclear war fighting'.[76] From this perspective, nuclear weapons improve the war-fighting capacity of the alliance and make its nuclear dimension more believable, because it involves more partners. This view is underscored by how the alliance itself calls for broadest participation of allies possible and also by initiatives such as the Conventional Support for Nuclear Operations (CSNO).[77]

Furthermore, for US officials, nuclear weapons have played an important role in stymieing the nuclear ambitions of allies. As argued, for successive US administrations since 1960s, preventing the spread of nuclear weapons was an important policy goal.[78] The US continues to be one of the key sponsors of the global nonproliferation regime and tried hard to co-opt its allies into it.[79] This goal is not absolute, but the US has spent significant political and financial capital preventing adversaries from acquiring nuclear weapons and dissuading allies from doing so. The US has gone far within its own alliance network to prevent allies from acquiring nuclear weapons – this applies to both allies, such as Germany and Italy, and partners, such as Sweden.[80]

Theorists have highlighted both military and political goals that nuclear sharing is supposed to accomplish. In Chapter 7, I will return to (some) of these goals, as I will study how and whether they are reflected in how elites justify their continued participation in nuclear sharing. However, understanding that the nuclear weapons are at the core of NATO politically *and* militarily helps us to grasp that nuclear sharing is not just some sideshow to NATO's core mission – it is a part of it.

---

[76] Schulte (2015, p. 113).
[77] CSNO was known as SNOWCAT (Supporting Nuclear Operations with Conventional Air Tactics).
[78] Gavin (2012, 2015).
[79] Gibbons (2022).
[80] On Germany, see Gerzhoy (2015) and, for a critical view, see Schneider (2016); on Italy, see Nuti (2017); on Sweden, see Jonter (2016).

2 Technocratic Responsiveness and Nuclear Sharing

INTRODUCTION

'If citizens don't want these things here, and if we are a democracy, how come these things are still here? Isn't that undemocratic?' So asked a leading scholar at a workshop in February 2023, after I had presented a paper on the German public opinion on nuclear weapons. Unsurprisingly, that paper concluded that Germany's continued reliance on nuclear deterrence, especially in its particular manifestation as nuclear sharing, has been (until very recently) deeply unpopular in Germany.[1] Up until Russia's invasion of Ukraine, the situation in other European host nations was very similar, as I will explain in depth in Chapter 3.

Faced with this unpopularity, the scholar's view was not new. Scholars have in recent years argued, time and again, that nuclear weapons (and nuclear sharing) in Europe lack the support of the general public and are therefore undemocratic.[2] Their understanding of democratic legitimacy is generally linked to overall public support. Put simply – policies are democratic if people like them. While appealing from the point of view of *volonté générale* as a source of policy legitimacy, such an understanding of democratic governance in the twenty-first century is somewhat simplistic. By continuing nuclear sharing, and continuing to invest billions in capabilities that they repeatedly expressed they hoped never to use, governments were often claimed to pursue technocratic policies unresponsive to the general public.

---

[1] The paper has now been published as Onderco (2024).
[2] Egeland and Pelopidas (2020); Perier (2019); Egeland (2019)

By contrast, in this book, I argue that nuclear sharing policies are best understood through the concept of 'technocratic responsiveness'.[3] This view recognises that policy is driven by technocratic considerations but shows responsiveness to popular pressures. Originating in the study of public administration, technocratic responsiveness is a concept that engages with how technocrats with expertise who make policies and are often insulated from the public *on purpose* react to conflictual pressures from different audiences.

In this chapter, I will provide a theoretical and conceptual account of technocratic responsiveness in foreign and security policy, contributing to our understanding of the democratic legitimacy of nuclear sharing. I want to underscore that this chapter does not deal with the democratic legitimacy of nuclear weapons as such but focuses on that of nuclear sharing, a much narrower question. While I will draw on literature on the democratic legitimacy of nuclear weapons in general, I will sidestep the discussion about nuclear decision-making in nuclear weapons states and other important but unrelated questions, such as the environmental and humanitarian impact of nuclear testing.[4] All of these issues can be – and are – scrutinised from the angle of democratic governance. Analysing whether policies are democratic, however, needs to go beyond what is popular with the general public and what is not.

To start thinking about technocratic responsiveness, we need to start from the beginning – the difference between responsiveness and responsibility in public policy. This is important because one key claim of technocrats – as I will explain later – is that they pursue a 'responsible' policy.

RESPONSIVENESS AND RESPONSIBILITY

The lack of public support for nuclear sharing and nuclear deterrence is often construed by civil society and academics opposed to

---

[3] van der Veer (2020)
[4] On decision-making in nuclear weapons states, see, for instance, Born et al. (2011). On the humanitarian and environmental impact, see Philippe and Statius (2021).

them as a reason to either withdraw them or rethink the nuclear policies.[5] Benoît Pelopidas and his collaborators developed this criticism through the concept of 'nuclear guardianship', which is supposed to signify the removal of nuclear weapons from public control over the policy, a key requirement of technocratic policymaking.[6] That concept was originally developed by Robert Dahl in his 1985 book.[7] Dahl's argument is disarmingly simple (but not trivial) – most of the policy questions related to nuclear weapons are too complex and too technical for citizens, so the natural solution is to turn them over to experts (whom Dahl labels 'guardians'). Yet these guardians often lack moral understanding of policy (which Dahl considers key), which might lead to preferring a technocratic approach over a view more attuned to public interests. A corollary is that these technocrats and bureaucrats usually spend a great deal of time working *only* on nuclear issues, making them much more specialised and knowledgeable but also giving them higher stakes in a given policy than elected politicians, for whom this is often not a priority. The argument about nuclear policy being developed especially by guardians and being hard to penetrate for elected policymakers, and hence largely immune from public preferences, has been made repeatedly in the US setting.[8]

Scholars of foreign and security policy have often discussed executive dominance in these fields. Executives dominate foreign and security policy for several reasons – the need to make swift decisions, secrecy surrounding many aspects (this applies even more in the nuclear field),[9] and technical expertise (which also often applies to other areas of foreign policy). All of these features make public – and legislative – oversight of foreign and security policy generally

---

[5] For civil society arguments, see ICAN (2019a, 2020).
[6] For academic work, see Egeland and Pelopidas (2020); Pelopidas (2021); Fraise (2022, 2023).
[7] Dahl (1985)
[8] Scarry (2014); Nolan (1989); Kaplan (2020)
[9] Wellerstein (2021); Mian (2009)

difficult and often translate into only very partial, and often incomplete, reflection of the views of the public.[10]

This reality of foreign and security policy clashes with the expectation that in a democratic polity, governments are expected to reflect public preferences.[11] As V. O. Key wrote over sixty years ago in his classic book, 'unless mass views have some place in the shaping of policy, all the talk about democracy is nonsense'.[12] The disparity between the views of the public and foreign policy (not only in the nuclear field) appears therefore prima facie problematic. Yet even in democracies governments have often institutionally shielded foreign policy from public opinion, and theorists of democracy have for a long time debated whether democratic politics is even good for foreign policy. They have argued over whether the public would be a source of prudence or impulse.[13] Once the study of public opinion became more prevalent, scholars have argued extensively that it is too fickle and based on moods rather than solid grounding, so it is best to ignore it.[14]

Over time, however, this view has given way to understanding that there is more substance to public opinion than initially assumed,[15] and, by now, it is generally accepted that it even has some coherence with foreign policy.[16] Political theorists have argued that a link between public opinion and foreign policy is necessary, as citizens ultimately pay for foreign policy – in both blood and treasure.[17] This view goes back to the argument related to the *volonté generale* as a basis for policy-making, as described by classical democratic theorists, such as Rousseau.[18] In public policy, this is called 'policy responsiveness'.

---

[10] Raunio and Wagner (2017). See also Curtin (2014). For a most recent take on this issue, see Saunders (2024).
[11] Dahl (2020)
[12] Key Jr. (1961, p. 7)
[13] Wagner (2020, pp. 15–20)
[14] Almond (1950)
[15] Holsti (1992)
[16] Everts and Isernia (2015); see also Baum and Potter (2015).
[17] Lord (2011)
[18] Clawson and Oxley (2021)

Most scholars of international politics will be familiar with a stream of inquiry that has placed policy responsiveness in its centre, even if it does not use that label. Democratic peace, the concept that democracies are less prone to fight wars with one another, rests on the idea that democratic governments are unwilling to carry the electoral costs of unpopular policies such as war.[19] The whole broader democratic distinctiveness research programme states that democracies behave differently in international politics because they are responsive to and representative of the broad public, the voters.[20]

Yet it is not uncommon in democracies to remove certain policies from democratic decision-making. Citizens, for instance, have only a limited impact on central bank interest rates, and central banks are sometimes completely insulated from democratic politics.[21] The withdrawal of certain policies from democratic politics links to leaving certain policies to technocrats. As American political scientist Douglas Foyle argues, leaders vary in how much they think that citizens *should* have a say in something as crucial as foreign policy.[22] Prominent political scientist Peter Mair developed a useful tool to understand this phenomenon in the early 2000s. As he argues, democratic policy-making is caught between two forms of control – responsiveness and responsibility.[23]

Responsiveness refers to a sympathetic response to 'the short-term demands of voters, public opinion, interest groups, and the media'.[24] Foyle calls this the 'delegate view of democratic representation'.[25] It usually works through one of two mechanisms – replacing

---

[19] Russett and Oneal (2001)
[20] Owen (2004); Geis and Wagner (2008)
[21] This is particularly a feature in the so-called Westminster systems. See Lijphart (1999). Recent work on central banks has, however, demonstrated that they are more responsive to public pressure than initially assumed. See Moschella (2024).
[22] Foyle (1999)
[23] Mair (2009)
[24] Bardi et al. (2014, p. 237)
[25] Foyle (1999, p. 2)

representatives through elections (turnover) and pleasing the electorate to improve one's chances in future elections (rational anticipation).[26] US political scientists Christopher Achen and Larry Bartels call this view a 'folk theory' of democracy, arguing that it reflects an 'everyday wisdom' about how democratic governments work.[27] By contrast, responsibility refers to the 'necessity ... to take into account (a) the long-term needs of their people and countries, which ... underlie and go beyond the short-term demands of those same people; (and) (b) the claims of audiences other than the national electoral audience, including ... the international commitments and organisations that are the root of their international credibility'.[28] Mair argues that one of the implications of responsibility as a form of control in democratic polities is that, in some cases, the leaders' hands are tied.[29] Foyle calls this 'the trustee view of democratic representation'.[30]

Yet what responsibility means is often hard to pin down. As political scientist Amandine Crespy and her co-authors note in their overview of the work on responsiveness, identifying what a 'responsible government' does is very difficult, oftentimes contingent, and dependent on power relations.[31] One very plausible argument is that technocratic and bureaucratic cadres and policy elites have a disproportionate impact on what is seen as responsible. Such elites tend to more often than not think alike, and while their views are often not uniform, less variation is likely.[32]

In the study of the EU, where the concepts of responsiveness and responsibility have been developed the most, the dynamic between them is often perceived as a dilemma or trade-off, often

---

[26] Zhelyazkova et al. (2019)
[27] Achen and Bartels (2017, p. 1). Achen and Bartels call this view also a 'populist ideal of electoral democracy' (p.14).
[28] Bardi et al. (2014, p. 237)
[29] Mair (2013)
[30] Foyle (1999, p. 2)
[31] Crespy et al. (2024)
[32] Saunders (2014); Kreps (2010)

leading to a gap.³³ 'Responsive responsibility' became a goal for policymakers, with a clear priority for responsibility, although responsiveness is seen as part of the package.³⁴

Mair worries that too much focus on responsiveness,³⁵ and competition in elections with growing polarisation makes responsible policy-making almost impossible in Western democracies. For instance, climate change is presenting European governments with massive challenges, but they face significant domestic opposition to their mitigation plans and often need to compromise to accommodate climate sceptics.³⁶ Too much responsiveness would make it impossible to create a responsible policy.

RESPONSIVENESS AND RESPONSIBILITY: NUCLEAR SHARING

While responsiveness and responsibility have been thus far mainly explored in the areas of economic governance, a good argument can be made to extend them to the study of security policy in general and nuclear policy in particular. These fields provide an especially fertile ground for arguments based on responsibility and not responsiveness.³⁷ Scholars of democratic policy-making, who have worked on responsiveness and responsibility, argue that the commitments made abroad and on behalf of others are those where arguments based on 'responsibility' are the easiest,³⁸ partially because the leaders can claim that their hands are tied.³⁹

---

[33] Crespy et al. (2024)
[34] Crespy et al. (2024, p. 4)
[35] Mair (2013)
[36] For the example of the Netherlands and the Farmer-Citizen Movement, see Henley (2023).
[37] For works on responsibility and nuclear weapons, see Sagan (2009); Sasikumar (2007). These, however, do not conceptualise responsibility as such. Brixley-Williams and Wheeler (2020, pp. 19–28) provide a historical overview of applying the 'responsibility talk' to nuclear politics. Note that the conceptual notion of 'responsibility talk' is somewhat different from responsibility in the work of Mair and other governance scholars; most literature on responsibility in the nuclear sphere focuses on external behaviour.
[38] Laffan (2014)
[39] On 'tying hands', see Fearon (1997).

The allied features of nuclear sharing make it easier for leaders to justify and continue the policy, while framing it as an alliance responsibility. Nuclear sharing, in Europe, is explicitly an alliance policy. While it is based on bilateral arrangements (between the host countries and the US), it creates effects for the alliance. An example of this is the last time that (some of) the host nations wanted to revisit nuclear sharing. In 2010, Germany, in a coalition of five European countries, including the Netherlands and Belgium, wanted to revisit the arrangements; it did so explicitly by calling on fellow alliance members to rethink nuclear sharing.[40] Despite being at its core a bilateral arrangement, alliance documents repeatedly highlight that nuclear sharing is a part of the alliance's deterrence mechanisms.[41] And while NATO's status as a nuclear alliance has been constructed over time,[42] it has created commitments for countries contributing to the nuclear mission. States (and policy elites crafting state policy) see nuclear deterrence as a 'responsible' policy because they feel a responsibility to assure the security of the state and, faced with nuclear-armed adversaries, view nuclear deterrence as a necessity.[43] In fact, the framework of responsibility to the alliance is very common in the Netherlands but also Germany.[44] Framing this policy as benefitting others – the rest of the alliance – makes positioning its continuation as a 'responsible policy' even stronger.[45]

---

[40] Nuti (2021)
[41] See, for instance, de Maizière et al. (2020); NATO (2020a, 2021, 2022, 2023b)
[42] Michaels (2022); Sayle (2020); Heuser and Stoddart (2017)
[43] Historically speaking, this has been the case for a long time. Historian Simon Miles, for instance, recalls that West German Chancellor Helmut Kohl was mistrustful of the German youth, whom he saw as spoilt and not recognising the risks to West Germany; see Miles (2020).
[44] Advisory Council on International Affairs (2019). See also Kabinetsreactie op AIV-adviesrapport 'Kernwapens in een nieuwe geopolitieke werkelijkheid' [Brief van de ministers van buitenlandse zaken en van defensie] (2019). On Germany, see Sonne (2018, pp. 4–5).
[45] One should not mistake political or normative responsibility for legal obligation. Critics of the argument of alliance responsibility often point to the lack of legal obligation to contribute to its nuclear mission. For an argument criticising the narrative of responsibility to the alliance, see Hummel (2024).

Three factors further weaken the pressures stemming from responsiveness. First, the salience of nuclear weapons among the public and political parties has declined. To be sure, low salience is not unique to nuclear weapons. As Achen and Bartels write, 'human beings are busy with their lives' and have generally little time to form sufficiently grounded views about different policy issues to evaluate politicians on them thoroughly.[46] It is therefore not surprising that, after over 90 per cent of nuclear weapons were withdrawn from Europe at the end of the Cold War and tensions between the East and the West eased, the salience in public discourse declined, at least until the start of the Russia's invasion of Ukraine in 2022 and Russia's associated nuclear threats. In the three preceding decades, many leaders had started to think about nuclear weapons as an old-fashioned problem, philanthropic funding for civil society in the field had declined, and the feeling that they were no longer a pressing issue had developed.[47]

Even more so, the electoral salience of nuclear weapons is declining. Except for a very rare occasion, the German federal election in 2021, where the replacement of the ageing Tornado fleet was raised, foreign policy issues are rarely salient in national elections.[48] In the Netherlands, for instance, foreign policy was not even an option in public opinion surveys that asked respondents about the most salient topics for the 2023 general election.[49] This is in stark contrast to the Cold War, when Western European leaders carefully considered how positions on nuclear weapons would pay off in elections.[50] Parliaments pay only limited attention to nuclear weapons, policy discussion tends to be rather shallow, and media generally ignore it.[51]

---

[46] For the quote, see Achen and Bartels (2017, p. 9). Chapter 2 of their book provides a more detailed treatment of the shortcomings of the populist theory.

[47] Egeland (2020b). On the decline of philanthropic funding in the field, see Onderco (2020).

[48] On German debate ahead of the 2021 elections, see Fuhrhop (2021).

[49] See, for instance, a report referenced by Dutch political scientist Simon Otjes: https://twitter.com/SimonOtjes/status/1695325361045672085.

[50] See, for example, Colbourn (2022).

[51] Parliamentary opposition and media attention are two criteria that make governments more likely to follow public opinion on foreign policy. See Baum and Potter (2015).

Hence, even if parties that have weapons withdrawal in their manifestos somehow get into governments, this topic is not important enough for them to break coalitions.[52] Again, declining public awareness, the level of knowledge about even the basics of nuclear sharing, and low electoral salience are not reasons for ignoring public preferences. However, salience is a key variable that explains when technocrats start paying attention to public preferences,[53] and its lack helps to clarify why it might be possible not to bring the views of the public into actual foreign policy.

Secondly, the governments in the host countries have developed policy that gives a semblance of policy responsiveness but avoids the core demands of the pro-disarmament voices. Such steps include, for instance, support for arms control negotiations, which these governments wholeheartedly embrace. Three host nations are members of the Non-Proliferation and Disarmament Initiative, a coalition of states working on transparency in disarmament that has not delivered any concrete proposal. The host governments with active and institutionally strong parliaments invite parliamentarians to join government delegations to major international conferences, creating an appearance of accountability.[54] Parliaments hold regular debates on nuclear topics, in which government representatives participate to explain and justify policy. Three of the five host nations (Belgium, Germany, and the Netherlands) attended the first Meeting of States Parties (MSP) to the Treaty on the Prohibition of Nuclear Weapons (TPNW) in Vienna in 2022, and one (Germany) also travelled to the second MSP/TPNW in New York in 2023.[55] Germany has had major discussions about contributing funds to compensate victims of nuclear testing – a further indication of steps that recognise public pressure without making concessions on key demands.[56]

---

[52] On coalition governments and foreign policy, see Oktay (2022).
[53] Rauh (2016)
[54] Onderco (2018)
[55] None of the host nations attended the third MSP in March 2025 in New York.
[56] Bündnis 90/Die Grünen (2022)

These steps are what Thomas Risse-Kappen called 'symbolic adjustments', and they allow governments to decrease the salience of the issue even further.[57]

And, last, nuclear sharing is a policy that is traditionally decided and managed by technocrats in prime ministers' offices, ministries of defence and foreign affairs, and NATO International Staff. Such technocracy bases its legitimacy on superior knowledge (which sets it apart from other forms of bureaucracy) and has independence from (and hence unresponsiveness to) the public mood, the representation of the interests of the whole of society, and rationally justifiable goals.[58] These technocrats "know" the minute details of their dossiers – doctrines, strategies, missiles, capabilities. They are the ones who embrace and nurture but also perpetuate the dominant strategic culture, which permeates how they (and hence the states) think about deterrence.[59] They are part of the epistemic community of experts, who meet in nice houses in the English countryside to talk about technicalities. The latest political science research in other fields has also shown that executives who consider themselves knowledgeable about policy details are more likely to be dismissive of contrary public views.[60] Those who criticise policy elites as unresponsive to public demands mistake a feature of this system for a bug.

That this policy pursues rationally justifiable goals does not mean that nuclear sharing is the only, best, or perennial choice. When it comes to 'the only' choice, alternatives exist – such as improving conventional armaments or pursuing global nuclear disarmament. But the NATO host nations have limited impact on the latter and are unwilling to invest (even more) in the former.[61] As experts have

---

[57] Risse-Kappen (1991, p. 502)
[58] Based on Caramani (2020, pp. 2–3)
[59] Lantis (2009)
[60] Pereira and Öhberg (2023)
[61] The impact of the host nations on US nuclear policy is a subject of intense debate, with numerous indications that the allies have *some* effect; see Brauß (2020). However, it is unlikely that they would have been able to push the US and other states possessing nuclear weapons into negotiations on nuclear disarmament.

stressed, compensating for a weapons withdrawal would require additional investment, including in advanced conventional weaponry and additional assurances to allies closer to Russia, perhaps through new institutional structures.[62] Nuclear sharing might not even be the best option – the debate about the technical capabilities of B61 tactical nuclear bombs is wide ranging.[63] Alternative arrangements could also continue to provide Europe with a nuclear deterrent but based on other means. Submarine-based ballistic missiles could be an option and have been contemplated by some scholars. While such options might be technically available, the European allies have historically shown a much higher need of assurance, which such solutions barely provide.[64] And they are certainly not a perennial choice but a policy that frontloads the benefits (nuclear protection), while underappreciating intergenerational risks.[65]

Critics of contemporary nuclear arrangements in Europe point to the many changes made in the past to step away from other nuclear practices. For instance, nuclear testing has been almost completely abandoned (with the exception of North Korea), and three countries (Kazakhstan, Ukraine, and South Africa) have given up nuclear weapons that were on their territory. However, these examples miss a key argument. For testing, alternatives were found that satisfied the technocrats and hence did not endanger the responsibility claim.[66] In South Africa, nuclear weapons were found not to be needed any longer.[67] In Kazakhstan and Ukraine, the situation

---

[62] Anthony and Janssen (2010)
[63] See also Kuhn (2023).
[64] For instance, Japan and South Korea continue to benefit from the US nuclear umbrella without any nuclear weapons stationed on their territory, thanks to a complex web of policy arrangements. However, these arrangements would fall short of the assurance requirements that European policymakers have historically voiced. For an overview, see Frühling and O'Neil (2017).
[65] I am thankful to Franziska Stärk and Matthew Rendall for introducing me to this line of argumentation. On nuclear weapons and intergenerational justice, see Rendall (2007, 2022).
[66] Krepon (2021)
[67] Möser (2019)

was very similar, and the new regimes did not have the means to maintain the weapons, which were a burden on the newly independent countries anyway.[68] Getting rid of them did not endanger but bolstered the "responsibility" claim.

Hence, the answer to 'How come these things are still here?' is in two parts – a weakened responsiveness claim and a strong responsibility claim. This makes nuclear policy similar to other areas, such as European integration, where the "democratic deficit" has been decried for years.

CONCEPTUAL MODEL

Even though nuclear sharing has been historically decided and managed by technocracies, defined as 'actors and institutions drawing legitimacy from their technical competence and administrative expertise',[69] this does not mean that societal pressures played no role in the actors' decision-making. On the surface, the demand for technocratic expertise is seductive because it gives an air of neutrality and expertise.

As I mentioned, the work on technocratic responsiveness has been most developed in the study of European economic governance. One important finding has been that technocratic policy-making in Europe initially focused on output legitimacy of its processes. In other words, technocracy led to economic growth, which in turn led to the legitimation of integration strategies.[70] However, starting in 1990s, the European Commission – the ultimate technocratic body – became increasingly responsive to public demands.[71] This process intensified and sped up as the EU became mired in economic crises, and as political contestation grew, the technocrats had to develop a different approach, such as technocratic responsiveness.[72] As recent economic policy studies by public administration scholars

---

[68] On Ukraine, see Budjeryn (2022). On Kazakhstan, see Kassenova (2022).
[69] Bickerton and Accetti (2017)
[70] Wood (2021)
[71] Rauh (2016)
[72] Wood (2021)

demonstrate, seemingly insulated technocratic institutions are actually sensitive to public pressure because they want to maintain their status and recognition by their "audience", which is often conceptualised as the general public.[73] This makes technocrats sensitive to protest and media coverage.[74] Further complicating matters, however, they might have to respond to different audiences. As Van der Veer argues in a recent work, technocracies may sometimes need to prioritise one audience because audience preferences are heterogeneous.[75] Engaging criticism is, however, not easy for technocrats – after all, they are the experts, and that gives critics legitimacy and political oxygen.[76] In such situations, technocracies seek to signal their independence and expertise rather than make policy concessions. Doing otherwise would signal that they are not experts but engaging in politics – something antithetical to their mission.

Technocrats must consider domestic audiences' influence for two reasons. The first is connected to electoral politics. Political parties, with their desire to keep or gain office, avoid unpopular policies, including in foreign policy.[77] They may also try to avoid rallying opposition around an unpopular cause.[78] More recently, scholars have argued that, even if not directly, public attitudes quietly shape what policymakers consider an appropriate policy choice in regard to nuclear weapons.[79] Experimental evidence suggests that technocrats take public attitudes into account when deciding appropriate policy choices in security policy.[80]

For technocrats to be responsive, we need to understand whom they are responsive to. Therefore, the theory I propose argues that

---

[73] Carpenter (2010); Carpenter et al. (2012); van der Veer (2021); Busuioc and Lodge (2016)

[74] On protests, see Alon-Barkat and Gilad (2016); on media coverage see Maor and Sulitzeanu-Kenan (2016).

[75] van der Veer (2021, 2020)

[76] Braun and Düsterhöft (2023)

[77] Schultz (1998); Kaarbo (2015); Hofmann (2013); Hofmann and Martill (2021)

[78] Bailey (2001)

[79] Press et al. (2013); Sagan and Valentino (2017, 2018)

[80] Lin-Greenberg (2021)

the technocrats who craft nuclear policies in the host nations seek to show signs of responsiveness but also pursue what is seen as a responsible policy. In formulating what such a policy is, they draw on their expertise but also on audiences beyond the nation-state, such as allies and partners. The final outcome – the policy that emerges – gives a nod to responsiveness demands while not compromising on what is seen as the core elements of a responsible policy.

For nuclear sharing, the technocratic and bureaucratic elites are faced with domestic but also allied actors, whom they must somehow be responsive to. Therefore, in the conceptual model, domestic and foreign audiences should matter. Domestically, public opinion and political parties attempt to influence policy outcomes. They are often aided (and spurred) by transnational civil society. But, ultimately, it is elites who craft the policy, as it is a technocratic, executive policy. Figure 2.1 captures the conceptual scheme. Not all relations are equally important for making policy. However, they all do exercise some form of pressure on elites.

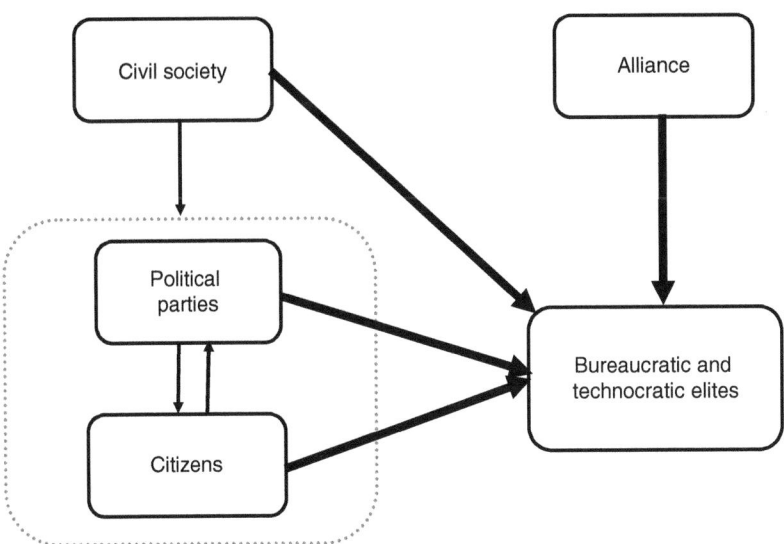

FIGURE 2.1 Conceptual model.

Starting with public opinion and political parties, three separate questions may need to be answered: what their preferences are, where these come from, and how they are considered by elites. And we barely understand the answers to these questions. Despite quite some public opposition to nuclear sharing – and political parties' criticism of the existing policies – the source of this opposition has been little studied. Therefore, I aim to map and explain how domestic audiences – parties and political parties – think about nuclear sharing and will try to explain where such preferences are coming from.

Transnational civil society, particularly nongovernmental organisations (NGOs), influences debates about nuclear sharing, both directly (by engaging technocratic elites) and indirectly (by influencing domestic audiences). We can think of the role of translational civil society as akin to that of other interest groups (lobbies).[81] Traditionally, civil society organisations are understood as a *transmission belt* between the public and policymakers.[82] In nuclear sharing, civil society is active at both global and local levels. At the global level, major NGOs, such as ICAN, act as lobbyists, often in coordination with states.[83] At the local level, they can act as agenda setters, norm generators, and advocates.[84] In recent years, NGOs have been active in Europe in attempting to persuade countries to give up nuclear sharing.[85] A vast majority of the recent work on NGOs in global nuclear disarmament, particularly in relation to the recently adopted TPNW, has been done by activists themselves and/or focused on the global level.[86] While some scholars looked at how policymakers influence civil society,[87] the much more straightforward question of local civil society's engagement with national

---

[81] And they understand their role as such as well, as will be shown in Chapter 5.
[82] Putnam (1993)
[83] Ruff (2018); Gibbons (2018); Acheson (2021)
[84] See, for example, the recent review of feminist activism in Eschle (2021).
[85] Ruff (2018)
[86] Acheson (2021); Docherty (2018); Gibbons (2018); Mekata (2018); Norman (2019); Welty (2020); Petrova (2018)
[87] Boncourt et al. (2020); Craig and Ruzicka (2013)

policymakers remains understudied. This gap means that many critical questions – such as how the representation and aggregation of individual interests or methods influences tactics, or the content of policy engagement – remain unanswered. Studies of another NGO that received a Nobel Peace Prize – International Physicians for the Prevention of Nuclear War – suggest that attention to the operation of activists is critical for understanding their actions.[88]

However, where the model diverges from the usual understanding of the democratic politics of foreign policy is that it considers the external audience (allies). Put simply, technocrats understand their responsibility to also lie with those who are *beyond* national borders. As I argued, commitments made abroad weigh heavily in their understanding of responsibility.[89] This is why I conceptualise the allied audience as a separate source of influence on elites and technocrats.

Ultimately, I wish to understand how technocratic elites consider these different audiences and balance their preference in developing policy. Therefore, I will also study elites, how they weigh these various pressures and demands, and what policy outcomes emerge.

---

[88] Day and Waltzkin (1985); Orient (1988); The Lancet (1991)
[89] Bardi et al. (2014)

3 Public Opinion

INTRODUCTION

Scholars have a broad agreement that European publics have been critical of the nuclear weapons umbrella; in fact, many memories of the tumultuous 1980s in European security are linked to unrest, protests, and parliamentary disquiet.[1] However, despite being historically unpopular, nuclear sharing continues, and governments still invest billions of euros to maintain the technical capability for its main mission – delivering a weapon that most people agree must not be used.

Nevertheless, our understanding of public views of nuclear weapons in Europe has major gaps. To start with, very few studies compare views across multiple countries. Some of them were done by activists, primarily ICAN, and others by academics.[2] However, none has compared attitudes across all five host nations. Furthermore, almost none tried to understand the roots of such views. Therefore, while appeal to public opinion abounds, we actually understand it rather poorly.

The purpose of this chapter is to rectify this shortcoming. I aim to not only map public views of nuclear weapons but also provide a theoretical framework, building on technocracy, populism, and foreign policy attitudes, to explain them – across the five host countries.

PUBLIC OPINION AND NUCLEAR WEAPONS

Public opinion surveys in Europe for a good part of the last two decades demonstrate, time and again, that nuclear deterrence and

---

[1] For instance, on Germany, see Risse-Kappen (1983); Müller and Risse-Kappen (1987); on the Netherlands, see Everts (1985a, 1985b).
[2] ICAN (2018a, 2019a, 2021); Smetana et al. (2021); Onderco et al. (2022)

nuclear sharing in Europe are unpopular, although the tide has started to change after Russia's invasion of Ukraine.[3] While the wording of individual questions might explain small variations, they do not explain the general pattern that emerges over time. The general dislike of nuclear weapons is clear in all surveys, which often ask respondents about their views of nuclear sharing and whether they would be willing to support nuclear disarmament or the use of nuclear weapons in a conflict.

In Germany, in repeated surveys, respondents consistently opposed nuclear sharing. For instance, in a 2005 survey, 75 per cent desired withdrawal.[4] These views have persisted over time in surveys conducted by activists and academics alike. In surveys for anti-nuclear activists, large shares of the population (often more than two-thirds) indicated a desire to have nuclear weapons withdrawn from Germany.[5] Surveys conducted on behalf of the Munich Security Conference had similar findings.[6] In academic surveys, citizens also reflected that they felt that Germany should seek nuclear abolition rather than nuclear allies.[7] Similar patterns can be found in Belgium; in 2014, over 60 per cent of respondents wanted nuclear weapons to be withdrawn. The share of the population wishing for this, however, declined and reached 49 per cent in 2019 and 57 per cent in 2020, still remaining below the 2014 percentage.[8]

Similarly, German respondents were opposed to any idea of nuclear use. They have demonstrated that repeatedly in surveys conducted by anti-nuclear activists and academic experts.[9] Germans have also opposed investment in maintaining the capacity to deliver

---

[3] Onderco et al. (2023)
[4] Der Spiegel (2005)
[5] ICAN (2018b, 2019b); IPPNW (2016); Greenpeace (2020, 2021)
[6] Bunde et al. (2020)
[7] Egeland and Pelopidas (2020)
[8] Coalition belge contre les armes nucléaires (2020); CNAPD (2019); Vlaamsvredesinstituut (2014)
[9] For anti-nuclear activists, see The Simons Foundation (2007); for academics, see Onderco and Smetana (2021); Smetana and Onderco (2022).

nuclear weapons stationed in Germany. If dual-capable aircraft were not replaced, Germany would technically lose that capability. In various surveys by proponents of nuclear disarmament, well over half of the population was opposed to replacing the fighter jets.[10] And Germany is not the only host country where the public dislikes nuclear weapons. In Belgium, 51 per cent of respondents felt that new aircraft should not be able to drop nuclear weapons.[11] In Italy, in 2007, almost 70 per cent of respondents stated that nuclear weapons use by NATO could never be justified.[12] A large majority of population was also opposed to equipping fighter jets with the capacity to deliver nuclear weapons and in favour of ending nuclear sharing.[13]

And, last, respondents in various surveys have generally supported the idea of developing global nuclear disarmament norms. In Germany, large majorities of the population supported destroying global nuclear arsenals and developing international laws banning them.[14] After the TPNW was opened for signature, large majorities of the public were in favour.[15] That would have had a particularly dire impact on the participation in nuclear sharing, as the treaty not only prohibits stationing nuclear weapons but also broader support for nuclear deterrence, which would in practice mean not only the end of nuclear sharing but also a much broader rethinking of participation in NATO's contemporary defence policy planning and exercises.[16] The situation was similar in Belgium, where over two-thirds of respondents supported signing the TPNW, a treaty inconsistent with Belgium's involvement in NATO nuclear sharing.[17] In Italy, almost two-thirds of respondents supported preventing the spread of nuclear

---

[10] ICAN (2018b, 2019b); Greenpeace (2019, 2021)
[11] ICAN (2021)
[12] The Simons Foundation (2007)
[13] ICAN (2017, 2018b)
[14] For surveys on destroying global nuclear arsenals, see Greenpeace (2019, 2020, 2021); on developing an international law, see IPPNW (2016).
[15] ICAN (2017, 2018b)
[16] Caughley and Mukhatzhanova (2017)
[17] CNAPD (2019)

weapons.[18] Similarly to Belgium and Italy, a large majority – almost three-quarters – of respondents were in favour of signing the TPNW.[19]

MAPPING THE ATTITUDES

To address shortcomings in the literature, I designed a new survey, fielded between 14–27 April 2023 in Belgium, Germany, the Netherlands, and Turkey, and in September 2023 in Italy by IPSOS, a leading global pollster.[20] A sample of approximately 1,000 respondents per country was drawn, representative of gender, age, educational structure, and geographical distribution in each country.

As I noted, in some host nations, this was one of many surveys, but in some – such as Italy and Turkey – this was one of the first to be done by independent academics. To map attitudes, the respondents were asked to respond to questions teasing out their views on nuclear weapons. For each country, the survey was translated by an academic specialising in international relations from English into the country's language, and each translation was checked by at least one other academic with expertise in nuclear weapons.

Nuclear Weapons Are Not Uniquely Unpopular

The gulf between what the government does and what the population would want it to do is not a unique challenge for governing nuclear weapons. A similar argument could be made about many other fields of public policy. After all, the nuclear field is not the only one where hypocrisy between pronounced commitments and government actions appears.[21]

To look for anything special about the gulf between public views and government actions for nuclear weapons, I included

---

[18] The Simons Foundation (2007)
[19] ICAN (2018)
[20] There was a small error in the translation of the nuclear use question in Italy. While all analysis indicated that this error had no practical consequences for the answers, I reran the survey in September 2023. The reported findings refer to the new survey, although the substantive differences are minuscule.
[21] On hypocrisy, see Finnemore and Jurkovich (2020) and Spektor (2023).

a question on whether respondents trusted 'the government to do the right thing when it comes to' a number of policy areas: climate change, educational policy, the EU, nuclear disarmament, taxes, and the welfare state. The question was deliberately vague, to be understandable to the broadest set of respondents, and required very little prior knowledge. The respondents used a seven-point Likert scale from 1 – strongly distrust to 7 – strongly trust.

The results are shown in Figure 3.1 and indicate that while citizens do not trust the government to do the right thing when it comes to nuclear disarmament, they generally tend not to trust it in other policy areas either. On average, trust on nuclear disarmament does not reach the mean of 4 in any host country, suggesting that respondents are, on average, not even *undecided*.

However, this score is not so much lower than in other areas. For instance, respondents have a similar or even lower trust in the government's ability to do the right thing for climate change, and the difference was even stronger for taxes. The only area where the trust in the government was consistently higher was the trust in the EU (but even then, in Turkey, the share of the population having trust in the government was lower compared to nuclear disarmament). Nevertheless, the mean trust was mostly below 4. Translated into

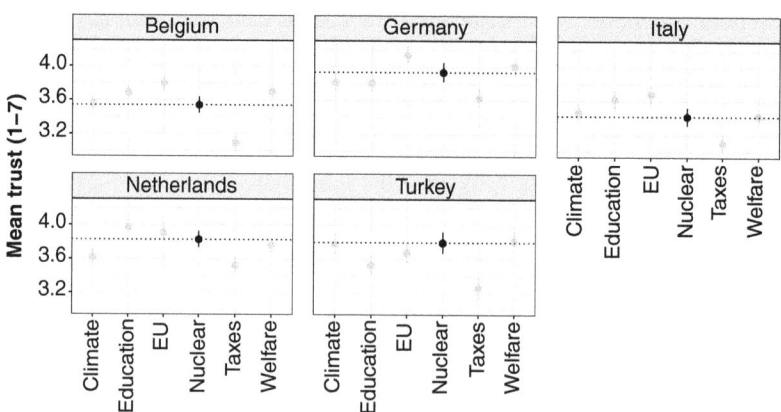

FIGURE 3.1 Trust in government to do the right thing.

the share of the population that trusts that the government will do the right thing in relation to nuclear disarmament, the percentage is 27–40 per cent in the host nations, much higher than for climate change and comparable with the welfare state.

This does not mean that somehow, miraculously, the disparity between government policy and public preferences does not matter or should not be concerning but rather that there are parallels between nuclear weapons and other areas of public policy. Arguing about public opposition to nuclear policy taps into public dissatisfaction with *everything* that the government does. The parallelism between nuclear policy and climate policy, for instance, is not surprising, given that both are areas where government action has been, for a long time, not living up to stated commitments.[22] Despite some specificities of the nuclear field, the key element remains – the public largely does not trust that the government will do the right thing in many key areas of public policy.

Knowledge on Nuclear Weapons Is Limited

This survey was in one way different from those conducted by other researchers (but also by me). Respondents were explicitly asked a number of knowledge questions first. These were supposed to test their knowledge about the basics of NATO and nuclear weapons, not to be an in-depth test of how well the respondents know the risks associated with nuclear weapons. There were three basic questions: first, respondents were asked to identify NATO countries in a list that included France, the survey country, a randomly selected country from the other host nations, and Russia. Second, they were supposed to say how many countries possess nuclear weapons today (5, 9, 15, or 20). And, last, they were told that the US is believed to station nuclear weapons outside its territory and asked to identify these countries. The responses included France, the survey country, a randomly selected country from other host nations, and Poland.

---

[22] See also Pelopidas and Verschuren (2023).

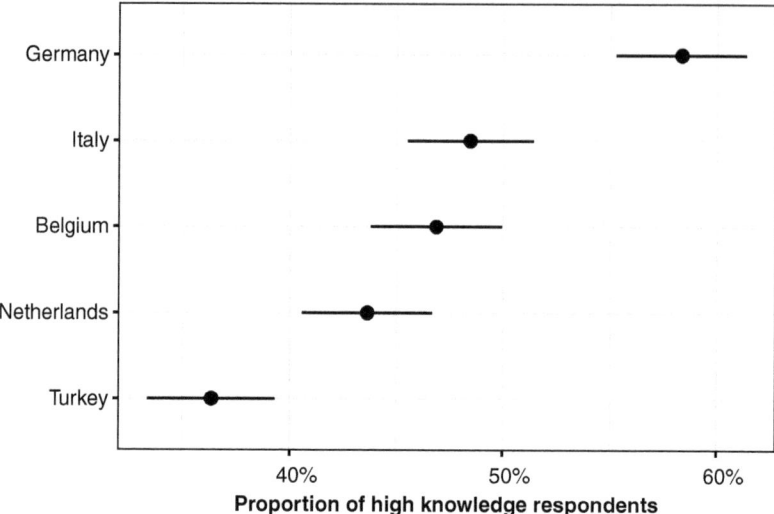

FIGURE 3.2 Public knowledge about nuclear weapons.

I used this scale to calculate the *knowledge* score, which was used in the analysis and ran from 0 to 9. Figure 3.2 shows the share of the population in each country that can be categorised as having high knowledge (a score of 5 or higher). German respondents had the highest level of knowledge and Turkish ones the lowest, which corresponds with the perception of salience of nuclear weapons in these countries.

After this knowledge element, respondents were informed that while the presence of nuclear weapons in their country has never been confirmed by its government or the US, researchers believe that this is true. A link to the most recent article from the Federation of American Scientists' overview, produced by Hans Kristensen and Matt Korda, was included.[23] Afterward, respondents were asked a few questions about their views of nuclear weapons.

First, they were asked whether they believed that the nuclear weapons stationed in their country deter nuclear and nonnuclear

[23] Kristensen and Korda (2023a)

attacks against NATO countries, on a six-point scale from 'disagree strongly' to 'agree strongly'. Second, they were asked to imagine a military conflict between NATO and Russia in the Baltics and whether they thought that the use of nuclear weapons stationed in their country would be legitimate in two scenarios:

- As a demonstrative explosion over an unpopulated area to de-escalate in an attempt to stop an ongoing Russian invasion of the Baltic countries
- As a demonstrative explosion over an unpopulated area to respond to a similar demonstrative nuclear explosion conducted by Russia

These offer a variation between the first and second use scenario but in a setting that is otherwise very similar. Again, respondents were asked to respond on the same six-point scale from 'disagree strongly' to 'agree strongly'. And, last, respondents were asked to reply (this time on a seven-point scale, thus with a midpoint) to five proposals about possible withdrawal:

- US nuclear weapons in [survey country] should not be withdrawn under any circumstance.
- US nuclear weapons in [survey country] can be withdrawn if there are additional reinforcements by US troops.
- US nuclear weapons in [survey country] can be withdrawn if NATO European countries, including [survey country], strengthen their military capabilities.
- US nuclear weapons in [survey country] can be withdrawn if the US and Russia agree on further arms control steps.
- US nuclear weapons should be withdrawn without any preconditions.

These questions build on batteries of questions asked in previous surveys and test – simply but reliably – how individuals think about three main questions related to nuclear weapons: whether they deter conflict, whether they would be willing to use them, and under what conditions they would want to have them removed.[24]

---

[24] These roughly track questions that I have used in published work with Michal Smetana and Tom Etienne.

PUBLIC ATTITUDES TOWARDS NUCLEAR WEAPONS

First, I begin with mapping how the public in the five host nations views nuclear weapons along the dimensions discussed. In the tables, I present the share of the population that holds favourable views – hence dichotomising responses from a more detailed scale.

However, it might be useful to remind the reader that this survey was undertaken after the start of Russia's invasion of Ukraine. The salience of nuclear weapons increased drastically, which also translated into more hawkish views of them among the general public.[25] One should therefore consider that the values measured in 2023 might be somewhat higher than if they had been measured earlier – as explained in the previous section.

Let us start with the first question, focused on the deterrent function. The results from the five host countries show some variation in how respondents view this. In Germany, the Netherlands, and Turkey, a majority (albeit not a very substantial one) sees that nuclear weapons deter both nuclear and nonnuclear attacks. In Belgium and Italy, a majority sees a deterrent function only against nonnuclear attacks. Table 3.1 indicates the spread across different countries.

These results are useful inasmuch as they indicate that the European publics are far from uniform on this issue. Diving deeper on patterns across the five countries reveals important differences. Belgium and the Netherlands show a decreasing trend with age in

Table 3.1 *Public views of deterrent function of nuclear weapons*

	Belgium (%)	Germany (%)	Italy (%)	The Netherlands (%)	Turkey (%)
Deters nonnuclear attacks	47	56	49	54	53
Deters nuclear attacks	52	56	49	56	56

[25] See, for instance, Onderco et al. (2023).

viewing the nuclear weapons as a deterrent, against both nonnuclear and nuclear attacks. The youngest respondents were most likely to see them as a deterrent. In Germany, Italy, and Turkey, young adults (aged 25–44) were most likely to see them as deterring attacks. Interestingly, for respondents aged 55 or older, the views are more or less similar across Belgium, Germany, Italy, and the Netherlands.

A similar difference is observed for gender. In Belgium, Germany, Italy, and the Netherlands, men are much more likely to see a deterrent value. The difference is sometimes rather stark – for instance, in the Netherlands, this was only 47 per cent of women but 62 per cent of men. When it came to deterrence against nuclear attacks, the difference was 10 percentage points (51 vs. 61 per cent). Turkey is the only country where such gender differences are not visible.

The differences between various groups based on education are not significant, except for Germany. There, about three-fourths of highly educated but only around 46 per cent of low-educated respondents think that nuclear weapons deter against nuclear and nonnuclear attacks.

Moving on to the views on the use of nuclear weapons, the differences between the five countries, surprisingly, almost disappear, as can be seen in Table 3.2. The approval rate is somewhat higher for a first-strike compared to a second-strike scenario, which might reflect considerations about potential escalation dynamics. The share of the population willing to consider some form of nuclear use is also higher compared to earlier surveys that I conducted with my collaborators. One potential explanation lies in the growing

Table 3.2 *Public views of nuclear weapons use*

	Belgium (%)	Germany (%)	Italy (%)	The Netherlands (%)	Turkey (%)
First strike	39	41	33	42	44
Second strike	39	42	32	39	42

salience of nuclear weapons during the war in Ukraine, and another might be the scenario of an explosion over an unpopulated area.

Again, a deeper dive indicates that in Turkey, the proportion of the public that would see nuclear use as legitimate varies very little across different age groups (with a somewhat lower support among respondents aged 45–55 in both scenarios). The situation is different in the other four countries. In Germany, support is relatively low in the youngest age category (34 per cent for the first strike and 41 per cent for the second), increases for 25–34- and 34–45-year-olds (to a rather staggering 67 per cent support for the second-strike scenario among the former), and then rapidly declines in the higher age groups. In Belgium, Italy, and the Netherlands, the decline is rather gradual with age, and young respondents are the most hawkish; the oldest respondents are the most reluctant to approve nuclear use.

The gender patterns are unexpected. In Belgium, Italy, and the Netherlands, men are more hawkish. However, the reverse is true in Turkey and Germany. The difference is quite large for Germany; female respondents were 4–7 percentage points more willing to find the use of nuclear weapons legitimate. However, there are no major differences across the different levels of education, except for Germany, where highly educated respondents were about twice as likely to approve the use of nuclear weapons.

Last, let us look at the withdrawal option. The answers to these questions indicate that it remains popular among Europeans. Support is also higher than in other public opinion surveys, especially in scenarios involving military reinforcements and unconditional withdrawal.[26] Again, the dynamic of the war in Ukraine might explain a part of the pattern. While Europeans show a relatively high level of readiness to support the use of these weapons (as shown), they are also rather supportive of withdrawal. A fairly puzzling picture emerges, as can be seen in Table 3.3.

---

[26] Compare with, for instance, Onderco et al. (2023) and Onderco (2024).

Table 3.3 *Public views of nuclear weapons withdrawal*

	Belgium (%)	Germany (%)	Italy (%)	The Netherlands (%)	Turkey (%)
Never withdraw	65	65	47	64	51
Withdraw with US reinforcements	63	66	54	62	64
Withdraw with European reinforcements	65	72	62	69	68
Withdraw with arms control	67	75	71	75	73
Withdraw unconditionally	63	69	70	67	80

Looking at the individual demographic categories does show only limited variation. When it comes to age, the only category with a consistent variation is withdrawal with US reinforcements and unconditional withdrawal. For the latter, support is consistently the highest among respondents aged 25–34 and 35–44 (which is interesting given that these groups are also among those most likely to support the use of nuclear weapons). For withdrawal with US reinforcements, in Belgium, support declines with age. In all other countries, the second-youngest group (25–34) is the most supportive, and relative support declines thereafter. In all countries and all scenarios, highly educated respondents seemed to be more supportive of withdrawal.

These data show that in 2023, public views of nuclear weapons in Europe were mixed. On the one hand, respondents see the deterrent function more clearly and are also more willing to support their use. At the same time, respondents would also like to see them withdrawn, often regardless of the scenario. This creates an image of a very charged and highly malleable situation, which might go in a number of different directions once the dust on the war in Ukraine settles. However, before talking about the war's effect, let us look at the possible explanations of these public views.

EXPLAINING PUBLIC OPINION

Scholars of international relations have often been dismissive of studying and explaining public opinion, as it is seen as too fickle and unstable.[27] The early Almond-Lippmann consensus (after its main proponents) held that public views on nuclear weapons were too volatile, unstructured, and ultimately inconsequential.[28] Scholars have only slowly started to challenge this view.[29]

One reason for this scepticism was the low level of knowledge about policy issues among the general public. This is true about major themes of foreign policy. Take the example of the EU – citizens are not only often poorly informed about what is happening in Brussels but also often incorrect about the basics of EU policy-making.[30] If this is true about the relatively more open world of the EU, it certainly applies even more strongly to the opaque world of nuclear policy. Scholars have, for a long time, decried the excessive use of secrecy when it comes to even most basic elements of nuclear policy, which has often made a reasoned discussion very difficult.[31] Just as an example, NATO did not declassify the *name* of its annual nuclear exercise ('Steadfast noon') until 2021, and this was after two years of debates in the NPG.

In the situations where citizens lack detailed knowledge, they rely on various heuristics to make sense of the world, which help develop views on individual policies even in the absence of detailed knowledge. They use such heuristics also to make sense of foreign policy, such as nuclear policy. As a result, public opinion becomes not only structured but also based on certain fixed principles. Individuals hold certain core beliefs, which tend to remain stable, but they translate these core beliefs into policy beliefs that are easier to change.[32]

---

[27] Almond (1950); Holsti (1992); Aldrich et al. (2006)
[28] Holsti (1992)
[29] Zaller (1992)
[30] Auel et al. (2018); de Wilde and Raunio (2018); Stoeckel et al. (2023)
[31] Dahl (1985)
[32] Hurwitz and Peffley (1987)

In this chapter, I test three potential explanations for how individuals think about nuclear weapons.

The first one links that viewpoint to fundamental foreign policy attitudes. As research has shown, including in Europe, individual views of international politics can be structured along a set of fundamental beliefs about the world.[33] The study of public opinion on foreign policy originated in the US. There, traditionally, the divide was among those who favoured involvement in the world (internationalists) and those who opposed it (isolationists). However, a shift in public view led to a discussion not about whether but *how* to be involved. As Wittkopf argued in 1981, the two faces of internationalism were militant and cooperative.[34] That framework became dominant in the study of foreign policy attitudes. It is likely that both cooperative and militant internationalism affect how individuals think about nuclear sharing. For cooperative internationalism (CI), the cooperation with other NATO countries is relevant, and nuclear sharing underscores this element. For militant internationalism (MI), the 'nuclear' element becomes dominant, which might influence views of nuclear weapons. Having said this, isolationism does remain an important and distinct element of worldviews – it is different from the lack of internationalism.[35]

I propose that these fundamental attitudes influence how individuals view nuclear sharing. Those who score high on CI will view the deterrent value positively, but CI will have no (or a negative) effect on use and the idea of withdrawal. Because individuals who score high on MI tend to be more positively attuned to the use of force in international politics,[36] I expect that they will have positive views on the deterrent value, use, and conditional but not unconditional

---

[33] Gravelle et al. (2017)
[34] Wittkopf (1981)
[35] Gravelle et al. (2017); Kertzer (2013); Gravelle et al. also argue that there is a fourth dimension – which they call the 'global justice dimension'. Unfortunately, in my survey, the factor analysis demonstrates only weak loading of items on this factor. I have therefore dropped this dimension.
[36] Rathbun (2013)

withdrawal. Respondents who score high on isolationism likely will have positive views on the deterrent value but negative views on the use, and view withdrawal positively under any circumstances.

The next two explanations link to the property of nuclear sharing as a policy decided by technocrats, with very little input from the general public. As I explained in the previous chapter, nuclear sharing carries signs of a technocratic policy.[37] Furthermore, it is undertaken on behalf of an international organisation – NATO – which further opens it to contestation. In principle, one could see this as a special case of contestation of international organisations – a very fruitful field of study in recent years.[38] This means that the policy can be opposed (or supported) based on how respondents view the idea of technocracy or how international organisations.

By contrast, positive views of technocracy are often associated with the most idealised elements of how international organisations should work. These are developed by states to depoliticise decision-making and put it at arm's length from everyday politics. Nuclear sharing is a perfect epitome of such depoliticisation. Individuals who view technocracy positively are also more supportive of removing governance questions from elected officials, often seeing them as corrupt and inefficient.[39] Distrust of representative democracy reflects a preference for technocratic governance.[40] Citizens with a positive view of technocracy are more likely to view nuclear sharing as being governed by expertise and impartiality, the key elements of technocratic governance.

Therefore, I hypothesise that a more positive the view of technocracy means a more positive view of nuclear weapons but also higher willingness to use them (supposedly because of expert decision-making). By contrast, I expect that respondents with pro-technocratic views are more likely to support conditional but not

---

[37] On the definition of technocratic policy, see Heyne and Lobo (2021).
[38] Börzel and Zürn (2021); van der Veer and Meibauer (2023); Tallberg and Zürn (2019)
[39] Chiru and Enyedi (2021)
[40] Bertsou and Pastorella (2017)

unconditional withdrawal (without replacement). I also expect that a high level of knowledge about nuclear weapons would reinforce those tendencies.

The most concrete contestation of technocracy comes from the populists, who, with their view of 'pure people' as being opposed to 'corrupt elites',[41] are in direct opposition to technocratic policy-making. Yet because populism is a thin ideology, its connection to foreign policy views is more complex. As the work on populism and foreign policy argues, populists come in many shapes and forms.[42] Emerging work on nuclear weapons and populism argues that they show strong pro-nuclear attitudes.[43] If so, views supportive of muscular foreign policy should clash with their relatively reserved views about international organisations and international policy.[44]

However, I also expect that the policy would vary depending on respondent knowledge. I expect that populist respondents will have positive views on the deterrent value of nuclear weapons and their potential use, driven by pro-militaristic views, and also that because populism is often about national control, they will be in favour of withdrawal. I expect that high knowledge would have a moderating effect on those trends.

Using the survey cited earlier, I measured all of these items. I relied on the established scales measuring all of the attitudes. To measure fundamental foreign policy attitudes, I used the scales developed by Gravelle et al.[45] To measure populism, I used the widely used scale developed by Akkerman et al.[46] To measure technocratic attitudes, I used the scale developed by Bertsou and Caramani.[47] All three use a multidimensional measurement, including 3–6 items per scale.

---

[41] Mudde (2004)
[42] Destradi and Plagemann (2019); Ostermann and Stahl (2022)
[43] Meier and Vieluf (2021); Herzog and Sukin (2023)
[44] See van der Veer and Meibauer (2023).
[45] Gravelle et al. (2020, 2021)
[46] Akkerman et al. (2013)
[47] Bertsou and Caramani (2022). Because in Bertsou and Caramani's model, two variables do not load properly on their scale, I also dropped them from the analysis.

For each of the variables, a separate model was run for each country, with a battery of controls for potentially confounding variables, including age, gender, ideology, knowledge about nuclear weapons, and level of education.

The results can be found in Figures 3.3–3.5, which represent the so-called coefficient plot. Dots represent estimates, and the lines around them represent confidence intervals. If a line does not intersect with the zero vertical line, the respective variable has a statistically significant effect on the dependent variable. Such figures offers easier readability (and save more space) than a set of regression tables but do not offer information about the control variables.

In Figure 3.3, we can see that across all countries, CI is associated with views that nuclear weapons deter attacks. In all countries, it is also associated with higher willingness to approve the use of nuclear weapons. Support for a conditional withdrawal is statistically significant, but the evidence is mixed for unconditional withdrawal.

The situation is somewhat different with MI. Unsurprisingly, respondents who score high on this are more likely to see nuclear weapons as providing deterrence. They are also more likely to

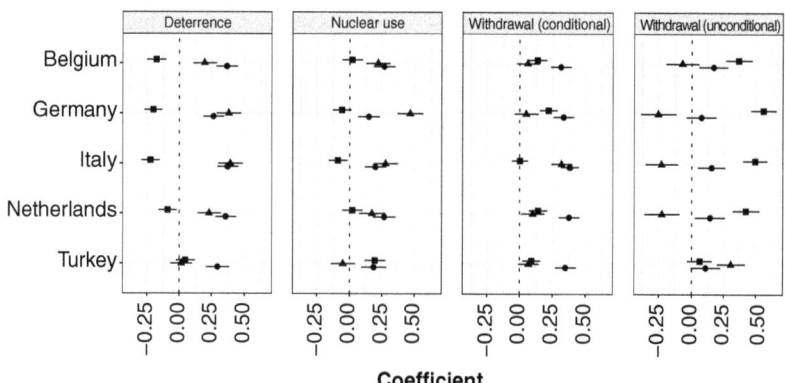

FIGURE 3.3 Coefficient plot: foreign policy attitudes.

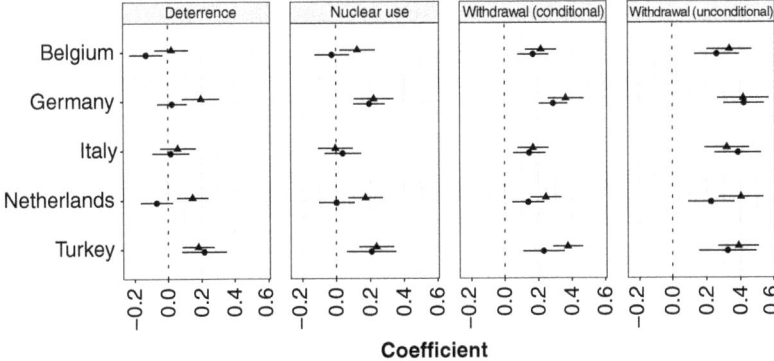

FIGURE 3.4 Coefficient plot: populism.

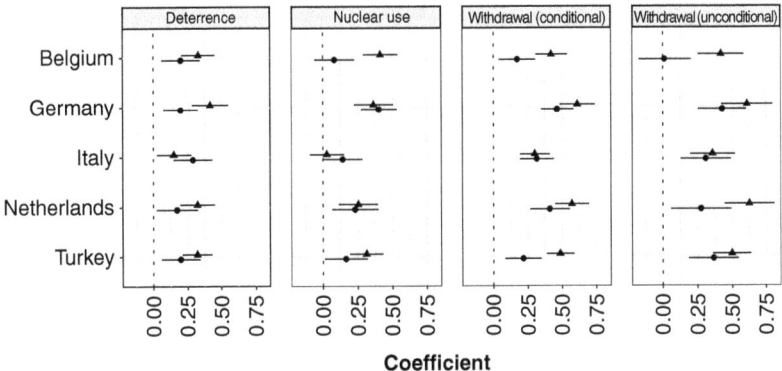

FIGURE 3.5 Coefficient plot: technocracy.

support nuclear use (though Turkey is an outlier in both settings). Surprisingly, respondents who score high on MI are also more likely to support conditional withdrawal, with the exception of Germany and Belgium. They are less likely to support unconditional withdrawal, save Belgium (where the result is not statistically significant) and Turkey (where they are more likely to support withdrawal). The association of MI with support for unconditional withdrawal from Turkey is not entirely surprising, given that the country possesses significant independent military force and on numerous occasions has been suggested as a candidate for nuclear proliferation.[48]

Isolationism is unexpectedly associated with the view that nuclear weapons do not provide deterrence (again, except for Turkey). It is also not associated with any particular views on nuclear use. In all countries but Belgium, isolationists are more likely to support a conditional withdrawal from their country's territory but not in other countries. However, with the exception of Turkey, they are significantly more likely to support unconditional withdrawal from their territory.

The results related to populism are not as straightforward as the scholarship would suggest. The results (Figure 3.4) related to the deterrent function are very mixed. In Germany, the Netherlands, and Turkey, populists with low knowledge about nuclear weapons see them as having stronger deterrent effect. In Belgium, Germany, and the Netherlands, the difference between the low- and high-knowledge populists is statistically significant. In Italy and Turkey, it is substantively very small and statistically insignificant. For use of nuclear weapons, in almost all countries (save Italy), low-knowledge populists are more likely to approve. However, the difference between the high- and low-knowledge populists is statistically significant only in Belgium and the Netherlands. In all countries except for Italy, populists are statistically significantly more likely to support using nuclear weapons. However, they are more likely to support a withdrawal in any scenario and in all countries. It is likely that the nationalism associated with populism kicks in here, and populists are driven by the desire to regain control and get rid of foreign weapons on their territory.[49]

Support for technocracy is associated positively with (almost) every single dependent variable. Supporters tend to see nuclear weapons as providing a deterrent function, exactly in line with the technocratic argument for nuclear sharing, and this trend is stronger

---

[48] Bugos (2019)
[49] Destradi and Plagemann (2019)

among those with lower knowledge about nuclear weapons. They are also likely to support nuclear use – a logical choice for someone who believes in deterrence, since successful deterrence requires a willingness to use the weapons. In four out of five host nations, the difference is very small; in Belgium, it is rather large and statistically significant. However, they are also more likely to support withdrawal, which might be linked to the idea that if any such step were to be taken, it would have been approved by the technocratic experts. Again, the difference between the low- and high-knowledge respondents is small, save for Belgium, where the trend is unexpectedly stronger for the former.

Overall, we observe some similarities among the host nations but also relevant differences. There are major similarities when it comes to the effect of populist and technocratic attitudes. However, the results are more mixed for fundamental foreign policy attitudes, underscoring that not only the distribution but also the effect of these attitudes varies across countries.

Russian Invasion of Ukraine and Support for Posture Changes
The Russian invasion of Ukraine has fundamentally changed how security is perceived in Europe. This is not entirely uncommon, as the role of focusing events in changing how individuals think about foreign policy is well known in the scholarship.[50] Political developments often lead to shifts in public opinion and often public views of what is good or bad.[51]

It is therefore not entirely surprising that the Russian invasion has led to a reconsideration of many foreign policy issues in Europe.[52] The most obvious was the desire of Finland and Sweden to enter NATO. In Germany, a special investment fund of 100 billion euros was announced as a central element of the *Zeitenwende*.[53]

---

[50] Kingdon (2014)
[51] Page and Shapiro (1992); Lambert et al. (2010, 2011); Erikson et al. (2002)
[52] Bunde (2022)
[53] Der Tagesspiegel (2022)

Last but not least, the war in Ukraine has led to significant shifts in how the European public has viewed international security, including nuclear weapons. Numerous surveys have demonstrated that European support for nuclear deterrence and nuclear sharing increased after the war's start.[54]

At the same time, the war has renewed debates about the need to adjust the nuclear deterrent posture in Europe. Arguments have been made in favour of expanding the nuclear sharing arrangements to Czechia and Poland.[55] In the latter case, even officials and policymakers came out in support of such a step, as did the public.[56] Experts have also discussed potential need for adjustment of the current nuclear deterrence postures.[57]

In this survey, respondents were given a set of questions about how they viewed nuclear sharing in the light of the war. They were asked whether they thought that the war showed that it was a good idea for the US to station weapons in Europe, it was important to do so, the current arrangements should be expanded, and their country should acquire nuclear weapons. They responded on a seven-point Likert scale.

The results, which can be found in Figure 3.6, are a mixed bag. When it comes to support for the current arrangements, the group of respondents who supported (agreed) and opposed (disagreed) that the war vindicated these were roughly equal. However, a significant group of respondents – in fact, a plurality – chose the midpoint, indicating that they neither agreed nor disagreed. This is the largest group for other questions as well.

The war is not linked to any increased support for proliferation. Neither vertical (acquisition of nuclear weapons by the respondents' country) nor horizontal proliferation attract much support. However, the midpoint is largely the most selected once again. What

---

[54] Onderco et al. (2023); Infratest-Dimap (2022)
[55] For Czechia, see Halás (2023); for Poland, see Kacprzyk (2023).
[56] Peters (2023); Sukin and Lanoszka (2022)
[57] Majnemer and Repussard (2023)

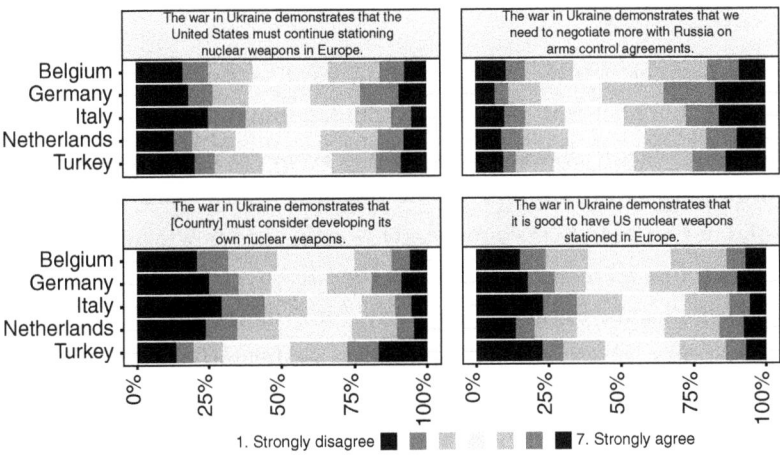

FIGURE 3.6 War in Ukraine, nuclear posture, and its adjustment.

citizens do support is arms control – arms control arrangements with Russia are highly and broadly supported, and Europeans clearly remain supportive of arms control agreements. The war might not have turned them completely against nuclear weapons, as some disarmament activists would prefer, but it has underscored the risks that highlighted the importance of arms control. In many ways, this public view gels with the view of many experts who note that arms control might be an option for rebuilding relations between the West and Russia after the war.[58]

Yet these findings also suggest that expanding nuclear sharing arrangements is likely to run into public opposition. While European publics do not see nuclear sharing as problematic, this might change rather quickly should the current arrangement expand. Furthermore, the plurality of respondents who place themselves in the middle, neither agreeing nor disagreeing, shows that public views are still somewhat fluid. This presents opportunities for governments and their public messaging but also for anti-nuclear activists and their campaigns.

[58] Pomper et al. (2022)

CONCLUSION

This chapter focused on the public view of nuclear weapons in Europe. I argued that, historically, public opinion has been squarely opposed, even if that stance was often based on insufficient factual knowledge. Nevertheless, public opposition has been strong and solid in European host countries. However, our knowledge about the attitudes in all host countries has been unequal. Despite abundant surveys in some of them – Germany, for instance – there have been almost none in others, such as Turkey. Comparative surveys across multiple countries were even scarcer. This created a real gap in our understanding of public opinion related to nuclear weapons.

Public opinion started to shift after the Russian invasion of Ukraine. Surveys have shown that at least in some European countries – such as Germany and the Netherlands – it changed significantly after the war. This chapter presented results from a unique and new public opinion survey that mapped attitudes towards nuclear weapons in all host nations. The main goal was to compare the main similarities and differences in public opinion in these countries and whether the drivers of such attitudes vary across the host nations.

The results indicate that, despite the public opposition to nuclear weapons, the public views are not uniform. This is highly important from the policy perspective, as it shows that various attitudes and experiences enable different communication styles from the policymakers. Similarly, the findings indicate that while differences between individual host nations exist, they are not dramatic. Italy came out as a country with the most nuclear-sceptic public, but it is not out of step with others when it comes to the preferences related to the withdrawal of nuclear weapons.

I tried to explain these public views, using fundamental foreign policy attitudes, technocracy, and populism. For the former, the results were somewhat mixed and not consistent across the five countries. However, I did show that both populism and technocracy are both strong drivers of public views of nuclear weapons, their use, and potential withdrawal.

The results confirm the theoretical expectations – the views of technocracy influence how individuals view nuclear weapons. This is not entirely trivial as it demonstrates that nuclear sharing faces not unique challenges but instead the forces that often oppose other activities of multilateral and international organisations. As a policy with signs of technocracy, it unsurprisingly draws opposition by those who dislike governance by experts and instead appeal to popular sovereignty.

In Chapter 4, I will discuss how public opinion overlaps with the views expressed by political parties and in the parliamentary debates, and in Chapter 7, I will return to this debate by looking at how elites reflect this contestation in public opinion.

4 Political Parties

INTRODUCTION

> Nuclear deterrence has never worked and cannot work at all because it cannot be credible. What should be the scenario in which we would use atomic bombs in Europe? ... What an absurd idea that German pilots would carry nuclear weapons from Büchel toward the East to drop them there, and in doing so kill millions of people and to contaminate the environment for generations? ... Nuclear deterrence is an aberration. NATO will have to abandon this aberration, and sooner rather than later![1]

Katja Keul, a German Green member of Parliament (MP) and its Defence Committee, was having her day in the plenary chamber of the German Bundestag. It was a cold winter January day, with some flurries in the sky, and the Bundestag was discussing whether Germany should join the TPNW, based on the request of the far-left Left party. The parliament did not vote that day, but the discussion was heated, as if a decision were to be made by the end of the day. Keul was the most passionate of all speakers, just like she had been many times before when issues of nuclear disarmament had been debated before the chamber. A few months later, Keul became the state secretary at the foreign ministry, responsible for relations with the Parliament.[2]

---

[1] Deutscher Bundestag (2021b, p. 21693)

[2] In this chapter, I refer to the members of legislative chambers as members or 'MPs', regardless of their official titles in their home countries. For variation, I refer to the different parliamentary chambers as Parliament, their official name, or their official English translation. Unless indicated otherwise, I always refer to lower chambers in the case of bicameral systems. Whenever referring to upper chambers, I denote these as Senate or their official name and their members as 'Senators'.

Keul's impassioned speech was both surprising – and not. It was surprising because the parliamentary role in foreign policy in Europe has been traditionally limited and circumscribed. While scholarship on their involvement in foreign policy has been steadily increasing in the last two decades, parliaments are generally not the locus of action for any foreign policy activity. By contrast, their role has been usually restricted, based on the understanding that governments need freedom to defend national interests, and secrecy is often preferred over public discussions. To US political scientists, the notion of 'politics stopping at the water's edge' will be familiar.[3] Often, the parliaments' role has been limited to ratifying treaties, and approving military deployments.[4] In the European setting, parliaments have been usually restrained to a handful of roles: limiting war powers,[5] participating in European affairs through specialised committees,[6] occasionally joining government delegations to support international negotiations,[7] and engaging in 'parliamentary diplomacy' – building relations with other parliaments.[8] However, compared to other areas of public policy, parliaments are usually significantly less involved with foreign policy. Foreign policy also lacks the distributional dimension, well known from the US, where base locations generate tangible material interests for elected politicians.[9] In Europe, where most parliamentarians are elected on the basis of party lists, such incentives are mostly lacking.

At the same time, parliaments have in recent years become more important in foreign policy execution. This is often linked to the growing pressure on governments to consider a broad set of opinions in formulating foreign policy, partially driven by the rise of

---

[3] For a paradigmatic statement applicable to Europe, see Keman (1986).
[4] Wagner et al. (2010); Peters et al. (2010); Raunio and Wagner (2017)
[5] Dieterich et al. (2010, 2015)
[6] Auel and Christiansen (2015); Karlas (2011)
[7] Götz (2011); Onderco (2018); Baehr (1969)
[8] Götz (2005); Weisglas and de Boer (2007); Stavridis and Jančić (2017)
[9] Eaves (2021)

populism in Europe.[10] The societal contestation of foreign policy has increased. While this applies to the greatest degree to the contestation of European integration, which has moved from 'permissive consensus' to 'constraining dissensus',[11] it also applies to other areas of foreign policy, including security policy. Therefore, the role of parties in foreign policy has increased significantly.[12]

This growing role of parties has also translated to the growing realisation that parties matter for nuclear weapons. Nuclear weapons were intensely debated during the Cold War, in the parliaments of all countries in which they were deployed, simply because they were an intensely salient issue at that time. This applied primarily in Europe but also in Japan.[13] Yet oddly enough, scholarship has neither reflected nor studied the role of parties in depth. Scholars have noted that in countries possessing nuclear weapons, parliaments do have a certain role, particularly in shaping the force structure through budgetary votes and approving officials who are then in charge of designing strategies, but they also, for instance, do not have powers linked to a nuclear launch.[14] Such work has not been done in the host nations. This is somewhat surprising given the now ample evidence that partisan ideology matters quite strongly for public views on nuclear weapons.[15] In the post-Cold War period, only scant attention was paid to parliaments, parties, and nuclear weapons based in Europe.[16]

In this chapter, I will look into the preferences and actions of political parties, and by extension of parliaments, on issues related to nuclear weapons since 2010. I will first explain what the scholarship and theory say about the role of parties and their hypothetical views on nuclear weapons. I will follow up by mapping their

---

[10] Henke and Maher (2021)
[11] Hooghe and Marks (2009)
[12] Hofmann and Martill (2021)
[13] Yost and Glad (1982); Colbourn (2022); Kurosaki (2020)
[14] Born et al. (2011)
[15] Baron and Herzog (2020); Onderco et al. (2022)
[16] See, for instance, Onderco and Joosen (2022)

preferences, on the basis of party manifestos and interviews with MPs. Last, I will look at parliamentary votes on issues related to nuclear weapons.

WHY AND HOW DO PARTIES VARY?

In recent years, scholars have demonstrated that parties vary in their views on foreign policy.[17] The differences reflect both the material preferences of parties – whether money should be allocated to guns or butter, to use a well-known analogy, but also, more fundamentally, how to think about the world. In this discussion, the left–right axis appears to have been the most appropriate to map the distinctions among the parties. As the pioneers in this field, Canadian political scientists Jean-Philippe Thérien and Alain Noël argue, the left–right axis remains dominant and is 'the most enduring and comprehensive way of mapping belief systems'.[18] Scholars argue that it has kept its explanatory power, despite the emergence of other competitors, such as the so-called gal versus tan dimension ('gal' stands for green-alternative-liberal, and 'tan' stands for traditional-authoritarian-nationalist).[19]

When it comes to security policy, the main distinctions seem to come down to the fundamental beliefs about the world. As US international relations scholar Brian Rathbun has argued in his numerous works, representatives in left-wing parties have a fundamentally different worldview compared to those on the right.[20] They seem to build it around what Robert Jervis called the 'spiral model', which underscores the deleterious effects of the security dilemma and calls for sensitivity to it. This sensitivity makes actors aware that their own actions might have effects on their counterparts and they therefore become more cautious about appearing too

---

[17] For the most fundamental works, see Rathbun (2004); Hofmann (2013); Wagner (2020).
[18] Noël and Thérien (2023, p. 151)
[19] Aspinwall (2007); for argument that the left–right dimension captures conflict over foreign policy better than gal–tan, see Wagner et al. (2018).
[20] Rathbun (2004, 2012)

aggressive, in order not to spook their counterparts into actions that would bring negative consequences to both parties.[21] Left-wing parties also tend to be more trusting of their counterparts and feel a moral obligation to cooperate in international politics.[22] This link has been abundantly shown to apply when it comes to security policy, where left-wing parties are generally more sceptical about military interventions and more likely to vote against them – with a notable exception when it comes to humanitarian interventions.[23]

The left-wing aversion to the use of force extends to nuclear weapons as well. During the Cold War, the left-wing parties and caucuses were often at the forefront of the contestation of nuclear weapons in Europe, especially in Germany but also in the Netherlands.[24] In studying public opinion, I have found with my co-authors that voters who identified as being on the political left were less willing to approve the use of nuclear weapons in a conflict compared to their right-wing counterparts.[25]

The right-wing parties, according to Rathbun, tend to espouse a different outlook on the world, rooted in a competing Jervis model – the so-called deterrence model.[26] It underscores preparedness for war, and by extension, focuses on armaments. Right-wing governments tend to see the world in more nationalist and sovereignist terms, which usually hinders international cooperation.[27] They are also more positive towards the military as a tool of foreign policy, therefore supporting military spending.[28] As Wolfgang Wagner and his collaborators show, right-wing parties are also more willing to support military intervention abroad.[29]

---

[21] For Jervis's spiral model, see Jervis (1976). For more work on security dilemma sensitivity, see Booth and Wheeler (2008).
[22] Rathbun (2012); Bayram (2017)
[23] Mello (2012); Wagner (2020); Fonck et al. (2019); Rathbun (2004)
[24] On Germany, see Risse-Kappen (1983); on the Netherlands, see Everts (1984).
[25] Onderco et al. (2022)
[26] Jervis (1976)
[27] Fordham and Flynn (2023)
[28] Wenzelburger and Böller (2020)
[29] Wagner et al. (2018)

Again, this general proclivity to support the use of force extends to nuclear weapons. During the Cold War, German conservative and right-wing parties were more strongly in favour of nuclear deterrence against the Soviet threat.[30] However, the pattern of right-wing voters (and voters of right-wing parties) being more positive about nuclear weapons applies in other settings too. Recalling my own work with the co-authors cited earlier, we found that the right-wing voters in Europe were more willing to support the use of nuclear weapons in hypothetical scenarios.[31] However, scholars working on other Western countries found similar results, particularly in the US.[32]

Therefore, I expect that the positions of political parties will yield significant voter differences on issues related to nuclear sharing that will mainly run along the left–right axis.

PARTY PREFERENCES

The scholarship on nuclear weapons in Europe has conspicuously avoided systematically studying the positioning of political parties on this issue. Even though mentions of party politics and partisanship abound, there is only a very limited attempt to measure them comparatively.

Comparative politics scholars would resort to one of the major quantitative databases to study party positions, such as the Comparative Manifesto Project (CMP) or Chapel Hill Expert Survey (CHES).[33] These two datasets represent the two major approaches to the study of party positions. Whereas the CMP bases its data on the analysis of party manifestos released ahead of elections, CHES relies on expert judgements to score party positions on various issues. Both are generally seen as reliable and valid approaches. However,

---

[30] Kelleher (1975)
[31] Onderco et al. (2022)
[32] Press et al. (2013); Sagan and Valentino (2017); Koch and Wells (2021); Haworth et al. (2019)
[33] For CMP, see Lehmann et al. (2023b). For CHES, see Jolly et al. (2022).

unfortunately, neither considered party positioning on nuclear weapons as a relevant factor. This oversight is not entirely surprising, as nuclear weapons are not an entirely salient issue for public debate, and party manifestos vary in length.

In the absence of readily available data, I use the approach of scholars who have comparatively studied party positioning on issues as diverse as the welfare state or Russia.[34] In particularly, I rely on the offshoot of the CMP, the Manifesto Corpus.[35] It slices all manifestos into 'quasi-sentences', which are meaningful chunks of text. Together with a small army of research assistants, we found all quasi-sentences that referred to nuclear weapons.[36] My assistants all were either native speakers of the languages of the host nations or had near-native fluency thanks to long-term residency in the country. We identified all the mentions and pruned those that used the word 'nuclear' but in a context that was not relevant (for instance, 'nuclear family'). The cutoff date for the manifesto collection was 15 May 2023, which meant that we did not include, for instance, those published before the late autumn 2023 elections in the Netherlands.

There were 148 quasi-sentences referring to nuclear weapons in the parties of all host nations since 2000. While a majority of these mentioned nuclear weapons in their national context or that of NATO, numerous references were made to Iran's nuclear programme or the general threat of nuclear proliferation. This showed that nuclear weapons are not a particularly salient issue for party competition. In most elections, only a handful of countries mentioned them at all. Figure 4.1 shows the distribution of these mentions over time and across parties. One pattern is that nuclear weapons are much more salient in some countries (the Netherlands, Belgium, and

---

[34] On the welfare state, see Horn et al. (2017). On Russia, see Onderco (2019).
[35] Lehmann et al. (2023a) Some party manifestos are missing from the database.
[36] As I discovered in an earlier project, the R package provided by the CMP does not properly split the manifestos into quasi-sentences, and some manifestos are entered as a single quasi-sentence. Therefore, using the R package is not suitable.

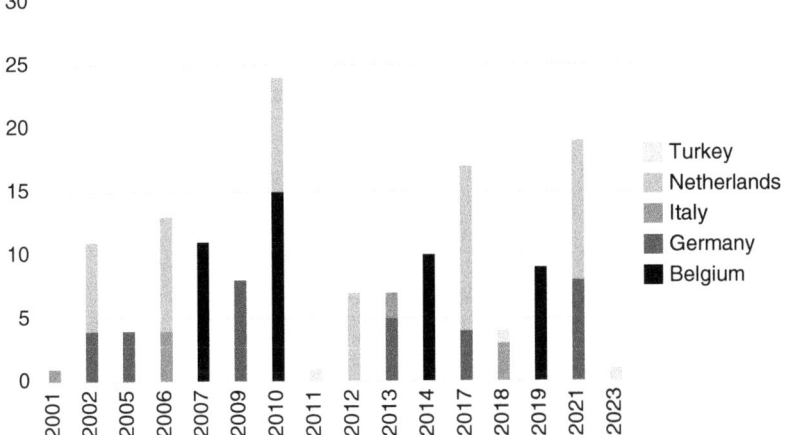

FIGURE 4.1 Distribution of mentions of nuclear weapons in party manifestos over time.

Germany are the top scorers) and that the pattern of salience changes over time, but there is no obvious logic to it.

Similarly, most of the mentions were made by parties leaning left. Using the classification provided by the CMP itself, a vast majority (91 out of 148) mentions were in the manifestos of ecological, left, and social democratic parties, compared to forty-five references found in the manifestos of liberal and Christian democratic parties.

Given the low number of quasi-sentences, it would be difficult to validly and reliably analyse them using quantitative tools, such as recoding. I have therefore opted to provide an overview of party positions via a qualitative analysis of the manifestos. However, I have also combined these insights with information from interviews with parliamentarians, civil servants, and experts that I conducted between September 2023 and March 2024. In the analysis, I will review the positions of the principal political parties from the five host nations since 2010 (from left to right); wherever relevant, I will note if these positions vary from those pursued in 2000–2010.

Radical Left, Socialist, and Green Parties

The category most to the left comprises the radical left, socialist, and green parties. Even though these parties are not among the key players in their national political systems (with a few notable exceptions), a full third of all mentions of nuclear weapons in party programmes comes from them. Most of them are strongly in favour of removing nuclear weapons from their home countries.

In Belgium, the Walloon green party Ecolo argued, in 2010, for building a European defence and security policy based, inter alia, on the 'rejection of nuclear weapons', 'bringing new life into ... disarmament on global scene' and a 'nuclear-weapon-free Europe'.[37] Its Flemish counterpart, Groen! held a similar but even more radical view. In its 2010 electoral platform, Groen! argued for 'Belgium to take a pioneering role in banning nuclear weapons from the world. A first step is the removal of tactical nuclear weapons from Belgium. ... We want Belgium to take active steps within NATO for the possibility of quick removal of nuclear weapons. ... During the review of the statute at the International Criminal Court we want the use of nuclear weapons to be labelled as a war crime.'[38] Groen! repeated this position in 2014, when its electoral manifesto argued that 'the nuclear weapons are, militarily speaking, entirely useless in Europe. Besides, they're expensive and dangerous.'[39] In 2019, Groen! again reiterated its position, arguing for banning nuclear weapons, signing the TPNW, and removing nuclear weapons from Belgian soil.[40] Groen!'s Walloon counterpart, however, did not reflect on these issues in its party platform. Both Ecolo and Groen! were represented in Parliament but in opposition to the ruling government. The Workers' Party (PVDA), the other left-wing party in Parliament that has been in opposition (but steadily growing since

[37] Ecolo (2010)
[38] Groen (2010)
[39] Groen (2014)
[40] Groen (2019)

its entry into Parliament in 2014), has also opposed nuclear sharing. In its 2014 manifesto, it labelled the nuclear weapons stationed in Belgium as 'outdated' and called for 'withdrawal … no modernisation … a ban' on nuclear weapons on Belgian soil.[41]

In Italy, too, parties on the left were supportive of nuclear disarmament. In 2013, Left Ecology Freedom, a radical left party created by breakaways from the former Communist Party, spoke out in favour of an international treaty to ban nuclear weapons.[42] Other radical left-wing parties, Free and Equal and Italy Europe Together, in 2018 committed to ratifying the TPNW.[43] That these parties were not very popular among voters is evidenced by how, at the time of writing, none of them still exist. The radical newcomer in the left-wing populist Five Star Movement has not discussed nuclear deterrence directly but been consistently opposed to procuring JSF. This has made it, by proxy, opposed to nuclear deterrence, but it never framed it that way.[44] As the Italian case shows, it is very possible that deterrence might be simply too conflictual for the parties or their principles.

In Germany and the Netherlands, these issues were also more contentious, because the parties at this end of the political spectrum are more plentiful and also attract a larger share of voters.

In the Netherlands, the green parties are represented by GroenLinks (GL). The GL is a fairly traditional green party in its foreign policy outlook. Since 2002, it has expressed strong opposition to nuclear weapons in the Netherlands and worldwide. In 2010, it called for an end to Dutch participation in the NATO nuclear weapon mission.[45] This was repeated in 2012 when it called for abolition of Dutch participation in the NATO nuclear mission and favoured the global ban on nuclear weapons.[46] Since 2017, it has

---

[41] Partij van de Arbeid (2014)
[42] Sinistra Ecologia Libertà (2013)
[43] Liberi e Uguali (2018); Italia Europa Insieme (2018)
[44] For its defence policy and curious pacifism, see Coticchia and Vignoli (2020b).
[45] GroenLinks (2010)
[46] GroenLinks (2012)

called for signing the TPNW and withdrawing from NATO's nuclear umbrella.[47] Although not a green party per se, the Dutch Party for the Animals (PvdD) is a small animal rights party. Unsurprisingly perhaps, the PvdD has been a consistently pro-disarmament party, advocated for the removal of weapons from the Dutch soil, and signing the TPNW.[48]

The Dutch Socialist Party (SP) holds similar views. In its electoral manifestos, the SP called for a worldwide elimination of nuclear weapons, including nuclear disarmament, and 'return[ing] the US nuclear weapons on Dutch soil'.[49] In 2012, it even called on NATO to abandon its nuclear doctrine 'because it does not contribute to maintaining and promoting peace and security'.[50] Since the TPNW was opened for signature, the SP has called for ratifying it and making sure that JSF aircraft are not assigned a nuclear mission.[51] At least in the case of the SP, the position is at least partially driven by the opposition to NATO, which it called 'an aggressive intervention force'.[52] What does set the SP apart from other parties, however, is that nuclear weapons are a salient issue for it.

In my research, I came across only a small handful of parties where nuclear weapons mattered – and the SP was one of them. As a former MP explained to me, the SP has three reasons for keeping this issue on the agenda. First, it pushed for openness in policy-making, linked to the secrecy surrounding nuclear weapons arrangements, especially in the Netherlands. Second, it was linked to nuclear weapons as a weapon that is indiscriminate. And third, the party believes that disarmament contributes to a peaceful world.[53]

As this former MP explained, the SP is a party that is traditionally pacifist. 'In leftist circles, it has also long been *bonton* to say:

---

[47] GroenLinks (2017, 2021)
[48] See, for instance, Partij voor de Dieren (2017, 2021).
[49] Socialistische Partij (2010)
[50] Socialistische Partij (2012)
[51] Socialistische Partij (2017, 2021)
[52] Socialistische Partij (2021)
[53] Interview with a former MP, December 2023

I am against the armed forces, I am against defence ... with the SP, it was *bonton* to say: I am conscientious objector.'[54] According to this MP, it was electorally beneficial for the SP to distinguish itself from other parties, including the Labour Party, which was in power in the Netherlands in the period between 2012 and 2017. Interestingly – and I will return to this in Chapter 7 when discussing elites – the MP also recognised that if the SP's proposals were actually executed, it would be bad for the country. 'The Netherlands would bring itself into a vulnerable position', the MP told me. Asked whether, during their time in the Parliament, people seriously considered the security consequences of such proposals, the answer was squarely 'no, it was more of a political discussion' that held a highly symbolic value.[55]

Since 2021, at the national level, the Dutch left-wing scene has a new entrant, Bij1. Bij1 is the most radically left-wing party in the Dutch political system, focused primarily on antiracism and equality. Although it has not mentioned nuclear weapons in its manifesto, it *did* mention its interest in stepping out of NATO. Bij1 supported the resolution in the Amsterdam Municipal Council to support the ICAN Cities Appeal, which I will mention in the next chapter.

In Germany, the group of radical left and green parties has two very specific parties. First, the radical left Die Linke was born of the former East German Communist Party. Die Linke is sometimes seen by German experts as a populist left party.[56] It called, in 2009, for the destruction of all nuclear weapons on German territory, in 2013 and 2017 for their withdrawal, and in 2021 for an end to German participation in the NATO nuclear mission, including training pilots and procuring dual-capable aircraft.[57] In 2021, Die Linke was also in favour of signing the TPNW.[58] Despite its pro-disarmament

---

[54] Interview with a former Dutch MP
[55] Interview with a former Dutch MP
[56] Thomeczek (2025)
[57] Die Linke (2009, 2013, 2017, 2021)
[58] Die Linke (2021)

credentials, Die Linke is in a rather specific position, as it is not a sought-out partner, as I will explain in the following subsection, due to its radical left background.

The other party at this end of the German political spectrum are the Greens (Bündnis 90/Die Grünen), another party for which nuclear weapons are a highly significant and salient topic, partially because the party base is split on how it views them.[59] The German Greens have come through the most significant transformation in the last five years, perhaps of all parties in all European host nations. As German expert Giorgio Franceschini, who was working for the Green Party's Heinrich Boell Foundation for a long time, wrote, based on the Greens' views, it was reasonable to expect that the German 'traffic light' coalition that had emerged from the 2021 elections would abolish German participation in nuclear sharing. Instead, the coalition doubled down on it by committing to procure the JSF, a decision driven in no small part by the Greens.[60]

The history of the Green Party is very deeply connected to the German peace movement. The connection, for instance, indicates that the Greens are still highly open to civil society. A German expert opined that there also seemed to be an overlap between membership in civil society organisations, such as ICAN, and the Green Party.[61] Despite no data for this, civil society representatives in interviews confirmed that they had succeeded in placing particular language into party resolutions at party congresses, which seems to support this expert observation.[62]

However, the party has developed a somewhat bifurcated position, split between the two wings of the party, so-called fundis and realos. The fundis were seen as the peaceniks, who were strongly in favour of disarmament. The realos got their name from the realist

---

[59] For a chapter-long treatment of the Greens' views on nuclear weapons, see Franceschini (2024).
[60] Franceschini (2024)
[61] Interview with a German expert, January 2024
[62] Interview with a NGO representative, January 2024

position, in which they were seen as not being fundamentally opposed to the military as a tool of nations' foreign policy. Following the merger with the moderate Bündnis 90, the realos improved their position within the party.[63] By the time of the Iraq War, the party still had a substantive fundi faction.[64] This was reflected in the party manifesto, which in 2002 still called for a 'new disarmament policy'.[65] In 2005, the position still included the withdrawal of all nuclear weapons from Germany and the creation of a nuclear weapons-free zone in Europe.[66] This position remained in the 2013 party manifesto.[67] In its 2017 manifesto, the Greens called for signing the TPNW, withdrawing all nuclear weapons from the Büchel Air Base, and ending participation in the NATO nuclear mission.[68] However, by 2021, this position, while reiterated, was placed very firmly in a long-term framework. 'Our aspiration is still nothing less than a world free of nuclear weapons', the relevant paragraph of the manifesto started.[69] The ambition to sign the TPNW was also represented by some party bigwigs, including Omid Nouripour, one of its most prominent thinkers on foreign policy.[70] However, the same manifesto indicated that 'a world without nuclear weapons can only be achieved through intermediate steps'. It committed Germany to participate in the TPNW MSPs as an observer, renew debates on nuclear deterrence, and introduce a no-first-use framework within NATO. However, curiously, it continued that 'we know that for this – also in view of Russia's conventional and nuclear armament – numerous talks are necessary within the Alliance, also with our European partner states, and above all the strengthening the security and reassurance of our Polish and Baltic allies'.[71]

---

[63] Frankland (1999)
[64] Kaarbo and Lantis (2003)
[65] Bündnis 90/Die Grünen (2002)
[66] Bündnis 90/Die Grünen (2005)
[67] Bündnis 90/Die Grünen (2013)
[68] Bündnis 90/Die Grünen (2017)
[69] Bündnis 90/Die Grünen (2021)
[70] Nouripour (2021)
[71] Bündnis 90/Die Grünen (2021)

As a German expert explained to me, there was a vigorous intraparty discussion, and while numerous realos who 'would never openly say, "I believe in deterrence", but they did believe in deterrence. ... And from that stemmed, I think, a more flexible stance when it came to nuclear issue. But they would never go out in public and say that we should keep nuclear sharing.'[72] The Greens believed 'you could have the cake and eat it too'. 'You could be for deterrence, you could be for some level of conventional armament, for less money, more European and still, you know, make progress on nuclear issues.'[73] While the shift in the Green Party started in 2014, it accelerated after 2022.[74] As a German Green MP explained in an interview, the party hosts numerous 'differentiated voices', and while it is pro-disarmament, it is also realistic in the face of the Russian threats to 'European security and peace'.[75] One of the main shifts is in the party base – the Greens have numerous young members, for whom NATO membership is not a salient issue.[76]

The transformation of the German Greens is one of the most important changes in Europe in this period. The party that was formally committed to nuclear disarmament has become one of the strongest supporters of the German participation in nuclear sharing. This turn is also visible in other areas of foreign policy – Greens have, for instance, become more hawkish on Russia and China. However, the policy shift on nuclear weapons in the last few years is exceptionally remarkable.

Overall, the parties in the left-most category show continued opposition to nuclear sharing and support for nuclear disarmament. Their positions show little development and very little adjustment to the changing situation in the world. The transformation of the German Greens is an exception to this rule and underscores that

---

[72] Interview with a German expert
[73] Interview with a German expert
[74] Franceschini (2024). Another German expert shared a similar insight.
[75] Interview with a Green MP, February 2024
[76] Interview with a German expert

parties might shift their position, partially in response to the domestic changes and partially because they want to be seen as responsible political actors.

Social Democratic Parties

Social democratic parties traditionally occupy the left-of-centre position in European politics. As opposed to the more left-wing parties discussed in the previous section, these have historically been more supportive of the military as a tool of foreign policy, and with the right-of-centre parties, they remain the steady pillar of their countries' commitment to international alliances.[77] As opposed to their more left-wing partners, however, they are also more successful in elections and more likely to feature in governments, sometimes even in leading positions.

In Belgium, in 2014, the Walloon Francophone Socialist Party in its 2014 manifesto argued that 'to ensure that nuclear disarmament is balanced, the reduction of nuclear arsenals can only be the result of multilateral negotiations in which Belgium will continue to play an active part'.[78] This statement places the party's desire to have nuclear weapons removed from Belgian territory (a goal stated in the next paragraph) firmly in a multilateral framework of arms control discussions. The Flemish Socialist Party (Sp.a) held an even stronger position. In its 2014 manifesto, it wrote that 'nuclear weapons are useless, expensive and dangerous mass destruction weapons. Sp.a wants them to be removed from Belgian territory as soon as possible and for our country to become nuclear-weapon-free'.[79] In 2019, the manifesto is even clearer, arguing in favour of 'push[ing] hard within all multilateral forums for binding agreements on ... dismantling of existing nuclear weapons', adding 'we want a nuclear-free Belgium, where no (modernised) US nuclear weapons are stationed.

---

[77] Wagner et al. (2018)
[78] PS (2014)
[79] Sp.a (2014)

In addition, the successor to the F-16 should have no nuclear capability. We immediately sign the … Ban Treaty.'[80]

A very similar view is held by the German Social Democratic Party (SPD). The SPD is the third of the parties where nuclear sharing and nuclear weapons are a salient issue. This comes partially because of its membership – over half of SPD members are over 60, which means that they were socialised during the major anti-nuclear protests in the 1980s.[81] A large portion of SPD members hold a strong anti-war sentiment, which percolates throughout the party to the highest echelons.[82] As Nils Schmid, the SPD's then-parliamentary speaker for foreign affairs, explained to me, the debate within the party does not prevent it from supporting participation in nuclear sharing or NATO.[83] However, the division within the SPD is visible to the outside world too. A Green MP, for instance, remarked that 'it really makes an enormous difference' whom one speaks to in the SPD.[84] Another SPD MP whom I interviewed, Ralf Stenger, who represented the party on the subcommittee for disarmament and arms control, insisted that the SPD 'always has been a peace party' and, therefore, the movement to get rid of nuclear weapons in Germany 'was very strong in [the SPD]'.[85]

The divisions and value placed on traditional peace politics within the SPD comes up very prominently in the party manifestos. In 2009, the SPD supported the goal of withdrawing nuclear weapons from Germany, arguing that 'they are a relic of the Cold War and as of today militarily obsolete'.[86] The same position, although in less critical terms, appears in the party's 2013 and 2017 manifestos.[87] In these, the SPD added a caveat that it was in favour of

---

[80] Sp.a (2019)
[81] Interview with a German expert, January 2024
[82] Interview with a German expert; interview with Nils Schmid, January 2024.
[83] Interview with Nils Schmid
[84] Interview with a Green MP
[85] Interview with Ralf Stenger, March 2024
[86] SPD (2009)
[87] Sozialdemokratische Partei Deutschland (2013); SPD (2017)

withdrawing nuclear weapons from Germany 'and Europe ... in the context of a pan-European disarmament treaty'.[88] In 2021, the SPD announced 'an arms control offensive' and supported US–Russian arms control negotiations to withdraw and destroy nuclear weapons from Germany and Europe. It has also advocated for a constructive engagement with the TPNW and observing the MSPs.[89]

Yet the SPD also ultimately pushed, together with the Greens and Liberals, for the JSF acquisition. This 'caused raised eyebrows' within the party, and its leadership had to approach the issue carefully.[90] However, that this ultimately happened without a major debate or pushback within the party speaks to two facts – the salience of nuclear weapons in 2023 was rather low, and interparty debate meant that the party needed a leader (such as Chancellor Olaf Scholz) to adjudicate between the wings.[91]

In the Netherlands, two parties are classified as social democratic – the fairly small DENK, which appeals mainly to the Turkish minority, and the mainstream traditional Labour Party (PvdA). Despite their differing constituencies, their outlook is remarkably similar. DENK is a committed opponent of nuclear weapons and rejected the reliance on nuclear deterrence in its 2017 and 2021 manifestos and vowed to ratify the TPNW in 2021.[92] The issue of nuclear weapons was more prominent for the Labour Party. The PvdA has supported a withdrawal in all of its manifestos since 2002, up to and including 2021. In 2010, it also advocated for a ban on investment in companies producing nuclear weapons,[93] which is a long-standing goal of NGO supporters of nuclear disarmament.[94] In 2012, it committed itself to 'actively pursuing further reductions of

---

[88] SPD (2017)
[89] Sozialdemokratische Partei (2021)
[90] Interview with a German expert
[91] The issue of low salience was confirmed to me in multiple interviews by experts but also by Ralf Stenger.
[92] DENK (2017, 2021)
[93] Partij van de Arbeid (2010)
[94] Don't Bank on the Bomb (2023)

tactical nuclear weapons' and consultations on the removal of these weapons 'in coordination with other EU countries'.[95] In 2012–2017, the party held the foreign ministry, and its foreign minister pursued other goals in the office, leading to party infighting. I will discuss this in more detail in Chapter 7. The party recommitted to the goal in the 2017 manifesto, in which it also called to an end of the long-standing secrecy around the presence of US nuclear weapons on Dutch soil.[96] And, in 2021, the party recommitted to the removal of the nuclear weapons from the Dutch soil and to signing the TPNW (and extending the INF and START treaties, something outside the powers of the Dutch government).[97]

Taken together, it is clear that even the more moderate left-of-centre social democratic parties are advocates of nuclear disarmament and withdrawal. The only exception to this, again, is the German SPD, which has been more moderate; while it has pushed for a world without nuclear weapons, it has noted the broader arms control context in these debates. Similarly, the Dutch Labour Party advocated for a coordination with allies on these issues but abandoned that position later.

Liberal and Christian Democratic Parties

The liberal and Christian democratic parties are the traditional right-of-centre parties in Europe, and, similar to the social democrats, they have been the pillar of alliances and security policy for decades. Compared to the social democrats, they do tend to be more in favour of the military as a tool of foreign policy, and they were traditionally more supportive of the alliance with the US.[98]

Only the liberals in Germany and the Netherlands have dealt with nuclear weapons to a significant degree. In Germany, the Free Democratic Party (FDP) is a traditional liberal force. In its 2009

---

[95] Partij van de Arbeid (2012)
[96] Partij van de Arbeid (2017)
[97] Partij van de Arbeid (2021)
[98] Hofmann (2013)

manifesto, it advocated for withdrawing the 'remaining American nuclear weapons from Germany'.[99] It also nominated Foreign Minister Westerwelle, who was the last to propose a serious initiative for a European withdrawal.[100] Once it failed, the FDP moderated its goals, refocusing on support for the NPT and the long-term goal of withdrawing tactical nuclear weapons from Europe.[101] In 2017, it advocated for 'a new diplomatic approach to arms control and disarmament' in which 'Germany should take a leading role here together with its close partners.'[102] This idea of new initiatives, but no firm commitments, reappeared in its 2021 manifesto.[103]

The situation was slightly different in the Netherlands, where the two liberal parties – the Democrats 66 (D66) and the People's Party for Freedom and Democracy (VVD) – occupied leading positions in the country, with the VVD leading the government since 2012. In its 2010, 2012, and 2017 manifestos, the D66 committed to withdrawing nuclear weapons from the Netherlands,[104] going as far as saying, in 2016, that they had no place in arsenals and opposing participation in the nuclear mission for JSFs.[105] In 2021, the party also committed to signing the TPNW.[106]

The situation is different for the VVD. It spends relatively little space in its party manifesto on nuclear mission participation, partially because this topic is seen as 'clear' and 'settled' for the party.[107] However, the party's commitment is clear. In 2017, it wrote in its manifesto that 'NATO is the cornerstone of our security policy. … As the Netherlands, we want to be a reliable ally. That is why we take our responsibility. This means that NATO

---

[99] Freie Demokratische Partei (2009)
[100] Sonne (2018)
[101] Freie Demokratische Partei (2013)
[102] Freie Demokratische Partei (2017)
[103] Freie Demokratische Partei (2021)
[104] D66 (2010, 2012, 2016)
[105] D66 (2016)
[106] In various off-the-record discussions, I was admonished to understand the difference between 'signing' and 'ratifying'. D66 (2021).
[107] Interview with a Dutch MP

tasks and obligations will not be unilaterally suspended. This also applies to the nuclear weapons task.' The manifesto continued by arguing that the party 'oppose[d] unilateral disarmament by NATO. This is reckless and makes us vulnerable.'[108] The 2021 manifesto similarly stated, 'with state-of-the-art F-35s capable of carrying nuclear weapons, the Netherlands fulfils an important role within the deterrent of the NATO. We support treaties on arms control and nuclear arms reduction, but as long as Russia has tactical nuclear weapons, the Netherlands does not impose any unilateral restrictions on itself.'[109]

What the VVD and the FDP have in common is that they are generally fairly right leaning. The VVD comes out as the strongest supporter of NATO nuclear sharing, but the FDP in practice sees disarmament primarily as an aspirational goal. By contrast, the D66 remains committed to that goal, which makes it more like the other left-leaning parties.

The position of the Christian Democratic parties was similar to that of their liberal counterparts. In Belgium, the Christian Democratic and Flemish in 2014 did not raise the issue of US nuclear weapons in Belgium and, in 2019, placed any disarmament discussions in a context of 'mutual disarmament'.[110] Its Walloon Christian democrat equivalent, the Humanistic Democratic Centre, advocated in 2010 to advance negotiations with NATO and EU members with 'their neighbours' to advance nuclear disarmament.[111] However, four years later, it also advocated for the withdrawal of nuclear weapons from Belgium.[112]

In Germany, the Christian democracy is represented by the CDU/CSU coalition, which governed from 2005 until 2021, and the

---

[108] Volkspartij voor Vrijheid en Democratie (2017)
[109] Volkspartij voor Vrijheid en Democratie (2021)
[110] Cd&V (2014, 2019)
[111] Centre Démocrate Humaniste (2010)
[112] Centre Démocrate Humaniste (2014); interestingly, it advocated banning nuclear weapons on humanitarian grounds in its 2007 manifesto, long before even academics started talking about this. See Centre Démocrate Humaniste (2007).

leadership of Angela Merkel. The CDU/CSU, in its 2013 manifesto, supported the goal of nuclear nonproliferation but also a 'fair and internationally responsible' approach to 'dismantling nuclear weapons', with the goal to use advancement on disarmament to support the goals of nonproliferation.[113] The party programme went even further in 2021; the manifesto stated clearly that 'NATO is the backbone of Euro-Atlantic security. This security is guaranteed by nuclear sharing.'[114] It continued that

> as long as there are states with nuclear weapons that actively challenge our community of values, Europe will continue to need the US nuclear umbrella and German participation in nuclear sharing within NATO will remain an important component of credible deterrence in the Alliance. We stand for Germany's resolute commitment to continue its nuclear sharing within NATO and to provide the necessary means for this.[115]

The CDU/CSU's commitment is one of the strongest from all European political parties, and its vision supporting national participation in nuclear sharing remains unmatched.

The Dutch Christian democratic parties carry complicated historical legacy, dating back to the Cold War, on nuclear disarmament. In that period, (dis)armament was one of the most contentious issues for them.[116] It is less so today, but various perspectives remain. Christian Democrats in the Netherlands have two main parties – the Christian Democratic Appeal (CDA) and the Christian Union (CU). The CDA is the larger party and has led coalitions for a significant portion of the post-World War II period. By contrast, the CU attracted primarily socially conservative but progressive issues on international politics and economics. This distinction also translates into their views on nuclear weapons. The CDA, for instance, in

---

[113] CDU/CSU (2013)
[114] CDU/CSU (2021)
[115] CDU/CSU (2021)
[116] van Dijk and Schaaper (2015); Everts (1984)

its 2010 manifesto, spoke of the role of the Netherlands as 'stimulating the debate on promoting nonproliferation and disarmament'.[117] However, it did not approach this topic in later manifestos, even though it remains supportive of NATO membership and higher defence expenditure.[118] By contrast, the CU in 2010 supported the idea of 'promot[ing] in the NATO context the active reduction of tactical-nuclear weapons'.[119] In 2012, it named nuclear weapons as 'the weapons that should not be used', and in 2017, it praised efforts 'being made to reduce the number of nuclear weapons'.[120] However, in 2021, it supported signing and 'complying with obligations' of the TPNW, while supporting global arms control.[121]

Taken together, the Christian democratic parties appeared to be somewhat split. The more established ones with experience of governing, like the CDU and the CDA, appear to be more supportive of the existing arrangements. By contrast, those representing smaller Christian democratic parties are more sceptical and appear more supportive of disarmament.

Nationalist and Far-Right Parties

Curiously, despite the growing appeal of the nationalist and far-right parties among the voters, they are not very outspoken on the issues related to nuclear weapons, at least not in their manifestos. In 2010, the Dutch Party for Freedom (PVV) opposed purchasing JSFs but has not spoken about nuclear sharing since.[122] The Alternative for Germany, the German far-right populist party, argued in 2021 in favour of the withdrawal of nuclear weapons from Germany but only in coordination with the destruction of missiles aimed at Germany, essentially endorsing an arms control framework for Europe.[123]

---

[117] Christen-Democratisch Appel (2010)
[118] Christen-Democratisch Appel (2021)
[119] ChristenUnie (2010)
[120] ChristenUnie (2012, 2017)
[121] ChristenUnie (2021)
[122] Partij voor de Vrijheid (2010)
[123] AfD (2021)

The party had, in late 2023, an internal debate spurred by the suggestion of the Young Alternative, the AfD's youth wing, to support Germany's independent nuclear deterrent, which was put down by the party leadership.[124] Belgian populists from the New Flemish Alliance (NVA) supported a world without nuclear weapons but not unilateral steps. The 2019 party manifesto read 'the N-VA strives for a world without nuclear weapons. The road to a nuclear-weapon-free world can't reduce our safety or that of our allies.'[125]

It is curious that the European nationalist and far-right parties do not discuss nuclear deterrence as a relevant topic. One explanation might be that, as opposed to more established parties, they can avoid such debates because they have less legacy to drive them. However, the recent manifestos from the Flemish and German far right demonstrate that they are surely no firm disarmers.

PARLIAMENTARY ACTIVITY

Another approach to study party politics on nuclear weapons looks at the activity of the parties in Parliament. Four out of five host countries have regular debates and votes in Parliament on related issues. Nevertheless, the number of such votes varies from country to country and is the highest in the Netherlands, emphasising its position as the country where Parliament is the most active on this issue, which also links to relatively frequent and common debates.[126]

The varying number of motions by country should be also understood as a reflection of different institutional rules and political norms. For instance, in the Netherlands, every MP can file a motion, which is voted on. By contrast, in Germany, roll call voting on individual motions is highly unlikely. Similarly, because motions are sometimes filed by a single MP, idiosyncratic reasons might prevent a party from voting in favour, even if it fits with the party platform. For instance, in Germany, parliamentary staffers mention that

---

[124] Schindler (2022)
[125] Nieuw-Vlaamse Alliantie (2019)
[126] For a case study of the Netherlands, see Onderco and Joosen (2022).

Die Linke often 'baits' other parties with pro-disarmament resolutions that also include peculiar wording that contradicts Germany's transatlantic orientation. For illustration, we can look at the motion 19/29960 filed by Die Linke on 20 May 2021 titled 'Dismantling instead of upgrading.' It called for not only ending participation in nuclear sharing but also 'to reject the NATO rearmament target of 2 per cent of GDP, to stop and reverse the rearmament programme for the Bundeswehr and to invest billions of euros in the resulting funds in the areas of education and health'.[127]

The variation in the number of parliamentary votes is enormous. By far, the most active Parliament is in the Netherlands, where the chamber votes on numerous motions annually. In interviews, Dutch MPs recognise this exceptional position.[128] It is orthogonal to how the German Parliament, for instance, has a specialised Subcommittee on Disarmament, Arms Control and Nonproliferation. One should, however, also recognise that this subcommittee is not per se a sign of strong salience of this issue. According to a German expert, the only reason it was not abolished a few years ago is that doing so would require a renegotiation of committee portfolios and therefore a negotiation with the far-right AfD, which all other parliamentary parties refused to do.[129]

For the analysis of parliamentary activity, I looked at all the votes taken in all five host nations since the year 2010 on issues linked to nuclear weapons. Sadly, there was no vote in Turkey, so this country cannot be analysed. As mentioned, the number of votes varies widely across individual countries. For instance, Belgium had no vote in most years, and the highest number of votes was four in 2019. Just next door, in the Netherlands, the House of Representatives voted fourteen times on related motions in 2016. What they do have in common, though, is that the votes are often taken by caucus (and not by individual roll call). As political scientist Simon Hug argues, roll

---

[127] Deutscher Bundestag (2021a)
[128] Interviews with a Dutch MP and a former Dutch MP
[129] Interview with a German expert, January 2024, Berlin

call voting biases findings because it might both discipline a party and allow more freedom.[130] Yet in systems that allow for a choice, choosing a roll call vote signals salience.

The advantage of analysing data taken by caucus is that the positioning becomes quite visible. Because the number of votes is too low for an analysis using standard quantitative tools, such as NOMINATE, consistently across cases, I resorted to another measure – I looked at who voted in favour, voted against, and abstained. Because the vast majority of the votes were critical of the policy, those who voted in favour were usually critics and those who voted against were usually supporters.

The key predictor variable is partisan ideology, and I measured left–right positioning of the parties voting in favour and against. To do so, I relied on CHES.[131] Its scale measures left–right ideology on a continuous scale from 0 (extreme left) to 10 (extreme right).

Figure 4.2 shows a violin plot with the distribution of ideologies by vote. Simply put, the thicker the area, the higher the number of votes by parties with the given ideology in a particular way. For the sake of simplicity, I dropped very small caucuses (five members or fewer) from the analysis.

The figure shows that Italy and Belgium have no clear patterns, in terms of relationship between ideology and voting on motions. Parties across the ideological spectrum might vote for or against motions, and the parties that are the strongest on the right, in both countries, are most likely to abstain. This pattern of abstention underscores that far-right parties are likely to keep quiet on these issues, which I discussed at the end of the previous section. In Italy, we see a pattern that is not completely different from what Italian political scientists found when it comes to other parliamentary activity in foreign and security policy, such as voting on military deployments. As these scholars have found, centrists are the most supportive of

[130] Hug (2010)
[131] Jolly et al. (2022)

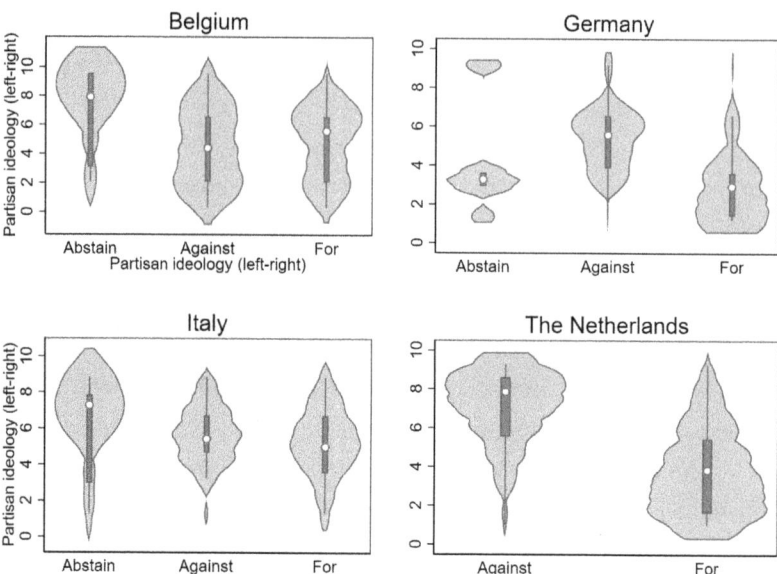

FIGURE 4.2 Parliamentary votes in host nations.

military deployments but on nuclear matters too. Interestingly, when it comes to nuclear weapons, the far left is not the strongest opponent, which is the case with military deployment, but this also has to do with its relative disappearance from Italian politics.[132] The pattern in Belgium is also similar to the findings of scholars studying military deployments – while the left is often opposed to foreign military entanglements, the right is divided and often more nuanced.[133]

In Germany and the Netherlands, however, we see a very clear left–right alignment on the motions related to nuclear weapons. In both countries, the left-wing parties are most often supportive (and hence critical of the existing arrangements) and the right-wing parties are most often opposed (and hence supportive of the existing arrangements). This pattern not exclusive, but it is rather strikingly similar between the two countries. It also confirms findings from the Netherlands, a very good case to study

---

[132] Coticchia and Vignoli (2020a); Vignoli (2020)
[133] Fonck et al. (2019)

voting on nuclear motions, because they are the most numerous there. And the alignment is almost a textbook example of the left–right divide. Of course, there is a small variation, because some left-wing parties (such as the PvdA) were in the government and therefore could not always vote against government policy. By and large, however, the left–right pattern persists.[134] The situation is similar in Germany, with a very similar alignment between the left and right on these issues. The rather large group of left-wing votes against nuclear motions might be explained by the SPD's participation in Parliament and intraparty debates within the SPD and the Greens, which prevent them from voting for the most extreme motions. The persistence of the left–right pattern in the Netherlands and Germany confirms the public opinion research that has found right-wing individuals and voters of right-wing parties to be more supportive of nuclear weapons use.[135]

CONCLUSION

In this chapter, I looked at the pattern of partisan and parliamentary activity on nuclear weapons in the parliaments of the five host nations. The chapter offers a number of findings that show similarities but also differences across the countries.

The first similarity is the relatively low salience of this issue among political parties. While nuclear weapons do appear regularly in the party manifestos, their salience is relatively low, which might reflect low priority for the parties. From those parties that do afford attention to nuclear sharing, the overwhelming direction is critical – by all, except for liberal and Christian democratic parties.

Interestingly, the issue is 'alive' in some of the European parties, where it has a higher salience. The German social democrats and Greens and Dutch socialists do care about this issue, because it is salient for their voters and party members. However, the salience

---

[134] On the Netherlands, see also Onderco and Joosen (2022).
[135] Onderco et al. (2022).

is much more limited in other parties in these countries. It is also very low in Italy and Turkey – in Italy, the political parties almost never discuss nuclear sharing, and in Turkey, they *never* do so. As Turkish political scientist Şebnem Udum explained to me, this lack of discussion comes down to a tradition that military affairs are often seen as too technical and 'only military can know it'.[136] However, the relative passivity of Parliament on foreign policy issues is relatively new. In the early 2000s, it very successfully intervened in the government's desire to allow the US to use Turkey as a base to open a Northern front in the invasion of Iraq,[137] but at least since 2010, its role has declined significantly.[138] As another Turkish political scientist, Mustafa Kibaroğlu, told me, 'the president makes the calls here'.[139] The domestic developments therefore lead to Turkey being in a stark contrast with the other countries where parliamentary debate is much more active.

The chapter has also shown that parliamentary activity has enormous variation among the countries, but, in most of them, nuclear weapons receive little attention. Turkey is one outlier, with no relevant vote since 2010. The Netherlands is the other outlier – it has had dozens of votes, with a peak of fourteen in 2016. The findings show that while Belgium and Italy have no clear patterns of voting alignment, Germany and the Netherlands usually have the left-leaning parties opposed to nuclear sharing but right-leaning parties mostly supportive. This pattern generally conforms with what the scholarship found about how left and right view nuclear weapons and military power in general. Nevertheless, the findings from this chapter underscore similarities but also differences and the intensely politicised nature of nuclear sharing in the European host nations.

---

[136] Interview with Şebnem Udum, November 2023
[137] Kesgin and Kaarbo (2010)
[138] I am grateful to Juliet Kaarbo for this insight.
[139] Interview with Mustafa Kibaroğlu, November 2023

5 Civil Society

INTRODUCTION

In 2019, the Dutch Society for Medical Polemology, also known as Doctors for Peace, or under its Dutch abbreviation NVMP, celebrated its fiftieth anniversary with a full-day conference. It took place in the modern grandeur of the Peace Palace Library in The Hague, the same hall as the summer sessions of the prestigious Hague Academy of International Law. Luminary after luminary appeared on the podium – including the UN Under-Secretary General of Disarmament Affairs Izumi Nakamitsu, Dutch Foreign Minister Stef Blok, and former Irish President Mary Robinson.[1] The event was festive and the lunch unusually good by Dutch standards. Then, Reynold Klooker, one of the peace activists in the hall, stood up and rolled out a banner that read, in Dutch, 'NL ALWAYS BEEN US VASSAL. JSF + NUCLEAR BOMB' (Figure 5.1).

While the argument that the Netherlands was a US vassal state was new to me, the anti-nuclear attitude was not. Dutch civil society was, for a few years by then, laser focused on Dutch participation on nuclear sharing arrangements. It has lobbied Parliament, collected signatures in the streets, and organised young people across the country. While civil society's focus on nuclear disarmament was not new, what was new was the renewed energy with which it, in a number of host nations, reiterated its activities. As opposed to the civil society of yesteryear, in the 2010s, Europe had a new concrete point to appeal to – the TPNW, more popularly known as 'the ban treaty'. The treaty, spearheaded by ICAN, became by the late 2010s a major discussion

---

[1] For the full programme, see NVMP Artsen voor Vrede (2019).

FIGURE 5.1 Reynold Klooker, an anti-nuclear activist.
Own photograph, published with Mr Klooker's consent.

point in the nuclear host nations (with the exception of Turkey), and ICAN became a major force to be reckoned with.

In this chapter, I seek to explain the role of civil society in shaping the debates about nuclear weapons in Europe, particularly the growing role of ICAN and the ban treaty. After outlining and analysing the origins and role of ICAN, I will zero in on its work in the European host nations, particularly the innovations it brought about. I will then look at one of ICAN's activities – the Cities Appeal, which was an initiative to attract as many cities as possible to call on their respective governments to sign the TPNW. Cities Appeal helps us to situate ICAN's disarmament work on the local level. I will look at its success in the host nations and any patterns that could help us to explain that. I will conclude with a brief outline of how the war in Ukraine transformed ICAN's activities in Europe (but also globally).

ICAN AND THE BAN TREATY

ICAN has become the epitome of European anti-nuclear civil society. It was originally founded in 2006 as an Australian organisation but soon developed into a paradigmatic transnational advocacy coalition or super-network.[2] We need not get deep into semantics – suffice it to say that ICAN has a multi-tiered networked structure. On top sits the headquarters in Geneva with what ICAN calls 'international staff'. Strategic guidance for the campaign is given by the international steering group (ISG), which is composed of leading organisations and 'issue professionals', to use the phrase of political scientists Laura Breen and Mette Eilstrup-Sangiovanni.[3] They represent their institutions, often in different campaigns, and their expertise is campaigning, although they sometimes also have expertise in the actual issue area. By their membership in multiple networks, they gain prominent positions for themselves but also their own organisations. The actual members of ICAN are called 'partners' – they are

---

[2] Breen and Eilstrup-Sangiovanni (2024); Schapper and Dee (2024)
[3] Breen and Eilstrup-Sangiovanni (2024)

organisations from across the world, although, as I will explain in the next section, they are disproportionately from Europe.

As international relations scholar Rebecca Davis Gibbons describes in her masterful account, ICAN's initial goal was not a nuclear weapon ban.[4] In fact, it pursued the idea of a nuclear weapon convention, which originated in late 1990s and was basically a model treaty that was supposed to provide all details for the path to disarmament. It ran over dozens of pages and often included minutiae. The project was picked up in the late 2000s by the International Physicians for Prevention of Nuclear War (IPPNW), which published a 186-page report titled *Securing Our Survival*.[5] Yet in the spirit of hope for disarmament in the late 2000s, pro-nuclear campaigners were looking for new ideas.[6] As another expert on disarmament, Bill Potter, writes, in this period, civil society, broadly speaking, was not particularly interested in it; it was seen as a niche issue where successes were hard to come by.[7] Partially for this reason, the Norwegian government, led by the Social Democrats, was interested in supporting new ideas on disarmament and supported a number of organisations, including the International Law and Policy Institute (ILPI) and ICAN.

One of the new ideas was to shift to a new frame, focused on banning nuclear weapons. This was, however, not fully embraced. As Gibbons recalls in her work, by the 2010 NPT Review Conference, ICAN was still pushing for the nuclear weapons convention;[8] however, the International Committee of the Red Cross managed to persuade three governments – Austrian, Swiss and Norwegian – to introduce a new language into the conference's final document, decrying the 'catastrophic humanitarian consequences' of nuclear weapons.[9] This insertion, after the committee reframed nuclear

---

[4] Gibbons (2018)
[5] On *Securing Our Survival*, see Dalaqua (2013).
[6] Gibbons (2018)
[7] Potter (2017)
[8] Gibbons (2018)
[9] Norman (2019)

weapons as a humanitarian problem, encouraged ICAN to shift its view. After securing additional funding, it established an office in Geneva and the structure we know today.[10] ICAN developed a full-fledged communications campaign, including for its partners and campaigners around the world, that refused the old framing of nuclear weapons as a diplomatic and security problem and pushed full on for the new framing. Denied their political and security value, the weapons came to be seen as a humanitarian burden.[11] This also made them a much more attractive issue for civil society.[12]

This reframing allowed its proponents to liken them to land mines.[13] Seen from the academic standpoint, it is not entirely surprising that this step succeeded; it created a possibility for what international relations scholar Richard Price called 'grafting'.[14] It essentially allows proponents of the ban to liken the weapons to others that have been banned and highlight their similarity (such as their indiscriminate effect).

The new frame received early support from governments. Norway sponsored the first in a series of three conferences on the humanitarian consequences of nuclear weapons. As Gibbons notes, the Norwegian government as a NATO member was particularly sensitive to any political message linked to these, which were initially meant as scientific meetings to discuss the humanitarian and health effects of nuclear explosions. However, the process ultimately morphed into a call to stigmatise, prohibit, and eliminate them, launched at the third conference in Vienna in December 2014.[15] After the failure of the 2015 NPT Review Conference, the momentum quickly picked up in the Open-Ended Working Group of the UN General Assembly towards starting negotiations on a legally binding instrument to ban nuclear weapons. Following the 2015

[10] Gibbons (2018)
[11] Bolton and Minor (2016)
[12] Potter (2017)
[13] Borrie (2014)
[14] Price (1998)
[15] Gibbons (2018); see also Potter (2017).

elections, the new conservative coalition in Oslo stopped all funding for nuclear disarmament, in a move broadly known in disarmament circles as 'Norpocalypse'.[16]

Not even the Norpocalypse, however, slowed down the momentum towards the ban treaty. The negotiations took place over four short weeks in spring 2017 in New York, attended by 132 states, including the Netherlands but no other NATO state.[17] Because of its prominence in the community and its role as an umbrella for virtually the whole of the relevant civil society, ICAN had a leading role in briefing the attendees, together with a small group of leading nations. These activities were a part of what Andrea Schapper and Megan Dee called ICAN's 'inside advocacy' – connecting with diplomats in support of the ban treaty. ICAN is also involved in 'outside advocacy', creating broad public pressure for it.[18] I discuss this in more detail in the third section of this chapter. The result of the negotiation marathon in New York was the TPNW, following a model of a 'simple ban treaty'.[19] The TPNW runs twenty short paragraphs and is devoid of any specific details on disarmament verification, for instance, which is reserved for later deliberation.

ICAN's main goal then became to be the chief cheerleader for the treaty. This meant different things in different regions. In the Global South, ICAN has provided information to local activists. However, the bulk of its activities – as I will show later in this chapter – have been in the Global North, primarily in Europe. ICAN's goals here have been clear – to persuade the political leaders in these countries to give up the US nuclear umbrella (and specifically the hosting role), get them to sign and ratify the treaty, and, failing that, persuade them to at least attend the treaty meetings.

ICAN is intimately connected to the TPNW. It is by now received knowledge in the field of nuclear disarmament that ICAN

---

[16] Gibbons (2018)
[17] For a diplomatic account of these negotiations, see Kmentt (2021). For a disarmament activist perspective, see Acheson (2021).
[18] Schapper and Dee (2024).
[19] On the downsides of a simple ban treaty, see Onderco (2017).

had an enormous impact on the form and content of and support for the ban treaty. Diplomatic memoirs,[20] academic papers,[21] and activists' own writings support this assertion.[22] Part of the success lies in the successful reframing of the debate as a humanitarian issue globally.[23] The humanitarian reframing also allowed ICAN to create linkage with other campaigns. For instance, ICAN's Director Melissa Parke, at its Campaigners Forum in 2025, connected disarmament with the fate of the civilian victims in Gaza, arguing that 'the issues are linked. It is the same ways of thinking that justify nuclear weapons and nuclear deterrence that justify the committing and facilitating of genocide, involving some of the same companies and countries. It is the same disregard for international law when it is.'[24] The forum included a session where disarmament activists explored opportunities to connect with other campaigns, often locally.

The ICAN's success does not mean that the campaign led to any tangible improvements in nuclear security. By the assessment of the Editorial Board of the Bulletin of the Atomic Scientists, seven years after the adoption of the TPNW, nuclear risks increased rather than decreased.[25] However, this is not a problem for ICAN. As international relations scholar Keith Krause wrote even before the ban treaty was adopted, 'as a general rule of thumb, one could argue that in the realm of international peace and security, the easier an issue is for civil society to focus on, the less important it is likely to be in generating tangible improvements in international (and human) security'.[26]

The reframing also allowed ICAN to attract younger generations, which came to nuclear disarmament from another angle.

---

[20] Kmentt (2021)
[21] Gibbons (2018); Schapper and Dee (2024); Breen and Eilstrup-Sangiovanni (2024); Norman (2019)
[22] Acheson (2021, 2023)
[23] Krause (2014)
[24] Parke (2025)
[25] Science and Security Board (2024)
[26] Krause (2014, p. 232)

A good example for this new blood is Emma Pike, a prominent advocate for nuclear abolition on TikTok, a social media platform. In a podcast interview, Pike linked her passion for abolition directly to her Buddhist background and associated care for every living creature.[27] While Buddhist movements have seen nuclear disarmament as important cause for decades, the reframing attracted a global audience and new followers.[28] However, Pike's professional path also underscores the idea that activists are becoming 'issue professionals'. More recently, Pike's online activism focused on the issue of lethal autonomous weapons systems,[29] against Israel's actions in Gaza,[30] or support for the pro-Palestinian protests at Columbia University in spring 2024.[31]

New Intellectual Energy

The new intellectual frame to think about nuclear weapons as a humanitarian issue is intimately tied to civil society's engagement with academia. Nick Ritchie, in his prominent database of TPNW literature, traces it back to two papers, one by Princeton-based expert Zia Mian[32] and the other by Chatham House expert Patricia Lewis.[33] They became the co-chairs of the TPNW Scientific Advisory Group upon its establishment in March 2023. While Lewis continued to advance the policy discussion until retiring; Mian, meanwhile, has focused on technical work – for instance, he co-authored a paper in which he outlined potential verification mechanisms for the treaty, which has become a blueprint for the treaty's own verification regime.[34]

---

[27] Buddhability (2022)
[28] Pike links her own interest in this cause to reading Daisaku Ikeda's book of conversations, Krieger and Ikeda (2002).
[29] See, for instance, www.instagram.com/emma_pike_/reel/C6Z5fuuMR0h/ and www.instagram.com/emma_pike_/reel/C6RwE-kpeC5/
[30] See www.instagram.com/emma_pike_/reel/C5jiZa1JOgy/
[31] See www.instagram.com/emma_pike_/reel/C57cl8gsO-j/
[32] Mian (2009)
[33] Lewis (2009)
[34] Patton et al. (2019)

However, the engagement with academia goes beyond the initial ideas. It also includes academic work that directly feeds into the reframing, which gives rise to new academic voices. ICAN is directly funding some of this work, often supporting projects that study the reframing or direct nuclear advocacy by academics.[35] The scholars supported by ICAN are often not the established names in the international relations field but rather younger academics, who develop new research directions.

However, the humanitarian turn also opened the door for new intellectual energy and new talent, which civil society extensively engages with. One such example is Kjølv Egeland, a young Norwegian academic with an Oxford doctorate in international relations and a dissertation on nuclear hierarchies. Egeland's published scholarly work made three contributions that are useful for civil society's work. First, he argues that the promise of consensus-based politics for nuclear disarmament is overrated and that even at the best of times, it was a pipe dream.[36] Second, and relatedly, he argues that adversarial politics is necessary to succeed in nuclear disarmament.[37] Third, with his co-author and postdoctoral supervisor Benoît Pelopidas, he advanced an argument that experts in the nuclear field are in conflict of interests due to research funding from nuclear weapons states and companies involved in the nuclear deterrence.[38]

In April 2018, less than half a year after submitting his dissertation, Egeland co-founded a network of researchers, the Norwegian Academy of International Law (NAIL).[39] Among the other co-founders were Gro Nystuen and Torbjørn Graff Hugo, both former Norwegian diplomats who Egeland previously worked with at the Oslo office of ILPI.[40] NAIL's goal was to 'contribute

---

[35] See ICAN's website for a list of supported projects, www.icanw.org/critical_nuclear_weapons_projects_2023_2024
[36] Egeland (2020b)
[37] Egeland (2017a, 2017b, 2021)
[38] Egeland and Pelopidas (2022)
[39] According to the Norwegian public register, the founding date of NAIL is 4 April 2018.
[40] Egeland thanks Nystuen and Hugo for 'for showing me the ropes' in the acknowledgements of his dissertation. See Egeland (2017b, p. 8).

with professional and procedural support for the development and implementation of rules of international law'.[41] Only six months after its founding, NAIL published a report *The TPNW: Setting the Record Straight*,[42] which has become a frequent touchstone for TPNW advocates and was cited in parliaments and diplomatic settings. ICAN was consulted on the preparation of the report and submitted to NAIL some of the (perceived) misconceptions about the treaty, which ICAN had received in the course of its lobbying campaign.[43] The report provided them with answers, which came with a cachet of an institution with a noble name – NAIL. Egeland quickly rose in prominence among the disarmament civil society – in interviews which I conducted only a few years later, numerous leading ICAN representatives named him as an influential thinker who impacts their work.[44]

Egeland is, however, not alone. Benoît Pelopidas's work on luck and avoidance of nuclear catastrophe has supplied a frequent speaking point for civil society and diplomats working for nuclear disarmament.[45] Another example of an academic who became closely linked to the humanitarian disarmament movement is Nick Ritchie, from the University of York. Ritchie's work in the early 2010s fostered the focus on normative delegitimation of nuclear weapons, which helped creating impetus, support, and justification of pursuing disarmament through a simple ban treaty route.[46] Ritchie is in many ways an intellectual steward of the ban treaty community, as he, for instance, maintains the hugely helpful and magisterial database of writings on the TPNW.[47] However, he also cultivated relationships

---

[41] The public register page of NAIL: https://w2.brreg.no/enhet/sok/detalj.jsp;jsessionid=OtpnrPo3TLFVDQJjwm0loc0rVxJJR-i7gc5UXw8c52V_BH8LZHoj!1231850988!-740609065?orgnr=920825516
[42] Nystuen et al. (2018)
[43] Interview with Daniel Högsta (2022)
[44] Interview with Beatrice Fihn (2022); interview with Ray Acheson (2023); interview with Daniel Högsta (2022).
[45] Pelopidas (2017); for a critical response, see Tertrais (2017).
[46] See, for instance, Ritchie (2013, 2014, 2016).
[47] See https://tinyurl.com/TPNWdatabase

with diplomats and even co-authored with them, particularly one Austrian diplomat, the chair of the first MSP and a key TPNW personality, Alexander Kmentt.[48] Ritchie also later co-wrote a report summarising the research findings on nuclear weapons for the Austrian foreign ministry,[49] which Austria promoted in diplomatic settings.[50]

Curiously, academic connections are much weaker in the European host nations, partially because the research in this area is more weakly developed. While all five host nations have academic researchers working on issues related to nuclear weapons, with very few exceptions, they are not particularly well connected to the NGO sphere. This is confirmed by the list of speakers at ICAN's Nuclear Ban Week in Vienna ahead of the first TPNW MSP in 2022. Even on the session on nuclear sharing in Europe, only one researcher from Europe spoke – Moritz Kütt, a physicist at the Institute for Peace Research and Security Policy in Hamburg.[51] In short, new intellectual horizons for fruitful engagement between civil society and academics opened thanks to the humanitarian refocusing of the nuclear debate.

Young Guns versus Old Guard

The rise of ICAN has led to a growing distinction between the 'young guns' and the 'old guard'. The young guns are often drawn from younger demographics but mainly distinguished by adopting new practices and doing things differently. The new practices are less afraid of confrontation and more open to adversarial politics – just as recommended by the new academic voices.[52]

This distinction applies at the international level. For instance, the ICAN's office in Geneva has a lot of young staffers for whom

---

[48] Ritchie and Kmentt (2021)
[49] Ritchie and Kupriyanov (2023)
[50] Melissa Parke, ICAN's executive director, mentioned both Pelopidas and Ritchie as important academic voices. See Interview with Melissa Parke (2024).
[51] Kütt was one of the first ICAN's interns at the time when it was still based in Australia. He also sits on the first TPNW Scientific Advisory Board and publishes on the TPNW in Germany. See Astner and Kütt (2024).
[52] Egeland (2021)

ICAN was either the first or the first major employer. Its former acting director, Daniel Högsta, started as an intern and rose through the ranks.[53] ICAN's advocacy coordinator, Florian Eblenkamp, followed a very similar path.[54]

Even the experienced hands were comparably young. Beatrice Fihn, a long-time executive director, was a think-tank analyst in Geneva. She was selected by Susi Snyder, the WILPF secretary general, for an internship position on human rights, only to be shifted to a disarmament internship position at the last minute. By her own admission, Fihn chose the latter position simply because it was paid.[55] Although initially not interested in the topic, she 'got completely sucked into it'. She was only thirty-five when she accepted the Nobel Prize on behalf of ICAN in 2017, but Fihn described herself as 'the elder in ICAN now', underscoring how young the environment in ICAN is. Other disarmament activists said that 'Beatrice was the best front woman you could have had now because she looked good, she spoke well, she was just like, everybody wanted to interview her.'[56] Involving young people, including in management and leadership, has been a distinguishing element of the organisation.[57]

ICAN is, of course, at pains to demonstrate that age does not play a role. Fihn, when still the executive director, said in her interview with me that 'there's a role for the 95-year-old nuns in this movement and there's a role for the 17-year-old TikToker in this movement, and everything in between'.[58] Both civil society leaders and experts recognise that ICAN's activism has brought many young people to nuclear disarmament. For instance, think tank expert Oliver Meier argued that ICAN's activities in Germany increased interest

---

[53] Interview with Daniel Högsta (2022)
[54] Eblenkamp's LinkedIn profile provides this information. See www.linkedin.com/in/florian-eblenkamp/
[55] Interview with Beatrice Fihn (2022)
[56] Interview with Xanthe Hall (2023)
[57] Interview with Beatrice Fihn (2022)
[58] Interview with Beatrice Fihn (2022)

in working in his institute,[59] and civil society leader Hirotsuku Terasaki opined that ICAN had 'inspired and empowered the young generation. So they have developed their ability and their knowledge. And to get these findings and scientific data as well as the discussion skills. They actually negotiate with the various diplomatic corps of the various countries. That was really wonderful.'[60]

Senior disarmament activists are very careful not to speak out about the generational divide at the heart of ICAN's rise. In interviews, for instance, the older members of the governing bodies at most speak with admiration and awe about the ability of ICAN to attract young people to the cause, something that even its critics acknowledge. And ICAN does not ignore the old guard. The ISG is composed of eleven different organisations. Some of these represent major actors in the humanitarian and disarmament field more broadly. For instance, the IPPNW is active in sixty countries and received the Nobel Peace Prize in 1985. It is represented on the ISG by Ira Helfand, a long-time pro-disarmament activist, who has been active in this field since around the time Fihn was born. By contrast, others are relatively small – the Acronym Institute, for instance, has been for a long time associated primarily with the activities of Rebecca Johnson, a British activist in the field since the time of the Freeze Movement in the 1980s.[61] On a global level, ISG epitomises this intergenerational connection, as it combines 'old hands' and younger generations.

In the national setting, the engagement between the older and younger generations can be cooperative too. Germany is a very good example. ICAN Deutschland, ICAN's German affiliate, has been led by the young guns but cooperated very closely with the IPPNW's German outlet, co-led by Xanthe Hall. The IPPNW provided mentorship to the group at its outset.[62] Hall likened ICAN

---

[59] Interview with Oliver Meier (2022)
[60] Interview with Hirotsugu Terasaki (2023)
[61] On the Freeze Movement, see Wittner (2003); Knopf (1998).
[62] Interview with Xanthe Hall (2023)

Deutschland to her own offspring: 'it's like having children, you have to let go of them at some point and let them do their own thing, which is why I can't see me staying on the board for that much longer, because I'm the only person that's over 40'.[63] ICAN Deutschland, for instance, worked in organising some events jointly with Greenpeace, a much more established civil society organisation. However, it also aimed at keeping its distance from Greenpeace, for instance, by not sharing all of its goals.[64]

However, the arrival of young guns often introduces fresh approaches, leaving the old guard puzzled about how to respond. The Netherlands provides a clear example of this dynamic. In 2009, IKV Pax Christi, an old and established civil society organisation active in the anti-nuclear protests in 1980s, decided to bring new life to its activities. It acquired substantial funding from Adessium, a private Dutch foundation established by the Van Vliet family that made its wealth in asset management and commodity trading. In 2002, the family sold its business and decided to start a foundation,[65] which hired its first staff in 2007.[66] IKV Pax Christi secured a long-term, sustainable financial commitment, ultimately resulting in the funding of approximately 1 million euros over a 10-year period. This support enabled PAX to expand its humanitarian disarmament team, hiring four new staff members to focus on nuclear disarmament, including Susi Snyder.[67] Snyder was a well-established figure before her arrival in the Netherlands. Born in Queens, she had become a nuclear disarmament activist soon after graduating from college. By 2001, she had been named Hero of Las Vegas, after her work with the local population in Nevada against the nuclear enterprise on Indigenous land.[68] She continued her work at WILPF, ultimately

---

[63] Interview with Xanthe Hall (2023)
[64] Interview with a civil society representative, January 2024
[65] Keidan (2017)
[66] Lévêque et al. (2017)
[67] Email interview with Miriam Struyk, April 2025
[68] Interview with Susi Snyder (2022); see also Snyder's personal bio at Snyder (2024).

becoming secretary general. Snyder came with a long track record and enormous wealth of knowledge and contacts.

Despite being a major hire with a potential to reinvigorate the debates, Snyder found that the integration in the Dutch disarmament environment was not smooth. Contrary to the German example, ICAN's main partner in the Netherlands, PAX (a renamed version of IKV Pax Christi) enjoyed much less close cooperation with IPPNW's Dutch outfit, the NVMP. Snyder described in a later interview that when she joined PAX, the Dutch NGO sphere was dominated by 'a handful of holdouts from the Mient-Jan Faber years' (who was the leading figure of the anti-nuclear protests in the 1980s). She also found the Dutch setting 'exclusive', which meant excluding her as coming from outside.[69] Snyder was, for instance, not invited to De Balieberaad, a meeting that took place in 2016 in De Balie theatre in Amsterdam, called for disarmament, and established an organised platform. This detail remains significant, because the organisers have since viewed themselves as *the* voice of the disarmament community in the Netherlands and are often invited to speak in public, including in Parliament.[70] Peter Buijs, a former chair of the NVMP, likes to list himself as a representative of De Balieberaad in speaking notes. However, Snyder was not impressed with it, labelling it 'a tiny afterthought', because 'it didn't entice or invite new people, it was more of the same'.[71] What PAX under Snyder did was to expand, attract new people, and focus on new areas, such as investment in nuclear weapons companies or funding in the disarmament field. PAX also teamed up with the Dutch MFA to fund four PhD positions in the Netherlands in the field.

Yet the reinvigoration brought new spirit to the Dutch nuclear debate. As a former Dutch MP summarised, 'what you found [among

---

[69] Interview with Susi Snyder (2022).
[70] See, for instance, the session of the Foreign Affairs Committee of the Dutch House of Representatives, on 15 February 2024, titled 'The Tensions in Europe', where De Balieberaad presented a position paper. See Tweede Kamer der Staten-Generaal (2024b). It is important to note that PAX, institutionally, did join De Balieberaad.
[71] Interview with Susi Snyder (2022).

the NGOs], at the hard core, were pensioners, that was true and that is still so. ... Those are true pacifists, "from swords to ploughshares", this sort of ideas. ... Old grey men and women who sit in with a set of principles ... if you want to breathe in a fresh air, you had to bring new people'.[72] Similar recollections came from a former leading Dutch expert on nuclear weapons Sico van der Meer, who later recalled in an interview that Snyder was 'able to shake things up' thanks to her 'very special personality'. Next to her personality, van der Meer recalled, Snyder was able to exercise influence because she 'knows what she's talking about ... she has a lot of knowledge. And it helps.'[73] That Snyder was a campaign professional who held full-time job on nuclear weapons while all other NGOs relied on volunteers (and rather elderly ones), gave her and her team at PAX an obvious advantage. As van der Meer recalled, she brought a wealth of expertise from her work in the US and Geneva, which made her a respected counterpart for discussions with policymakers. Hiring Snyder elevated PAX in international networks.[74] But it also exacerbated the generational conflict between the young guns and old guard at the national level.

The generational tension in the Netherlands did not have a single defining feature but instead varied among different ways of doing things. The old guard preferred writing op-eds for newspapers, whereas the young guns would not hesitate to lobby directly in Parliament.[75] The old guard would prioritise broad appeal, demonstrated by the fact that De Balieberaad includes organisations as broad as the Council of Churches and the NVMP, whereas the young guns were in favour of decisive action, alone, if needed. They were also ready to use new tactics, such as petitions. Their communication with the world was also different. The NVMP, for instance,

---

[72] Interview with a former Dutch MP, December 2023
[73] Interview with Sico van der Meer (2022)
[74] Interview with Sico van der Meer (2022)
[75] Supported by the fact that one of the members of the PAX's new nuclear disarmament team was Krista van Velzen, a former parliamentarian and parliamentary staffer for the Socialist Party, who actively used her parliamentary networks for lobbying. See Interview with Susi Snyder (2022).

preferred to coordinate things through the IPPNW; PAX would leapfrog intermediaries and directly become active globally. Buijs, the NPMP's long-time chair, would communicate using papers in academic journals or opinion pieces in national newspapers.[76] Snyder would call out people on Twitter.

The gap ultimately shrunk. In 2021, Snyder left PAX for a position at ICAN's Geneva office. The pandemic – and the shift in Dutch and international politics – meant that the salience of nuclear disarmament decreased. At the time of writing (June 2024), one could no longer speak about the old guard and young guns in the Netherlands. While all formally support ICAN and its leadership, the young guns' spirit has disappeared from the Dutch scene.

ICAN'S ACTIVITIES IN EUROPE

Despite being a global campaign, ICAN's predominant focus lies in the Western countries. The campaign's institutional partners are predominantly found in the West. In Figure 5.2, I show a world map; different shades represent the number of ICAN partners in a given country.[77] Table 5.1 shows a simplification of that information;

Table 5.1 *ICAN partners across regions*

Region	Partners
African Group	96
Asia-Pacific Group	85
Eastern European Group	22
Latin American Group	24
Western European & Others Group	452
Total	679

[76] Buijs (2018)
[77] ICAN also has a set of 'international partners', which are other international NGOs. As these NGOs are not representing or active within a particular country (and because they are often based in UN capitals, such as Geneva or New York), I have omitted them from the map.

FIGURE 5.2 ICAN partners by country.

I report the number of partners by UN regional group, using data scraped from ICAN's website.[78]

This very simple table demonstrates that while ICAN does have global footprint, its partners are predominantly Western organisations. Fully two-thirds of members come from the UN Western European & Others Group (WEOG). This extraordinary number of partners from the West is partially represented by ninety-six Australian, fifty-five French, and seventy-nine US organisations. In other regions, most countries are represented more modestly, although there are thirteen Nigerian organisations, thirteen from the Democratic Republic of Congo, and fifteen from Japan. Yet looking at the map, it is inescapable that ICAN is focused on Western countries.

The perception of ICAN as an organisation focused on Western countries was shared by external observers. For instance, in an interview, Hirotsuku Terasaki from Soka Gakkai International observed that ICAN 'ha[d] very European characteristics. Especially ... it's ... mainly acting in Europe'.[79] He also added that into the next decades, ICAN's leadership needed to strive to have 'more universality or more diversity'.[80] However, even academics have noticed

---

[78] At the time of writing, ICAN's website stated that it had 650 partners. By scraping the website, I found 679 partners. This discrepancy is likely because ICAN does not actively maintain a database of partners – when organisations register, they are simply added to their country's section on the website.
[79] Interview with Hirotsugu Terasaki (2023).
[80] Interview with Hirotsugu Terasaki (2023).

that ICAN's global aspirations sometimes conflict with the policy preferences of European anti-nuclear NGOs, which are numerically dominant within it.[81] The focus on Western countries is also partially a strategy; ICAN finds it easier to function in democratic settings with a developed civil society.[82]

When it comes to the host nation settings, ICAN's activities vary, depending on the national context. In all countries, ICAN engages in inside advocacy, lobbying foreign ministries and parliaments. In Germany and the Netherlands, for instance, local partners directly lobbied parliamentarians. A German Green MP confirmed in an interview that she is in regular contact with ICAN and let it co-write a major speech.[83] In the Netherlands, PAX, ICAN's local partner, relied on lobbying in Parliament, including by Krista van Velzen, a former Socialist MP. In Italy, local ICAN affiliate Rete Pace e Disarmo regularly meets with parliamentarians and even met directly with the defence minister Guido Crossetto from the far-right Brothers of Italy.[84] Some of this lobbying has had *some* effect. For instance, in Germany, the humanitarian narrative has taken firm root in discourses in Parliament.[85] However, one needs to recognise that ICAN often preaches to the converted. An NGO representative, for instance, told me that it is obvious that some are more receptive to their message.[86] By contrast, a Dutch MP told me that early in his tenure, local ICAN affiliates came for a visit, but both sides soon recognised the gulf between them.[87]

Some of the more established ICAN partners have been active in pacifist messaging for a long time. A good example comes from Italy. Francesco Vignarca, campaign coordinator of the Italian network for Peace and Disarmament and a leading TPNW campaigner,

---

[81] Futter and Samuel (2024).
[82] See, for instance, interviews cited in Gibbons and Herzog (2024).
[83] Interview with a German Green MP
[84] Interview with Francesco Vignarca (2023)
[85] Astner and Kütt (2024); Franceschini (2024)
[86] Interview with an NGO representative, January 2024
[87] Interview with a Dutch MP, November 2023

was previously a strong pacifist opponent of the purchase of JSFs in Italy.[88] Vignarca, in his work against that purchase, mainly argued that it was unnecessary and the money would be better spent on welfare or healthcare.[89] Yet only a few years later, he published a book aiming at promoting nuclear abolition in Italy, which predominantly adopted a humanitarian frame.[90]

The most interesting example of ICAN's campaigning, however, comes from the Netherlands and the experience with the 'Citizens Initiative'. Since 2009, a law allows the Dutch population to make a proposal for 'making, changing or withdrawing legal rules'.[91] Along with basic requirements (the proposal must touch on issues that Parliament decides, cannot deal with constitutional or tax issues, and must have not been decided in Parliament in the last two years), it requires 40,000 signatures by Dutch citizens. Dutch civil society uses this mechanism to deal with contentious issues (there was, for instance, a proposal to allow euthanasia based on a 'fulfilled life') or changes brought about by modern life (for instance, internet bullying).

In 2014, PAX started collecting signatures for the Citizen Initiatives 'Sign Against Nuclear Weapons' (Teken tegen Kernwapens).[92] The goal was a ban on Dutch territory. At the end of September 2015, the initiative was submitted with 45,608 signatures. While this appears impressive, one needs to take into account that signature collection was a joint effort by three organisations (the Dutch Red Cross and socially responsible ASN Bank joined in). That it took PAX almost a year, while Parliament actually debated hotly about participation in the OEWG and mandated government to do so,[93] testifies to rather low issue salience. Dutch expert Sico van der Meer,

---

[88] See Catanzaro and Coticchia (2018).
[89] Coticchia (2016); Catanzaro and Coticchia (2018)
[90] Vignarca (2023)
[91] Tweede Kamer der Staten-Generaal (2024a)
[92] The word 'teken' in Dutch carries both the literal and figurative meaning of 'sign' and can be also used as 'draw'. I have written in more detail about the initiative and the subsequent debate in Onderco (2021).
[93] Tweede Kamer der Staten-Generaal (2015)

who worked for the Clingendael Institute and was not involved in the effort, reminisced

> It took them so [much] time. If you start a signature action [for] sick cats, you would have the same number of signatures in one month. When we talk about nuclear weapons, people say, 'what do I need to sign? I don't know anything about it.' You know, I think they did a lot of efforts going on the streets telling people about the topic. And then people signed. So, it was a great effort of them. And it worked. There was a parliamentary debate.[94]

The proposal prominently placed humanitarian concerns as the second most important reason for adopting a national ban (after proliferation concerns but before 'growing worldwide support for legal ban on nuclear weapons').[95] The parliamentary debate, in April 2016, was rambunctious. With the exception of the VVD and the populist far-right PVV, all parties spoke against continuing the nuclear sharing arrangements. Thirteen motions were filed, of which eleven pushed for unilateral steps. Four were adopted: to publish all bilateral agreements with the US related to nuclear weapons,[96] push for global nuclear disarmament,[97] participate in the OEWG,[98] and phase out nuclear weapons hosting.[99] The parliamentary activism, spurred by the Citizens Initiative, later forced the government to take part in the TPNW negotiations and the first TPNW MSP. It is therefore no wonder that PAX, and ICAN, like to see the Citizens Initiative as a success.[100]

Yet that success also comes down to a fairly open institutional rules in the Netherlands that allowed for it to happen. Such rules do not exist in other countries, and therefore ICAN cannot organise such activities elsewhere. Where they exist (for instance, Italy has

---

[94] Interview with Sico van der Meer (2022)
[95] PAX No Nukes (2016)
[96] Tweede Kamer der Staten-Generaal (2016c)
[97] Tweede Kamer der Staten-Generaal (2016b)
[98] Tweede Kamer der Staten-Generaal (2016d)
[99] Tweede Kamer der Staten-Generaal (2016e)
[100] See, for instance, Interview with Susi Snyder (2022), Robinson (2019).

an equivalent law), they have not been used thus far. Furthermore, PAX's success in the Netherlands in dominating the national debate, albeit briefly, comes down also to the paucity of the local expertise. For instance, when the Dutch Parliament debated nuclear weapons in 2019, from over a dozen speakers, only three were not affiliated with any of the ICAN partners.[101] This was different from the Bundestag debates, where experts and university professors are often invited.[102] However, at the 2024 debate about nuclear weapons, only one of the four speakers was affiliated with ICAN.[103]

The ICAN Cities Appeal

ICAN partners across Europe have various ways of engaging with the public against nuclear weapons. PAX in the Netherlands, for example, claimed credit for major pension funds divestment from nuclear weapons investment.[104] In four out of five countries, local ICAN partners organise events to bring attention to nuclear weapons through debates. In Italy, for instance, Senzaatomica organises exhibitions showing the horrors of nuclear weapons use.

However, the Cities Appeal has become ICAN's major effort to provide bottom-up pressure on the host governments. This is not the first effort to rally cities to support nuclear disarmament – during the Cold War, Mayors for Peace provided a major outlet for the East–West partnership. It continues to be relevant today; in recent decades, for instance, almost one thousand Iranian cities joined it.[105] The Cities Appeal is different – it has signatures primarily from Western countries. The only non-WEOG countries are Argentina (2 cities), Croatia (2 cities), India (1 city) and Japan (2 cities).[106]

---

[101] Tweede Kamer der Staten-Generaal (2019)
[102] See, for instance, Deutcher Bundestag (2023).
[103] Tweede Kamer der Staten-Generaal (2024b)
[104] PAX No Nukes (2018)
[105] On Mayors for Peace, see Jakobi (2025).
[106] Again, these data are taken from ICAN's website at the time of writing. However, ICAN does not have a regular and systematic policy for updating its website, and therefore these data may be outdated.

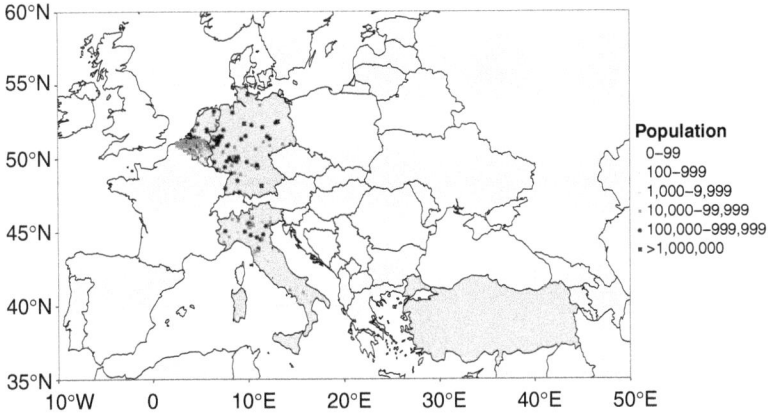

FIGURE 5.3 Location of cities that signed the ICAN Cities Appeal.

Cities Appeal has attracted signatures of hundreds of cities, 297 of them in the five European host nations (Figure 5.2). These cities are, however, very unequally distributed. A plurality of them – 137 – are in Belgium, with only one in Turkey – Fındıklı joined in October 2023. Local mobilisation also varies. While, for instance, Fındıklı signed the appeal 'on its own', without any coordination with ICAN, Italy saw a concerted effort to get municipalities to sign.[107] Figure 5.3 shows the location of these cities in the European host nations.

Table 5.2 compares the distribution of the size of municipalities across the five host nations. One obvious pattern is the variation across countries. In Italy, for instance, 54% of cities are under 10,000 inhabitants. By contrast, in Germany, 65% are major cities above 100,000 inhabitants, and 6% are even above one million inhabitants. In Belgium, 98% of participants are mid-sized cities of up to 100,000 inhabitants.

Given the lack of data about the municipalities that have *not* signed the Cities Appeal (surprisingly enough, no reliable social science databases contain data on all municipalities), it is difficult to analyse what makes some municipalities more likely to sign.

[107] Interview with Francesco Vignarca (2023)

Table 5.2 *Population of cities that signed the ICAN Cities Appeal*

	Population						
Country	Under 100 (%)	Over 100 (%)	Over 1k (%)	Over 10k (%)	Over 100k (%)	Over 1 mil (%)	Total
BE	0	0	27	71	2	0	137
DE	0	0	4	30	59	6	69
IT	1	7	46	32	13	0	82
NL	0	0	0	38	63	0	8
TK	0	0	0	100	0	0	1

However, we might look at the population of the cities and their characteristics to understand features of those who *did* sign.

Because most of the endorsements of the Cities Appeal are made by municipal councils, I have examined their composition and ideological leaning. I applied a standard formula that is used in comparative politics, taking the measure of the ideology of an individual party and then weighting them by its share in the council. Because of the popularity of local parties in Europe and because it is virtually impossible to measure their ideology, I analysed only municipalities where at least 50% of seats were occupied by national parties. To measure party partisan ideology, I relied on the left–right measure from CHES, a standard source for measuring ideology in political science.[108]

The results, found in Figure 5.4, indicate that the municipalities that endorsed the Cities Appeal tend to be led by centrist and centre-left municipal councils. Figure 5.4 shows a violin plot, where relative thickness indicates frequency distribution of the data. Very few municipal councils led by extremist leaders endorsed the Cities Appeal, but it is also unusual to have municipal councils with right-wing majorities do so. The exception to this rule is the Netherlands, where only a handful of local municipalities did, but they were solidly left-wing. These findings somewhat confirm the

---

[108] Jolly et al. (2022)

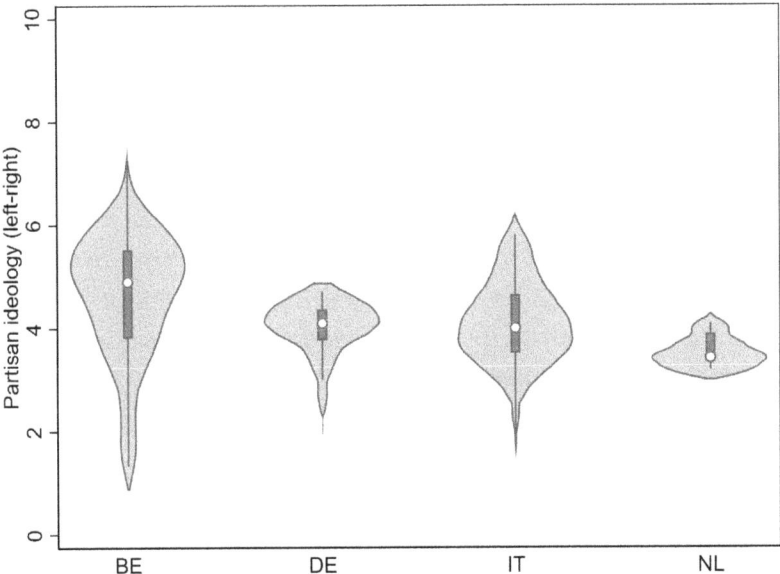

FIGURE 5.4 Left–right ideology and support for the ICAN Cities Appeal.

findings from the previous chapter that parties on the political left are more likely to support pro-disarmament messages.

While the activities of local ICAN partners are often important in encouraging municipal councils to endorse the appeal, I can already make some generalisation about its supporters. In Belgium, these are usually mid-sized cities led by centrist municipal councils. In Italy, they tend to be smaller towns led by centrist and centre-left municipal councils. In Germany and the Netherlands, they tend to be bigger cities with left-leaning (in the Netherlands, leftist) governments.

The experience of Amsterdam being in support of the Cities Appeal illustrates nicely how particular municipal dynamics might actually lead to support it. In Amsterdam, the initiative to sign was filed by five members of the municipal council (*gemeenteraad*, in Dutch), of which four came from left-wing parties the PvdD, GL, BiJ1, and SP, with the fifth from the Social Democratic DENK.[109] As the

[109] Gemeente Amsterdam / Gemeenteraad (2019)

proposal makes clear, the main motivation for filing was to address tax avoidance by weapons producers – including Lockheed Martin, Boeing, BAE, General Dynamics and United Technologies – that used shell companies headquartered in Amsterdam's Zuidas business district to exploit the Dutch tax system.[110] The initiative from the Municipal Council of Amsterdam started in 2016, when the leftist and centre-left parties in the council wanted to address tax avoidance by the weapons companies. This, however, did not lead to tangible results.

Cashing in on the growing concern about international security, members of the municipal council tried again in 2019. The effort was led by Femke Roosma, a municipal councillor from the left-wing Green Left party, whose portfolio included welfare and housing. As Roosma said later in an interview, addressing the tax avoidance angle was a key motivation for them. Only then did they start discussing with PAX, which, through its contacts with the Socialist members of the municipal council, alerted them to the existence of the Cities Appeal.[111] In September 2020, the municipal executive (*college*, in Dutch) responded to the organisers. The letter very clearly indicates the reservations the municipal executive had. It mentions that the issue at hand is at its core a competence of the national government and not the municipality.[112] However, recognising the potential of sending a message by joining an initiative with other capitals around the world, the municipal executive indicated it was willing to take this point. In January 2021, the municipal council debated and approved a modified initiative, which included the suggestion to sign the appeal.[113] Two days later, Deputy Mayor Rutger Groot Wassink signed.[114]

In Rotterdam, the motion to join the Cities Appeal was put forward by a small group of municipal council members from the left-wing and religious-right parties and led by a Green Left councillor,

---

[110] Gemeente Amsterdam / Gemeenteraad (2019, p. 2)
[111] Interview with Femke Roosma, April 2024
[112] Gemeente Amsterdam (2020)
[113] Gemeente Amsterdam / Gemeenteraad (2021)
[114] GroenLinks Amsterdam (2021)

Stephan Leewis. Leewis was responsible for the portfolio including energy transition and sustainability.[115] The proposal itself had a very strong focus on environmental damage caused by nuclear weapons. The council debated the proposal along with a motion to ban armament expos from taking place in Rotterdam Ahoy, a giant conference centre owned by the municipal executive.[116] That motion failed, but the motion to adopt the Cities Appeal was passed after the so-called two-minute debate.[117] The municipality informed the council, on 8 December 2020, in dry bureaucratic language, that it told PAX that the municipality would sign the Cities Appeal.[118] Ultimately, the experience of the two largest Dutch cities shows that left-leaning municipal councils are crucial for taking action and that often other issues – such as tax avoidance or environmental concerns – are key in motivating their actions.

Taken together, this underscores the similarities but also differences between cities and their support for the ICAN Cities Appeal. It also shows that while ICAN has used the initiative in all five host nations, it has not been equally successful in all five of them, and the initiative continues to be driven by varied dynamics on the ground.

CONCLUSION

In this chapter, I have looked at the reinvigorated civil society working on nuclear issues in the European host nations. I have described a pattern where civil society organisations renewed their activities in early 2010s, particularly under the aegis of ICAN. Through their various actions, globally but also locally, they have rallied the cause in support of nuclear disarmament, against nuclear sharing, and in favour of the TPNW. This effort has led to only very limited

---

[115] GroenLinks Rotterdam (n.d.)
[116] See agenda item 17.4 in Gemeente van Rotterdam (2020).
[117] Allocation of two minutes to this issue also indicates the relative importance of this agenda for the municipal council.
[118] Gemeente Rotterdam/College van Burgemeester en Wethouders (2020)

domestic political impact but inspired public debate and enabled ICAN to spread its message across domestic publics. ICAN and its affiliates worked very diligently with parliaments, particularly in the Netherlands and Germany, where they managed to develop solid relations with parliamentarians. However, ICAN was also successful in developing relations with other actors, such as civil society in cities.

Writing this chapter in spring 2024, I noticed that ICAN's activity has changed since the Russian invasion of Ukraine. In the European host nations, their activities have quieted down. There have been very few additions to the list of Cities Appeal signatories (although quite a few in Italy). In the Netherlands, ICAN has almost stopped campaigning for signing the TPNW,[119] which is partially linked to the changed tone of the national debate; public views of nuclear deterrence shifted significantly.[120] In Germany, civil society recognised that now was not the time to lobby for joining the TPNW and satisfied itself with lobbying for the participation in future MSPs.[121]

However, as political scientists and nuclear disarmament experts Stephen Herzog and Rebecca Davis Gibbons wrote in 2023, the current swing in public attitudes is not definitive.[122] It is likely that, as the war in Ukraine slows or reaches a stalemate, the calls for nuclear disarmament will return. The pro-nuclear swing in public opinion has already started to dampen, and public views of nuclear weapons have somewhat returned to the pre-war normal.[123] Therefore, it is not completely impossible to expect that ICAN will return.

In Chapter 7, I will look at how technocratic elites engage civil society's activities, what arguments they use in such engagement, and how they seek to deflect and reflect some of the criticism.

[119] However, during a recent parliamentary testimony, the PAX representative did call on the government to sign the treaty. See Tweede Kamer der Staten-Generaal (2024b).
[120] Onderco et al. (2023)
[121] Interview with a civil society representative
[122] Gibbons and Herzog (2023)
[123] Onderco (2024)

6 Allies

INTRODUCTION

'Going forward, there will be a need for a stronger focus on NATO as a nuclear alliance.' One would hardly expect such a sentence in a national security strategy of a Scandinavian nation, known for their support for disarmament. Yet it appears on page 39 of the *Danish Security and Defence Towards 2035* report, a strategic document issued in 2022.[1] In 2016, an earlier report spoke of Danish security being 'ultimately guaranteed' by NATO through a 'nuclear deterrence coupled with robust conventional forces'.[2]

A book about NATO nuclear sharing needs to consider how the allies view the practice. This matters for three reasons. First, from the standpoint of theory, as I explained in the second chapter, it matters immensely that nuclear sharing is not just a bilateral policy but an alliance policy. These commitments made abroad should allow elites to deflect domestic pressures. Second, therefore, we need to study how the allies think about nuclear deterrence and whether they think explicitly about the nuclear sharing as a relevant factor. Third, we also need to consider where this pressure is mostly coming from and whether it happens at the level of individual allies or of the alliance.

In this chapter, I will look at how the NATO allies see nuclear deterrence within the alliance and whether they specifically consider the role of nuclear sharing. In particular, I will examine three categories – the US as the country stationing the weapons, the individual allied countries, and the alliance documents themselves. Taken

[1] *Danish Security and Defence Towards 2035* (Denmark) (2022, p. 39)
[2] *Danish Diplomacy and Defense in Times of Change* (Denmark) (2016)

together, they represent three angles through which the alliance underscores the continuous importance of nuclear sharing.

Methodologically, I focus on the strategic documents published by these three groups. For the US, I focus on the successive Nuclear Posture Reviews (NPR) and other documents published by various administrations. For the alliance, I look primarily at the Deterrence and Defence Posture Review, successive summit communiqués as the highest-level strategic guidance documents, and various study group documents. For the allied states, I look at national defence and strategy documents published in individual countries. For this task, I largely rely on the corpora of strategic documents collected by Jordan Becker and his collaborators over time.[3]

THE US AND NUCLEAR SHARING

Since the weapons stationed in Europe are controlled by (and legally belong to) the US, it must be seen as one of the actors whose views on nuclear sharing matters, and separately so from those of the allies and the alliance. After all, for the host states, nuclear weapons are an important element of strengthening their bilateral relationship with the US.

At the beginning of the 2010s, the US considered withdrawing the remaining weapons from Europe. This was in line with President Obama's vision of a world without nuclear weapons. Those in Europe were seen by many around the president as militarily obsolete, and his appointed ambassador to NATO, Ivo Daalder, was often seen as having a mission to achieve that withdrawal.[4] Early in his career, Daalder published a paper in which he advocated for a complete withdrawal,[5] and many inside and outside the administration saw him as holding on to such views.

Obama's Nuclear Posture Review, published in 2010, started by stating that the 'the presence of US nuclear weapons – combined with NATO's unique nuclear sharing arrangements under which

---

[3] Becker and Malesky (2017); Becker et al. (2024)
[4] Interview with Brad Roberts, January 2024
[5] Daalder (1993)

non-nuclear members participate in nuclear planning and possess specially configured aircraft capable of delivering nuclear weapons – contribute to Alliance cohesion and provide reassurance to allies and partners who feel exposed to regional threats'.[6] The strategy, however, also committed to retaining this capability and proceeding with the full-scope life extension of the B61 bombs.[7] The 2010 NPR also committed not to make any changes 'without continued close consultation with allies and partners'.[8]

Trump's NPR, published eight years later, found the world dramatically different. It committed the US to 'maintain, and enhance as necessary, the capability to forward deploy nuclear bombers and DCA around the world' and 'with NATO to best ensure – and improve where needed – the readiness, survivability, and operational effectiveness of DCA based in Europe'.[9] However, it explicitly placed the role of non-strategic nuclear weapons in Europe in the context of 'correct[ing] any Russian misperceptions of advantage and credibly deter[ring] Russian nuclear or non-nuclear strategic attacks'.[10] It went further than Obama's NPR and called them 'an essential political and military link between Europe and North America and ... the supreme guarantee of Alliance security'.[11]

When President Biden was elected, many commentators expressed hope that he would continue Obama's pro-disarmament policies. Among many European allies, fears were raised that the administration could adopt either a no-first-use strategy or the sole-purpose policy, which would effectively rule out NATO's use of nuclear weapons in scenarios other than those after the first nuclear use by an adversary.[12] However, the Biden administration ultimately changed very little. Biden's NPR, for instance, proudly stated that

---

[6] Department of Defense (2010, p. xii)
[7] Department of Defense (2010, p. xiii)
[8] Department of Defense (2010, p. 28)
[9] Department of Defense (2018, p. XII)
[10] Department of Defense (2018, p. 31)
[11] Department of Defense (2018, p. 36)
[12] For an overview of national concerns, see Arndt et al. (2021).

'United States strategic nuclear forces and forward-deployed nuclear weapons provide an essential political and military link between Europe and North America. ... US nuclear forces remain essential to the Alliance's deterrence and defence posture. Since Russia's invasion of Ukraine and occupation of Crimea in 2014, NATO has taken steps to ensure a modern, ready, and credible NATO nuclear deterrent.'[13]

The importance and relevance of nuclear sharing has been underscored in the 2023 report of the US Strategic Posture Commission, which confirmed that the views of the allies related to the relevance of the US deployment of nuclear weapons in Europe and associated updates to 'nuclear sharing mechanics' advance NATO's 'steadfast commitment to the defence of its members'.[14]

US pressure on allies is often assumed, but there are very few explicit signs of this. One clear example happened during the TPNW negotiations, when the Obama administration circulated a memo to NATO allies, arguing that the ban treaty would 'hurt the alliance'.[15] These pressures were repeated by the Trump administration, which had also circulated a letter to the signatories of the treaty, asking them to withdraw their signatures (no NATO members signed).[16] Lobbying can also take more informal forms. For instance, in 2020, the US defence policy grandee Michele Flournoy co-published an op-ed, warning Germany not to lose a seat at a 'very exclusive table', which would happen if the DCA mission were not extended.[17]

THE ALLIES AND NUCLEAR SHARING

In addition to the US, pressure comes also from the allies whom the nuclear umbrella is supposed to protect. Scholarship has, however, paid only limited attention to the positions of these countries and how they view nuclear sharing.

[13] Department of Defense (2022)
[14] Creedon et al. (2023, p. 78)
[15] Gibbons (2017)
[16] Lederer (2020)
[17] Flournoy and Townsend (2020)

The most recent study to take a look at their views was the 2018 European Council on Foreign Relations (ECFR) study of how European countries view nuclear deterrence. The study, published in a report with the telling title *Eyes Tight Shut*, classifies European countries into five categories: True Believers, Neutrals, Conflicted, Pragmatists, and Conformists.[18] The authors indicate that the following countries belong to each of the groups:

> True Believers: France, the United Kingdom, Poland, Romania
> Neutrals: Austria, Cyprus, Finland, Ireland, Malta
> Conflicted: Germany, the Netherlands, Sweden
> Pragmatists: Belgium, Bulgaria, Czechia, Estonia, Lithuania, Latvia, Italy
> Conformists: Croatia, Denmark, Greece, Hungary, Luxembourg, Slovakia, Slovenia, Spain, Portugal

The ECFR's classification is, of course, a snapshot in time. Finland, for instance, was classified as neutral, with the argument that 'the nuclear threat is not a priority in its strategic assessment of its environment' and 'deterrence remains marginal to Finland's defence strategy'.[19] This assessment would not be correct in 2024, when Finland was in NATO, and deterrence had been an important element motivating its request to join.[20] The group of Neutrals contains only the countries outside NATO and so is not terribly relevant for this discussion. Nevertheless, the ECFR classification offers a useful heuristic to understand that countries within the alliance view nuclear deterrence's importance differently. For the moment, I will set aside the non-NATO countries, and France and the UK, whose nuclear deterrents are seen as 'independent' by the alliance.[21]

---

[18] Rapnouil et al. (2018)
[19] Rapnouil et al. (2018)
[20] See, for instance, Fedina (2024); Pesu and Juntunen (2023).
[21] NATO's documents officially state that '[t]he independent strategic nuclear forces of the United Kingdom and France have a deterrent role of their own and contribute significantly to the overall security of the Alliance. These Allies' separate centres of decision-making contribute to deterrence by complicating the calculations of any potential adversaries.' See NATO (2023a).

Among the True Believers, Poland is of course the most prominent. This was not always the case. In the first decade of the third millennium, Poland teamed up with Norway to develop ideas for the elimination of tactical nuclear weapons in Europe.[22] This effort extended to a joint op-ed in the *New York Times* by Polish Foreign Minister Radosław Sikorski and Swedish Foreign Minister Carl Bildt calling on the US and Russia to 'commit themselves to early measures to greatly reduce so-called tactical nuclear weapons in Europe', with the goal of a 'total elimination of these types of weapons'.[23] Sikorski issued a similar statement with the Norwegian foreign minister Jonas Gahr Støre.[24] Various analysts disagreed why Poland placed such attention on tactical nuclear weapons in that period. Some argued that the focus was purely military and had to do with its vulnerability as a likely battleground state and the growing Russian militarisation of Kaliningrad.[25] Others agreed but said that the focus on disarmament was a function of warming Polish–Russian relations, which the Polish government tried to translate into arms control steps.[26] Others disagreed and saw the Polish concern as a primary function of the fundamental distrust in the US commitment to the NATO alliance.[27] Still others felt that Poland, like other Central European countries, actually viewed nuclear weapons in Europe as a useful political bargaining tool for the intra-alliance engagement with the US and as an additional assurance from the US.[28]

Polish national security documents reflect the developing priorities. The ones from the early 2010s underscore arms control initiatives, such as the Polish–Norwegian initiative discussed in the earlier paragraph.[29] This view shifted over time. By 2017, Poland noted the

---

[22] Government of Norway (2009)
[23] Bildt and Sikorski (2010)
[24] For an overview of these statements, see Péczeli (2013).
[25] Somerville et al. (2012)
[26] Valášek (2011)
[27] Péczeli (2013)
[28] Horovitz (2014)
[29] White Book on National Security of the Republic of Poland (Poland) (2013)

relevance of the Russian nuclear threats, including the risk that Russia might use tactical nuclear weapons.[30] These concerns were repeated in the 2020 National Security Strategy.[31] Poland became much more hawkish when it came to nuclear hosting and saw the weapons as a fundamental element deterrence.[32] As I will discuss further in the conclusion, with the invasion of Ukraine, Polish concerns have increased so much that by 2024, serious voices advocated for its inclusion in nuclear sharing.[33]

Among the Pragmatists from the ECFR report, nuclear weapons are often listed as the ultimate backdrop. In the early 2000s and 2010s, they appeared in national security strategies primarily through the prism of commitments to nuclear nonproliferation or security. Such commitments can be found, for instance, in various Czech strategic documents.[34] Concerns about 'dirty bombs' or terrorists using nuclear weapons also appear, exactly in line with the literature and worries at that time. For instance, Latvia's strategic documents are clear about such concerns.[35]

The strategic documents of these countries provided fewer references to nuclear weapons as a deterrent. In 2012, Latvia's State Defence Concept said that 'taking into account the international security situation, Latvia believes that NATO must maintain the nuclear posture also further on. An appropriate mix of nuclear and conventional forces is an important basis for military response of the Alliance.'[36] The 2015 Czech Security Strategy says something similar.[37] This lukewarm wording has intensified in recent years, certainly after Russia's invasion of Ukraine. For instance, the 2023 Czech

---

[30] The Defence Concept (Poland) (2017)
[31] National Security Strategy (Poland) (2020)
[32] Sus and Kulesa (2024)
[33] Kacprzyk (2023)
[34] Ministry of Defence of the Czech Republic (2015); Security Strategy of the Czech Republic (Czechia) (2011)
[35] National Security Concept (Latvia) (2002)
[36] The State Defence Concept (Latvia) (2012)
[37] Ministry of Defence of the Czech Republic (2015)

Security Strategy not only discusses Russia's attempts at nuclear coercion at length but states plainly that 'a strong, operational, and cohesive NATO, based on a firm transatlantic link, capable to deter and resist a technologically advanced adversary thanks to its effective and credible nuclear deterrence capability ... is a "strategic interest of our State"'.[38] Interestingly, the document also denounces the TPNW by stating that 'Czechia is against non-systemic initiatives calling for a complete ban on nuclear weapons, such as the [TPNW], as these initiatives are not consistent with the operative [NPT].'[39] Similar statements can be found in other national strategies. Latvia's 2016 National Defence Concept argues that 'maintenance of the alliance's nuclear arsenal as well as support to the current placement of the alliance's nuclear weapons in Europe is imperative to retain NATO's nuclear capacity and is in Latvia's interests as long as nuclear weapons exist in the world'.[40] Estonia's 2017 National Security Concept contains similar language, arguing 'NATO's ultimate security guarantee is its nuclear deterrent. This must be credible and available in the Alliance's European territory.'[41] Similar preferences were voiced by Lithuanian officials, who, for instance, in 2020 expressed that they were opposed to the withdrawal of US nuclear weapons from Germany, in the midst of that debate.[42]

Among the Conformists, one finds countries that have also recalibrated their views of nuclear weapons. Denmark, in the early 2000s, for instance, considered them primarily in the context of radiological emergencies (that is, also primarily as a risk of dirty bombs used by terrorists).[43] This had shifted by 2016, when Danish strategic documents decried that 'Russia is underway with a comprehensive of its armed forces and apparently also lowers the threshold

---

[38] Ministry of Foreign Affairs of the Czech Republic (2023, p. 11)
[39] Ministry of Foreign Affairs of the Czech Republic (2023, p. 23)
[40] National Defence Concept (Latvia) (2016, p. 8)
[41] National Security Concept (Estonia) (2017, p. 12)
[42] Saldžiūnas (2020)
[43] The Danish Defence Agreement 2005–2009 (Denmark) (2004)

for the use of its nuclear military capabilities.'[44] In response, the document mentioned that Russia's modernisation challenges the NATO posture with its strict distinction between conventional and nuclear means, before concluding that 'Denmark's security is ultimately guaranteed through NATO's collective defence, [which includes] nuclear deterrence coupled with robust conventional forces.'[45] Prior to 2014, the strategic documents of Hungary, Greece, Portugal, or Slovakia also primarily discussed nuclear weapons in the context of nonproliferation and terrorism.[46] Interestingly, both Slovakia and Hungary underscored around the same time that Russia continued to be a factor in European security through its nuclear capacities, but this argument has never been developed further.[47] Spain, for instance, in 2011, 'embrace[d] NATO's doctrine for harmonising minimum nuclear deterrence with disarmament commitments' in its Security Strategy.[48]

These views started to change over time, for some. In 2016, Slovakia's White Paper on Defence contemplated possible Russian use of tactical nuclear weapons in a conflict.[49] In 2021, the Defence Strategy went as far as to say that 'The deterrence of an armed attack against the Slovak Republic is based on NATO's collective deterrence and defence potential and on the resolve to defend itself. Allies' nuclear weapons play a key role.'[50] The 2022 Danish strategy concluded that 'With the growing importance of nuclear weapons, there is also reason to consider whether we must once again prepare for the worst.'[51] Not all strategic documents changed, however. In Hungary,

---

[44] Danish Diplomacy and Defense in Times of Change (Denmark) (2016)
[45] Danish Diplomacy and Defense in Times of Change (Denmark) (2016)
[46] National Security Strategy (Hungary) (2004); The Defence Strategy of the Slovak Republic (Slovakia) (2005); White Paper (Greece) (2014); Defense in 2020 (Portugal) (2013)
[47] The Defence Strategy of the Slovak Republic (Slovakia) (2005); National Security Strategy (Hungary) (2004)
[48] Spanish Security Strategy – Everyone's Responsibility (Spain) (2011, pp. 56–58)
[49] Government Office of the Slovak Republic (2016)
[50] Obranná stratégia SR 2021 (2021)
[51] Danish Security and Defence Towards 2035 (Denmark) (2022, p. 78)

nuclear risks continued to be primarily associated with terrorism.[52] These developments are completely in line with the Conformists' role; they do not emphasise deterrence. Denmark and Slovakia, having started to give more attention to nuclear deterrence in strategic documents, might be an exception.

THE ALLIANCE AND NUCLEAR SHARING

The alliance itself provides an additional source of pressure. Allied documents speak, by now rather clearly, about the nuclear dimension of deterrence and the role of nuclear sharing therein.

Next to the doctrinal sources, discussed further on, the social sources of the allied pressure are equally, if not more important. All allies, except for France, take part in the NPG. It was established in 1966 to involve the allies in US planning for nuclear employment within the alliance.[53] The NPG meets once a year, works on the basis of consensus, and aims at very high-level debates. It is supported by the High-Level Group (HLG), a group composed of senior-level national civil servants (usually at the level of the security policy director, in Europe). The HLG's work is supported by the NPG Staff Group, which meets at least weekly and is composed of national diplomats accredited at the NATO Headquarters in Brussels.[54] Scholarship extensively argues that this arrangement was primarily meant to give them a voice in the debate in case of a war, even if it would significantly complicate an actual employment of nuclear weapons.[55] The NPG maintains political control over NATO nuclear deterrence at all times and under all circumstances, and the North Atlantic Council (NAC) defers to the NPG on decision-making on nuclear issues. In war, the NPG's role would be much greater than that of the NAC for conventional weapons, as

---

[52] National Security Strategy (Hungary) (2020)
[53] Sayle (2020)
[54] An overview of these groups can be found in Bunn (2022, pp. 206–208)
[55] Michaels (2022); Sayle (2020)

it would be involved down to the level of particular weapon use. The reinvigoration of the NPG in recent years (especially after Russia's 2014 occupation of Crimea) gave NATO members an even greater stake in the alliance's nuclear mission.[56] However, the fact that these countries meet regularly in an institutionalised setting means that they also create social pressure towards one another, especially the one described in the previous section.

In terms of strategic documents, the alliance's post-Ukraine nuclear strategy has been encapsulated in the summit communiqué released at the NATO summit in Vilnius in July 2023. The document's money quote can be found in three brief paragraphs:

> 43. The fundamental purpose of NATO's nuclear capability is to preserve peace, prevent coercion and deter aggression. Nuclear weapons are unique. As long as nuclear weapons exist, NATO will remain a nuclear alliance. NATO's goal is a safer world for all; we seek to create the security environment for a world without nuclear weapons. The circumstances in which NATO might have to use nuclear weapons are extremely remote. Any employment of nuclear weapons against NATO would fundamentally alter the nature of a conflict. The Alliance has the capabilities and resolve to impose costs on an adversary that would be unacceptable and far outweigh the benefits that any adversary could hope to achieve.
>
> 44. The strategic nuclear forces of the Alliance, particularly those of the United States, are the supreme guarantee of the security of the Alliance. The independent strategic nuclear forces of the United Kingdom and France have a deterrent role of their own and contribute significantly to the overall security of the Alliance. These Allies' separate centres of decision-making contribute to deterrence by complicating the calculations of potential adversaries. NATO's nuclear deterrence posture also

---

[56] I am relying on information shared in various Track II settings. Note that this account is consistent with the information provided in NATO (2025, p.14).

relies on the United States' nuclear weapons forward-deployed in Europe. National contributions, by Allies concerned, of dual-capable aircraft, as well as the provision of conventional forces and military capabilities in support of NATO's nuclear deterrence mission, remain central to this effort.

45. NATO will take all necessary steps to ensure the credibility, effectiveness, safety and security of the nuclear deterrent mission. This includes continuing to modernise NATO's nuclear capability and updating planning to increase flexibility and adaptability of the Alliance's nuclear forces, while exercising strong political control at all times. The Alliance reaffirms the imperative to ensure the broadest possible participation by Allies concerned in NATO's nuclear burden-sharing arrangements to demonstrate Alliance unity and resolve.[57]

These paragraphs offer a lot to unpack. The first paragraph is meant to set NATO apart from Russia, which attempted to use nuclear coercion during its war in Ukraine; NATO called out Russia for that in the same communiqué. NATO wants to separate itself from Russia by signalling that it does not intend to use its own nuclear forces for coercive purposes.[58] The first half of this paragraph also contains a famous assertion that 'as long as nuclear weapons exist, NATO will remain a nuclear alliance'. This sentence was inserted into NATO communiqués for the first time in 2010 in Lisbon, partially in response to pressure from Germany and others to open discussion about the end of nuclear sharing.[59] The second part of the first paragraph is meant to signal to adversaries that NATO would respond to all nuclear attacks but not necessarily have to do so by using nuclear means.

---

[57] NATO (2023b)

[58] NATO's argument also challenges some countries' interpretation that all nuclear states engage in threatening rhetoric. The final statement of the first TPNW MSP reflects this view. See United Nations (2022).

[59] NATO (2010)

The second paragraph is similarly important because it discusses how NATO assures nuclear deterrence. The second half has direct relevance to nuclear sharing, as it speaks about forward-deployed nuclear weapons in Europe and the contributions of the allies that host dual-capable aircraft. The wording of this paragraph is unique, since, as discussed earlier, the categories of the host nations and dual-capable aircraft providers do not fully overlap. More countries provide DCA aircraft than host nuclear weapons, and not all host nations supply aircraft.[60]

The third paragraph is important because it underscores the commitment to modernise nuclear capability, which includes providing the new fighter jets. However, the second half is key because it speaks about the 'broadest possible participation by Allies', which makes NATO's nuclear mission the responsibility of not only the nuclear allies and DCA nations but also each ally. One way NATO countries could contribute to such mission is by contributing to the alliance's CSNO mission, but countries can contribute in multiple ways.[61]

In a subsequent paragraph, the Vilnius summit communiqué also rejects the TPNW, arguing that it

> stands in opposition to and is inconsistent and incompatible with the Alliance's nuclear deterrence policy, is at odds with the existing nonproliferation and disarmament architecture, risks undermining the NPT, and does not take into account the current security environment. The TPNW does not change the legal obligations on our countries with respect to nuclear weapons. We do not accept any argument that the TPNW reflects or in any way contributes to the development of customary international law.[62]

---

[60] See the discussion in Kristensen et al. (2023).
[61] Hosting the annual NATO Nuclear Policy Conference in nation's tourist hotspot is a popular way for some NATO nations to contribute to NATO's 'nuclear burden sharing'.
[62] NATO (2023b, para 54)

This statement is a strong example of how the NATO communiqué provides an argument for the host nations, especially those with a strong civil society, with a ready-made language that can be used in domestic settings. However, it also binds the member states and discourages them from attending the TPNW MSPs. As one senior government official told me in an interview, attending the MSPs 'is a strange pastime and we cannot fully understand it'.[63]

Last but not least, the Vilnius communiqué provides an argument that the existing NATO nuclear arrangements are fully consistent with the NPT, countering another argument often advanced by NATO's critics in diplomatic settings, that nuclear sharing arrangements violate NPT.[64]

The Vilnius statement develops and structures earlier thoughts. The key elements were stated in the 2022 NATO Strategic Concept,[65] 2021 Brussels Summit Communiqué,[66] 2018 Brussels Summit Declaration,[67] and 2016 Warsaw Summit Communiqué, which appears to be the first to also underscore the role of the DCA partners.[68] Similar language can be also found in the report of the NATO reflection group, which argued that

> NATO continues to have a critical role to play in maintaining both conventional and nuclear deterrence and defence through Allied arsenals and via US forward deployments in Europe. Nuclear weapons have been a critical pillar of NATO's collective defence since its inception. Moreover, nuclear sharing arrangements play a vital role in the interconnection of the Alliance and should remain one of the main components of security guarantees and the indivisibility of security of the whole Euro-Atlantic area.[69]

---

[63] Interview with a senior government official, March 2024
[64] NATO (2023b, p. para 53)
[65] NATO (2022)
[66] NATO (2021)
[67] NATO (2018)
[68] NATO (2016)
[69] de Maizière et al. (2020, p. 36)

However, not all earlier communiqués have been so explicit. The 2019 London Statement, for instance, repeats the line about remaining a nuclear alliance but does not discuss the special role of NATO's DCA countries.[70] Similarly, the line about that special role does not appear in the 2014 Wales Summit Declaration.[71]

Similarly, NATO allies have been unequivocal about their rejection of the TPNW. On 20 September 2017, the day when the TPNW was opened for signature, the NAC published a statement that denounced it. 'Seeking to ban nuclear weapons through a treaty that will not engage any state actually possessing nuclear weapons will not be effective, will not reduce nuclear arsenals, and will neither enhance any country's security, nor international peace and stability. ... The ban treaty, in our view, disregards the realities of the increasingly challenging international security environment.'[72] A similar view was repeated in 2020, when the TPNW came into force.[73]

As discussed in the first chapter, the explicit insistence on NATO's identity as a nuclear alliance can be traced back to the 2010 Strategic Concept.[74] However, that came in an interesting time, at the heels of a major discussion about the presence of non-strategic nuclear weapons in Europe. This also meant that the Strategic Concept, similarly to the Deterrence and Defence Posture Review (DDPR) published two years ago, maintained the position that nuclear weapons were relevant but their role and numbers should diminish.[75] Obama's ambassador to NATO Ivo Daalder has been identified as a 'supporter of disarmament in the Obama camp', and it is therefore not a surprise that he did side with those who wanted to diminish the role of nuclear weapons in Europe.[76] The 2012 DDPR, for instance,

---

[70] NATO (2019)
[71] NATO (2014)
[72] NATO (2017)
[73] NATO (2020b)
[74] NATO (2010)
[75] Kristensen (2015)
[76] On Daalder, see Borger (2010a).

still discussed conditions for reducing the alliance's 'reliance on non-strategic nuclear weapons based in Europe'.[77] Interestingly, the DDPR does mention that non-strategic nuclear weapons are stationed in Europe, but it assigns the concern for them not to the DCA nations but to all the members of the NPG.[78]

CONCLUSION

In this chapter, I have discussed how the NATO allies think about and discuss nuclear sharing. I have shown that in the early 2010s, not only was little attention given to nuclear sharing but there was also hope in many circles (among US diplomats but also some European NATO allies and at the level of the alliance itself) that the non-strategic nuclear weapons deployed in Europe would be withdrawn.

The position started to shift around 2014, when Russia invaded Ukraine for the first time and started occupying NATO. Stronger wording related to nuclear sharing started to appear in NATO documents around 2016, roughly coinciding with the momentum picking up in the OEWG towards negotiating a nuclear ban. Not only did some allies (e.g., Estonia) start to include explicit language highlighting the role of nuclear sharing in their security, but NATO also started to explicitly discuss its role and that of nuclear weapons stationed in Europe. For instance, while in 2012, DDPR still spoke about all NPG members having the responsibility for nuclear deterrence, and 2014 Wales Declaration did not discuss the host nations in any particular way, the 2016 Warsaw Communiqué was for the first time explicit about their role. This was also a moment when the importance of the host nations became more visible. As a former NATO official told me, a few years ago, 'states acted from the lack of knowledge [and] a political, not policy, debate'.[79]

---

[77] NATO (2012, p. para 12)
[78] NATO (2012, p. para 11)
[79] Interview with a NATO official, September 2023.

Almost all subsequent NATO documents were explicit about this role, whether issued by NATO leaders (such as summit statements) or experts (such as reflection reports and strategic concepts). This underscores that the timing matters and that the allies are becoming an important and influential force, exercising some form of pressure on the host nations. They are also becoming increasingly aware of the role of nuclear sharing in the alliance. In the next chapter, I will explain how this pressure is interpreted by the elites in the host nations.

7 Elites

INTRODUCTION

It was a freezing and wet January day when I was visiting my interlocutor. Crossing a small courtyard, I regretted the choice of shoes with a flat sole, as the ground was slippery and my mind was laser-focused on not falling. A few short minutes later, I was seated in a leather chair in a well-appointed office of the government official whom I was meeting. As my eyes scanned the room, I noticed a small printed sign above the standing table, right at eye level, as the desk was in the standing position. The sign read 'SI VIS PACEM, PARA BELLUM' – if you want peace, prepare for war.

A few short years before, such a sign would have certainly shocked me. European host nations' security policy was everything but preparing for war. Defence budget cuts were à la mode, and the military was meant to be used for expeditionary wars rather than national defence.[1] In such a world, it was no wonder that nuclear weapons came to be seen as an expensive and perhaps questionable tool.

In this chapter, I will study how elites in the host nations engage the contestation of nuclear deterrence and nuclear sharing. As I explained in Chapter 2, nuclear politics is particularly well shaped for making arguments based on responsibility rather than responsiveness. This is primarily because it is a policy designed by experts, who are *meant* to be isolated from public pressure, and concerned with the long term and linked to engagements made abroad.

In this chapter, I seek to look at three elements: first, how elites interpret public pressure; second, how they justify continuous

---

[1] For a good overview of just how much European militaries shifted in the period leading up until the mid-2010s, see Meijer and Wyss (2018).

participation in nuclear sharing; and third, what steps they take in response to public pressure, that is, what bureaucratic responsiveness looks like in practice.

In doing so, the chapter will extend the work on NATO as a "nuclear alliance". Scholars have argued that the definition of NATO's work as a nuclear alliance has almost magically given carte blanche to policymakers in NATO countries to construe any opposition to nuclear weapons as anti-NATO.[2] By contrast, I will argue that foreign policy elites see the nuclear dimension as a natural part of their NATO commitments. In other words, rather than seeing nuclear sharing as an instrumental operationalisation of the alliance membership, they view it as a real contribution to the alliance in the context of the international commitments that their country has made. This is entirely in line with the argument that policymakers and elites are under two forms of control – responsiveness and responsibility – and balance the two in their decision-making. Therefore, as I will show, the international dimension of nuclear sharing allows them to deflect the criticism that their responses are insufficiently 'responsive' by claiming that they more than compensate for that by being 'responsible'. Furthermore, as I will explain, leaders do not ignore the public pressure but rather deflect it, using steps that I label "symbolic adjustments", which are meant to show that they are aware of the public pressure without giving in to its core demands.[3]

FACING PUBLIC PRESSURE

Choosing whether and how to face public pressure carries a political cost for policymakers and technocrats. These costs might be tangible or intangible – they might have to make concessions, engage in horse-trading (exchange progress in one area in favour of concessions to other fields), or at least spend time on addressing them.[4] All

---

[2] Egeland (2020a)
[3] The notion of symbolic adjustments comes from the work of Thomas Risse-Kappen; see Risse-Kappen (1991).
[4] On these three mechanisms, see Saunders (2024).

this makes elites less willing to engage the public, but often they have no choice but to react.

One solution is to ignore the problem. From my research, Turkey and Italy seem to be the countries where this is the preferred method. As a NATO official told me, speaking in general and without reference to any particular country, elites often try to avoid conversations: 'If we do not engage, if we say "it's classified", it'll go away.'[5] Especially political elites in DCA countries are not well-versed in nuclear deterrence, so they are 'afraid of getting asked questions'.[6] However, secrecy is a real issue in the nuclear field – both its overuse and the need to maintain it around certain issues.[7] As one former MP explained, 'there are agreements made ... the minister is in a difficult situation, because he knows. And maybe he even wants more openness. But he cannot [give it]. So he sits in the chamber [Parliament] where he knows our views, and we know his'.[8] However, the same MP added 'from the point of view of democratic decision-making, so from a politics point of view it is a real problem, because there's legitimacy missing. However, from the military point of view, I find [the secrecy] completely logical.'[9]

However, in some countries, a deliberate withdrawal from public pressure is a strategy. A senior government official told me that in Italy, the presence of nuclear weapons on national territory is a *segreto di Pulcinella*, or Pulcinella's secret.[10] Pulcinella is a traditional Napolitan artisanal puppet. One of his features is that he cannot keep quiet about his secrets. So Pulcinella's secret is something that should remain secret but everyone knows about – an open secret. Yet it remains, formally, a secret. The Italian debate about the procurement of the JSF is, for instance, a good example of how

---

[5] Interview with a NATO official, September 2023
[6] Interview with a NATO official, September 2023
[7] On overuse, see Wellerstein (2021).
[8] Interview with a former Dutch MP, December 2023
[9] Interview with a former Dutch MP, December 2023
[10] Interview with a senior government official, March 2024

this works. The replacement of the ageing supersonic fighter jet fleet with the JSF was a major point of debate in Italy. Parliamentary debates were very lively, and civil society was heavily involved and opposed.[11] However, the dual-capable nature of the aircraft was never discussed, by the government or opponents in civil society.

The secrecy has historical roots, reaching back to the Cold War period, when Italy was the Western European country with the strongest Communist Party, and the government preferred not to raise controversial issues. However, it persisted even after the end of the Cold War, when societal support for NATO increased.[12] As numerous interlocutors explained to me, doing so would simply raise the political costs and could open Pandora's box.[13] As a result of this deliberate strategy, the societal salience of the issue is unexpectedly low. As Italian disarmament researcher and sociologist Fabrizio Batistelli told me, 'people in Italy, at the moment, do not know, ... in a blatant way, the exact terms of Italian involvement in' deterrence.[14]

Curiously enough, not even the opposition or populist parties wish to raise this issue. The lack of salience might partly explain it. Furthermore, most Italian elites working on the issues of security are 'pessimistic by default', as one interlocutor told me, which further dampens interest in nuclear disarmament.[15] The institutional inertia, at national and international levels, is seen as immense. And, last, for the elected policymakers, the fear is that promising and not following up could become politically costly. As an Italian expert explained to me, (some) Italian politicians are wary about making promises they know they would not be able to keep in the real world.[16] Changing anything about the sharing

---

[11] For an overview, see Coticchia (2016); Catanzaro and Coticchia (2018).
[12] Interview with Alessandro Marrone, March 2024
[13] Interviews with Alessandro Marrone, Fabrizio Batistelli, an Italian expert, and a senior government official, March 2024
[14] Interview with Fabrizio Batistelli, March 2024
[15] Interview with Alessandro Marrone, March 2024
[16] Interview with an Italian expert, March 2024

arrangements would require a sustained political focus and a lot of political capital. Another Italian expert, Alessandro Marrone, told me that the average time an Italian foreign minister lasts in their post is around eighteen months and so they are unlikely to be able to carry an agenda through two NATO ministerial summits.[17] This makes nuclear disarmament an unpopular agenda item and also an unlikely one to be raised by politicians.

Italy is by no means unique, however. In Turkey, the issue is also discussed very little, primarily because the ministries of foreign affairs and of defence are in the leadership position, together with the Permanent Representation to NATO in Brussels. Even among elites, because of the lack of public salience and very small circle of involved experts, debates are usually held in a 'very limited elite discussion' setting that has 'no reflection on the broader public'.[18] However, the situation is similar in other countries – in all five host countries, the nuclear sharing dossier is handled by the missions to NATO, security policy departments of foreign ministries, or defence ministries. By contrast, it is not uncommon for the nonproliferation and disarmament departments to even be in different units and staffed differently.[19]

By contrast, in countries with more openness, such as Germany, the government often prepares for public interaction. As a German expert explained to me, 'sometimes you can tell that they're not giving you the whole truth', but the expert refused to see that as 'an illegitimate exercise of power'.[20] Numerous interlocutors also mentioned that the government often approached coalition and opposition parties differently. Coalition parties would get more information and better access, and opposition sometimes 'piggybacked' on those.[21]

---

[17] Interview with Alessandro Marrone, March 2024
[18] Interview with Sinan Ülgen
[19] The Netherlands is an exception here, as the Nuclear Policy Department within the Ministry of Foreign Affairs hosts the full range of nuclear-related topics.
[20] Interview with a German expert, January 2024
[21] Interview with a German expert, January 2024; interview with a Green MP, February 2024

Therefore, even if the government did not directly reflect civil society's views, these would trickle up through the party structures and political systems and, through party representatives, reach policy elites.[22] Yet salience matters. German think-tanker and a former parliamentary assistant Pia Führop, for instance, wrote that prior to 2020, there was very little debate about deterrence issues in the Bundestag.[23] However, this was partly because of a 'lack of demand' from the Bundestag.[24]

German government officials confirmed these views. In interviews, they mentioned a number of contravening factors, such as the 'traditional pacifist streak', but they also held strongly pro-transatlantic views and had a lack of knowledge about strategic questions in general.[25] They also expressed that the role of Parliament was seen as desirable, because it gives legitimation and support for the government policy.[26]

However, in countries where the salience of national participation in nuclear sharing is higher, such as in Germany or the Netherlands, the most common form of engaging public pressure is responding to parliamentary action. In the Netherlands, as was discussed in Chapter 4, Parliament hosts a debate on the topic annually on the topic, and the foreign minister often attends. Most policy elites regularly visit parliaments to meet with MPs and engage extensively in drafting letters, which are sent to parliaments on behalf of either a ministry or minister. Policy elites also participate in numerous debates, often with other speakers. Last, they also try to shape the public debate, such as by inviting external speakers. In 2019, for example, the Dutch MFA invited several speakers to address parliamentary committees but also provided a public lecture on nuclear deterrence.[27]

---

[22] Interview with a German expert, January 2024
[23] Fuhrhop (2021)
[24] Interview with a German expert, January 2024
[25] Interview with a government official, January 2024
[26] Interview with a senior government official, January 2024
[27] The invitation can be still found online at www.clingendael.org/event/public-lecture-natos-nuclear-deterrence

Therefore, we see an interactive relationship with the audience – where salience and public involvement are low, elites are not unexpectedly in favour of such arrangements. However, where salience is higher and parliamentary action more lively, elites tend to engage on bureaucratic terms (the use of letters, for instance) but also more directly. This indicates that the level of salience generates response patterns that do tend to be self-reinforcing.

JUSTIFYING PARTICIPATION

Elites are pro-sharing, and therefore there is less point in understanding what policy position they have. It is more interesting to understand why they think that such participation is important.

In Chapter 1, I discussed that the scholarship has raised numerous reasons the allies would be interested in having nuclear weapons on their territory. It was therefore interesting to see which, if any, of the reasons would come back in the interviews with elites.

Responsibility

Some interviewees mentioned that participation in nuclear sharing is a sign of governmental responsibility. Nuclear sharing 'underlines our support for nuclear deterrence within NATO ... not only benefitting, but also actively contributing to ... the risk and burden sharing', a German expert told me in January 2024.[28] Similarly, another German expert explained to me that politicians start speaking about nuclear weapons differently once in office because 'in the very moment you take on government responsibilities, you speak differently'.[29] The sense of responsibility is also linked to knowing 'where are the limits', 'what they can do, what they can say'.[30] In an interview with me, an Italian expert linked this to issues related to the anti-EU attitudes among some politicians – once they reach public

---

[28] Interview with a German expert, January 2024
[29] Interview with a German expert, January 2024
[30] Interview with an Italian expert, March 2024

office, they want to stay there, and that requires a certain manner of handling partners and allies. Italian expert Alessandro Marrone told me something very similar, that seeing government responsibilities makes politicians speak differently.[31] And a senior government official in an interview confirmed, the issue 'puts a sense of responsibility into national leaders'.[32]

Alliance Commitments

The sense of alliance commitments is much more commonly referenced. This appears, for instance, in the national security documents of the host countries. In 2016, the White Paper on German Security Policy repeated the NATO line that 'NATO remains a nuclear alliance' and continued that 'through nuclear sharing, Germany continues to be an integral part of NATO's nuclear policy and planning'.[33] Similarly, the 2018 Dutch Integrated International Security Strategy clearly indicated that the Netherlands would 'continue to meet its commitments regarding NATO's nuclear task'.[34]

However, the part of the alliance responsibilities also comes out very clearly in the interviews. A NATO official told me that nuclear weapons are a part of the 'raison d'être' of the alliance, being the glue that holds the two ends of the alliance together.[35] Similarly, others reasoned that nuclear sharing is an embodiment of political commitment within the alliance.[36]

Very often, nuclear sharing is seen as something that the alliance asked the country to do, and the agreement continues to be a part of the commitment to the alliance. A Dutch MP told me that nuclear sharing is a part of the 'alliance commitment' and the

---

[31] Interview with Alessandro Marrone, March 2024
[32] Interview with a senior government official, March 2024
[33] White Paper on German Security Policy and the Future of the Bundeswehr (Germany) (2016, p. 64)
[34] Working Worldwide for the Security of the Netherlands – An Integrated International Security Strategy 2018–2022 (Netherlands) (2018, p. 31)
[35] Interview with a NATO official, September 2024
[36] Interview with a government official, January 2024

commitment to 'the free world'.³⁷ As the MP reasoned, 'if you expect from the United States to offer you a nuclear protection, and they ask us, the Netherlands, to provide a small contribution, then I think that we have to take the responsibility, which cannot be automatically passed on to others'.³⁸ Nils Schmid, a German MP and SPD's foreign policy then-speaker argued that 'being part of a defence alliance based on nuclear deterrence and not participating in nuclear sharing is also a little bit, um, how shall I call it? [It] is dishonest.'³⁹ This way of thinking sees nuclear deterrence as necessary and also as a way to compensate for conventional weakness. However, it makes a specific argument that this is an alliance contribution rather than a specific defence contribution.

However, the alliance framework also helps to excuse insufficient investment in conventional defence. Belgian strategic documents, for instance, constantly debate the low investment in conventional defence and whether Belgium is at least an average member in terms of defence expenditure,⁴⁰ but contributing to NATO nuclear sharing balances that. Belgium is not the only country with such logic. A former Dutch MP told me that if his country stopped participating in nuclear sharing, it would 'bring itself into a difficult position within the alliance and surely with the Americans' because the country already has an image that it participates in the alliance just for show.⁴¹ As a German expert explained to me,

> We want to be a trustworthy ally for our NATO partners, especially those in Eastern Europe, especially those who are the most vulnerable, the most insecure ones, who will legitimately

---

³⁷ Interview with a Dutch MP, November 2023
³⁸ Interview with a Dutch MP, November 2023
³⁹ Interview with Nils Schmid, January 2024
⁴⁰ See, for instance, The Strategic Vision for Defence (Belgium) (2016); Security Environment Review (Belgium) (2019).
⁴¹ Interview with a former Dutch MP, December 2023. The interviewee used the expression *voor spek en bonen*, which literally means 'for bacon and beans'. The expression is used to describe situations when someone participates in an activity but without caring about the outcome and with no meaningful impact on the activity.

look at a country like Germany and say 'What can you offer us in terms of security? You're the richest ones. If you spend 2% of GDP, you would have the biggest defence budget all over Europe. You have a responsibility. You are benefitting from the EU market most of all.' So there are expectations, on Germany, in terms of projecting security.[42]

This alliance framework is a two-way street, however. The presence of nuclear weapons is sometimes seen as a tangible example of belonging to the alliance. In Turkey, for instance, it is concrete proof of belonging to the West.[43] This is particularly important for an ally such as Turkey, which is geographically on the border of the alliance but also often seen as the odd one out. For Turkey, being part of nuclear sharing strengthens its bond with the West. 'It's a kind of a sense of belonging to the West, you know. NATO is just a powerful organisation', Turkish expert Mustafa Kibaroğlu said.[44] Other experts voiced a similar argument, stating that participation in nuclear sharing is a sign of their country's 'loyalty to' the US and NATO.[45] 'It is very important for Italy to stay with the NATO membership, with friends', said Italian MP Giangiacomo Calovini.[46]

Seeing participation in nuclear sharing as a part of the alliance commitment can be undoubtedly constraining. For instance, the US repeatedly used the argument that nuclear sharing is an alliance policy in discussions with allies seen as acting contrary to such policy. The US's response to the German effort to have nuclear weapons withdrawn from Europe in 2010 is a good example. Making the argument that nuclear sharing is an alliance policy and therefore the allies would have to agree with it made the stakes much clearer. As the former Obama administration official Brad Roberts told me, allies are often 'knowledgeable about their policies and the

---

[42] Interview with a German expert, January 2024
[43] Udum (2020)
[44] Interview with Mustafa Kibaroğlu, November 2023
[45] Interview with an Italian expert, March 2024
[46] Interview with Giangiacomo Calovini, March 2024

logic supporting their policies, [but not] particularly well-informed about the views of the others within the alliance'.[47] Any opposition to the existing policy can be then seen as undercutting the alliance. Again, as Roberts said, 'especially on a topic as sensitive as this one[,] any indication that the agreement isn't very deep and can easily unravel ... is contrary to our interest'.[48]

That the alliance commitment and its symbolic value matters for the policy elites is not lost on to pro-disarmament NGOs either. As one NGO representative told me, 'established bureaucrats ... do not want to show up to a next ... NATO coordination meeting and say "well guys, we're getting rid of nuclear weapons" and then be criticised'.[49]

Nuclear sharing therefore fulfils the role of a magic wand, demonstrating countries' commitment to NATO but also their belonging to it. Again, it is interesting that proof of belonging to NATO matters less for some countries but is an important part of the narrative in others, such as Turkey or Italy. By contrast, in Germany and the Netherlands (and, to a lesser part, in Belgium), the narrative focuses on the commitments made within the alliance.

Status within the Alliance

The status of individual countries within the alliance is also frequently mentioned as an argument for participating. During the 2020 Tornado renewal debate in Germany, for instance, both domestic and US observers made arguments that it raises the country's status within the alliance.[50]

Formally, such arguments are often found lacking on empirical grounds (it is difficult, for instance, to find examples where status helped any of the host nations empirically), but arguments

---

[47] Interview with Brad Roberts, January 2024
[48] Interview with Brad Roberts, January 2024
[49] Interview with an NGO representative, January 2024
[50] For domestic, see Brauß (2020). For US observers, see Flournoy and Townsend (2020).

based on status in international politics are often found to be difficult to substantiate.⁵¹

Yet policy elites often make arguments based on status. Some of these appear in the previous section, as they are linked to the argument of belonging to a powerful organisation. However, nuclear weapons are also meant to enhance their voice in a seemingly egalitarian organisation. Being part of the nuclear decision-making within the alliance and having their voice heard is an essential element of the status for these interviewees. Policy elites in numerous countries underscored this. 'It's a sign of Turkey being … an integral part of the nuclear planning and potential nuclear response', said Sinan Ülgen, a former Turkish official and a think-tanker today.⁵² Similarly, German MP Nils Schmid told me that Germany should be a part of the nuclear sharing as 'the most important European member state of NATO'.⁵³ Schmid continued that participation in nuclear sharing is good for a German reputation. In the same vein, a Dutch MP told me what could happen if the Netherlands stopped participating: 'if you are not taken for a serious actor, that has consequences, so it'd be bad for the Netherlands … from the position of the government'.⁵⁴

While all NATO members except for France are members of the NPG, the nuclear host nations are often assumed to have a better insight than others – in words of one German expert, they become *'primus inter pares'*.⁵⁵ A senior government official, in a separate interview, told me that he believed that nuclear sharing 'puts countries in a category of its own', arguing that within NATO, 'all animals are equal but some animals are more equal'.⁵⁶ Another senior government official reasoned that hosting nuclear weapons gives his

---

[51] See, for instance, Larson et al. (2014).
[52] Interview with Sinan Ülgen, November 2024
[53] Interview with Nils Schmid, January 2024
[54] Interview with a former Dutch MP, December 2023
[55] Interview with a German expert, January 2024
[56] Interview with a senior government official, March 2024

country 'a seat at the table on these very special issues'.⁵⁷ Italian experts were, in particular, very adamant that for Italy, its main concern was being left out of the decision-making, and therefore withdrawing from nuclear sharing would further undercut its centrality to alliance decision-making.⁵⁸ Although it did surprise me, Italian experts pointed out that the last Italian NATO secretary general was Manlio Brosio, who left office in 1971, which was cited as evidence of sidelining of Italy within NATO.⁵⁹

Very closely related to the status symbol and the alliance commitments is the supposed link that nuclear sharing creates directly with the US. In other words, next to the alliance effects, stationing US nuclear weapons is meant to create a specific bond with the US.

Rather than having specific goals, such an activity can be seen like collecting chips in a casino. Chips can be exchanged, but they can be also spent on other goods or expensive bets. Hosting weapons 'gives, if you want, a leverage to Turkish policymakers as they're discussing defence matters with the US', said Sinan Ülgen.⁶⁰ A similar argument was used by another Turkish expert, Mustafa Kibaroğlu, who said that nuclear sharing is a sign of US commitment to Turkish security.⁶¹

Others saw it in a somewhat broader context. 'The United States is in a difficult phase of its political living, and [having weapons on national territory] gives some more security that the United States stays engaged in Europe', said a German expert.⁶² A different expert said that having US nuclear weapons is a backbone between Germany and the US.⁶³ A government official similarly argued that

---

⁵⁷ Interview with a senior government official, January 2024
⁵⁸ Interviews with two Italian experts, March 2023
⁵⁹ NATO was also led by an Italian deputy secretary general for brief interregnum periods since.
⁶⁰ Interview with Sinan Ülgen, November 2023
⁶¹ Interview with Mustafa Kibaroğlu, November 2023
⁶² Interview with a German expert, January 2024
⁶³ Interview with a German expert, January 2024

the US is interested in having (sensitive) security conversations with Germany.⁶⁴ These bilateral relations are supposedly different from the alliance considerations but add to a particular status of a given country within the alliance.

Deterrent Value

Given that the nuclear weapons are primarily supposed to have a military function to deter attacks on the alliance, it is somewhat surprising that the deterrent value does not appear more prominently in the experts' answers.

Some scholars state that the weapons have no military purpose. Kibaroğlu, for instance, wrote this twenty years ago and maintains that it is still valid.⁶⁵ Şebnem Udum argued that they are 'like a buoy for a swimming person', only adding a feeling of safety.⁶⁶ Similarly, a Green MP in Germany matter-of-factly stated that 'nuclear sharing [is] not really a strategic asset anymore anyway'.⁶⁷

Others said that nuclear deterrence helps their country to deter threats without much investment. We saw the argument that the Netherlands participated in the NATO nuclear mission to avoid appearing participating in the alliance for show. A German expert, similarly, said that

> we profited from [nuclear protection] enormously for the last thirty years, longer, obviously, but especially for the last thirty years. We had the chance to organise our security under the nuclear umbrella at a very low cost, [we] could reduce our troops. We ... had less spending on military and security affairs. We just could do trade, you know, and rebuild, uh, part of our country after reunification. Yeah. This was possible because of the nuclear protection from the United States, obviously.⁶⁸

---

⁶⁴ Interview with government official, January 2024
⁶⁵ Kibaroğlu (2005); interview with Mustafa Kibaroğlu, November 2023
⁶⁶ Interview with Şebnem Udum, November 2023
⁶⁷ Interview with a Green MP, February 2024
⁶⁸ Interview with a German expert, January 2024

And many, especially NATO and US officials, reasoned that nuclear sharing underscored the unity of the alliance. 'I am not sure, when it comes to nuclear weapons, where the dividing line is between the military and the political', said Brad Roberts.[69] A NATO official said that nuclear sharing increased the credibility of the alliance deterrence posture.[70] Similar views were held by a senior government official, who also noted a 'broad understanding' that nuclear sharing 'interlink[s] European and American security with the ultimate tool for deterrence and defence [and] this symbolism is broadly understood'.[71] In even plainer terms, an Italian expert told me that nuclear deterrence is 'essential for avoiding war in Europe, between NATO and once upon a time the Soviet Union and now possibly Russia', continuing that the 'nuclear arsenals of France and United Kingdom [are not] really enough for this'.[72]

SYMBOLIC ADJUSTMENT

In early 1990s, German political scientist Thomas Risse-Kappen coined the phrase 'symbolic adjustment' to describe a situation where policy elites make some policy adjustments without compromising on the core elements.[73] It is the outcome that policy elites choose if they believe that the policy is fundamentally a 'responsible' one but also feel the need to respond to public pressure. As the scholarship in political science shows, policy elites are often reluctant to follow public pressure if they feel that they know the policy well and think that the public views are misguided.[74]

For the European host nations, the symbolic adjustments depend on the level of salience but also the positioning of the policy elites. As we have seen in previous chapters, the host nations differ significantly in some but not all aspects. For instance, despite differences

---

[69] Interview with Brad Roberts, January 2024
[70] Interview with a NATO official, September 2023
[71] Interview with a government official, January 2024
[72] Interview with an Italian expert, March 2024
[73] Risse-Kappen (1991)
[74] Pereira and Öhberg (2023)

between nations and factors explaining public views across the five countries, they are broadly somewhat similar. Similarly, the patterns of party contestation are very similar across the host nations, with some notable exceptions. Parliamentary activity does vary significantly, though, as do the activity of civil society and its ability to influence parliaments and have access to policy elites. Italian and Turkish civil society is much less successful in influencing policy elites, and Belgian civil society is much weaker compared to the one in the Netherlands and Germany.

This variation also explains how far policy elites feel the need to respond to public pressure and engage in symbolic adjustments. The forms of those adjustments vary from country to country.

In Germany, the first form of symbolic adjustment was the debate about the renewal of the Tornado aircraft. The problem was that it clearly needed to be replaced. While a lifetime extension would have been theoretically possible, it would have been very costly, possibly exceeding the cost of some of the other solutions. It would also be ultimately unsatisfying, as it would kick the can down the road and was seen as undercutting German reliability within the alliance.[75] The intermediate solution was to purchase F-18 fighter jets.[76] However, this was not ideal. Experts called the solution adopted by the German defence ministry 'a poor one'.[77] Germany's own air force saw the JSF as the best idea. After all, the F-18 fighter jet was at the end of its development life cycle, which would serve for a few more decades but not longer. By contrast, the F-35 is a platform with an expected lifespan of at least six decades.[78]

The chief of staff of the air force, Karl Müllner, was sent into early retirement after expressing this view, which was broadly seen as an affront to the political leadership.[79] The issue of selecting the

---

[75] For an overview of the debate about the Tornado replacement, see Bunde and Onderco (2023).
[76] Sprenger (2020)
[77] Bronk (2020)
[78] Leonard (2023)
[79] Morcinek (2018)

JSF was so sensitive that, at the time, policy elites in the government would not speak on open lines about it but talked about 'the big bird'.[80] Even afterward, however, it was not clear whether the F-18 would be able to fulfil the nuclear sharing tasks, as it was not originally certified for a nuclear strike mission. This uncertainty was resolved only in the coalition agreement of 2021, which clearly stated that the Tornado replacement would be a dual-capable aircraft.[81] In 2022, after the Russian invasion of Ukraine, the plans were updated, and Germany committed to purchasing the JSF.[82]

While the dual capability was not the only or the dominant reason the Tornado was not renewed, it was a major consideration together with other domestic industrial considerations. However, for numerous opponents of nuclear sharing, this was an opportunity to push Germany *technically* out of nuclear sharing. As a German expert explained the situation to me,

> you had the, I would say, the very realist defence people, who would say, 'look, we don't necessarily like nuclear sharing, but probably we will have to make a decision on that one'. And then I think people would have been happier to say, 'let's buy the F-18 instead of the F-35'. Then you had the [pro-disarmament] camp ... who would say, 'no, we can wait it out' and we can fly [the Tornado] for a while and then make a procurement decision, you know.[83]

Waiting things out would have been a solution that would have allowed Germany to more easily create conditions for withdrawing nuclear bombs from Germany and Europe, if it actually did not have the capacity to deliver them.[84] The position, pushed by some of the more pro-disarmament minded parliamentarians and some experts,

---

[80] Interview with a senior government official, January 2024
[81] Mehr Fortschritt wagen: Bündnis für Freiheit, Gerechtigkeit und Nachhaltigkeit. Koalitionsvertrag zwischen SPD, Bündnis 90/Die Grünen und FDP (2021)
[82] Sprenger (2022)
[83] Interview with a German expert, January 2024
[84] Fuhrhop et al. (2020)

was essentially designed to push Germany out of nuclear sharing. For instance, Oliver Meier, a German think-tanker, advocated for postponing the decision until 2030, which the German air force clearly indicated would be the very end of the Tornado's life.[85] The decision to procure the F-18 as an intermediate solution was a symbolic adjustment that conceded some of the demands (not committing to a US solution for many decades).

However, the main forms of symbolic adjustment can be found in how the governments in the host nations approached the TPNW. As discussed in previous chapters, numerous political parties, repeated parliamentary motions, and civil society did demand that they join the treaty, but this would be in direct contrast with the political commitments made within the alliance and make participation in an alliance backed by a US nuclear umbrella impossible. Therefore, elites had to find a way to respond to those demands without conceding to the core demands.

The Netherlands participated in the TPNW negotiations, as the only NATO country, in 2017.[86] This decision, however, can be traced back to a parliamentary motion passed in 2015, which compelled the government to substantively contribute to international disarmament negotiations.[87] As discussed in Chapter 5, this motion gave rise to the civil society-driven citizens' initiative to ban nuclear weapons in the Netherlands.[88] Following the submission of the successful initiative, parliamentary rules required the government's response, which arrived in February 2016 and made it clear that new opportunities for disarmament will arise 'only if the participants remain ready [for dialogue] and adopt a constructive attitude'. The government also highlighted that any unilateral steps would have consequences for NATO as a whole and Dutch participation in the different arms control

---

[85] See https://twitter.com/meier_oliver/status/1457298380971991047
[86] For a detailed account of how the Netherlands ended up in these negotiations, see Shirobokova (2018); Onderco (2021).
[87] Tweede Kamer der Staten-Generaal (2015)
[88] PAX No Nukes (2016)

mechanisms, such as the NPT, NPDI, IPNDV, and FMCT talks.[89] The debate in Parliament led to four successful motions, three linked to phasing out sharing,[90] and one linked to participation in the disarmament negotiations.[91] While the government voted against the start of the TPNW negotiations in the OEWG, it did ultimately participate, which is largely seen as appeasing Parliament.[92] The Netherlands ended up being the only country that voted against the treaty draft.[93] However, when ICAN received the Nobel Peace Prize 'for its work to draw attention to the catastrophic humanitarian consequences of any use of nuclear weapons and for its ground-breaking efforts to achieve a treaty-based prohibition of such weapons',[94] the Dutch MFA congratulated it on Twitter.[95] Participation in the TPNW negotiations, and then voting against, was a sign of symbolic adjustment from the government, which conceded that it wished to reflect demands from Parliament but did not reflect the core demands.

The participation of Belgium, Germany and the Netherlands in the first TPNW MSP in 2022 is the latest example of a symbolic adjustment. For each of these countries, the decision to participate was made for a different constellation of domestic reasons.

In Belgium, the decision was a compromise between the coalition parties, at the very last minute, following a contentious parliamentary debate.[96] For the Netherlands, the dynamic was very similar. Only a week before the meeting, Parliament had adopted a motion that requested the government to take part in the first MSP.[97] While it did so, the minister of foreign affairs and minister of defence also sent a sharply worded letter to Parliament afterward,

---

[89] Tweede Kamer der Staten-Generaal (2016a)
[90] Tweede Kamer der Staten-Generaal (2016c, 2016b, 2016e)
[91] Tweede Kamer der Staten-Generaal (2016d)
[92] Shirobokova (2018)
[93] Kingdom of the Netherlands (2017)
[94] Nobel Prize Outreach (2025)
[95] See https://x.com/MinBZ/status/916251534127714304
[96] De Kamer (2022)
[97] Tweede Kamer der Staten-Generaal (2022)

which stated plainly that 'membership in this treaty is not reconcilable with our membership of NATO'. The letter continued that 'the Netherlands is a member of the NATO alliance, which our national security is dependent on. NATO is a nuclear alliance as long as nuclear weapons exist. Furthermore, the Netherlands has a nuclear weapons task in the context of the alliance'. It concluded by stating,

> Based on participation in the first meeting of state parties of the TPNW, the Netherlands concludes for the time being that further participation as an observer is not useful. The absence of a substantive discussion on verification and the security concerns and future membership of non-TPNW member states (in particular the nuclear weapons states), again underlined for the Netherlands the limited added value of this treaty.[98]

Indeed, the Netherlands did not take part in the second MSP in New York in late 2023, or the third one in New York in March 2025.

The situation was somewhat more complex in Germany. The commitment to attend the MSP was included in the coalition agreement of 2021.[99] The decision of political parties to go ahead with this choice was a result of the explicit desire to balance domestic political pressures. As a senior government official told me, the decision 'was a consequence of party politics'.[100] As one expert explained, at the time of the coalition agreement negotiation, the choice was between committing to a DCA as a Tornado replacement and attending MSP or not attending and not having a commitment that the Tornado replacement would be a DCA. 'If you compare that, it's better to stay in nuclear sharing and be an observer than to leave nuclear sharing and stay out at the ban treaty.'[101] The logic was even more clearly explained by a German expert:

---

[98] All citations from Ministerie van Buitenlandse Zaken (2022)
[99] Mehr Fortschritt wagen: Bündnis für Freiheit, Gerechtigkeit und Nachhaltigkeit. Koalitionsvertrag zwischen SPD, Bündnis 90/Die Grünen und FDP (2021)
[100] Interview with a senior government official, January 2024
[101] Interview with a German expert, January 2024

> The Greens would like to be trustworthy allies of NATO. And NATO is a nuclear alliance. And therefore ... we have to do our nuclear homework. But at the same time, they would like to be advocates of nuclear disarmament. And how do you combine it? Somehow you shift nuclear disarmament to an aspiration. It's not everyday politics, because that is we have to purchase F-35 and we have to modernise our contribution within nuclear sharing. But at the same time, we would like to show, or pay credit to this global movement and nuclear disarmament. And how do you do that? You don't actually disarm, but you do, for example, [an] observer in in the TPNW.[102]

Indeed, within the Green Party, nuclear disarmament has shifted from an immediate policy goal to a long-term aspiration. This is why attending MSP appeared to be a doable concession.[103] Domestically, the German government keeps its participation 'totally under the radar'. As one German expert summarised it, the Foreign Office 'treats it like "can we change topics? Can we not talk about it?"'[104] Yet it also provides them with an opportunity to let parliamentarians and civil society be heard during the pre-conference consultations.[105]

Three host nation governments (Belgium, Germany, and the Netherlands) attended the conference with Norway, as did another NATO country and Finland and Sweden as membership candidates. However, their statements at the first MSP were among the sharpest and strongest. In a quantitative analysis of their speeches conducted with my colleague Valerio Vignoli, we found them to be among the most extreme presented at the conference.[106] Therefore, while these governments do attend the MSP, that does not lead to any bridge-building because, for diplomats, it is an exercise

---

[102] Interview with a German expert, January 2024
[103] Franceschini (2024)
[104] Both citations from interview with a German expert, January 2024
[105] Interview with a Green MP, February 2024
[106] Onderco and Vignoli (2022)

in futility. The Dutch MFA has put it on paper, but government officials have complained in interviews that the conferences do not lead to improved dialogue with the Global South.[107] At the same time, as one government official told me, 'there is no cost to be paid with the US', only with Paris and London.[108] Attendance is therefore an excellent example of a symbolic adjustment – something that does not require a lot of political capital or any long-term political costs but appeases domestic audiences.[109]

CONCLUSION

In this chapter, I looked at how policy elites respond to pro-disarmament pressures. As I explained at the beginning, in some host countries, public pressure is minimal, and therefore elites do not feel the need to respond. At least a part of the strategy is to keep the contestation deliberately low. By contrast, in others, the pressures cannot be overlooked, and then elites do have to respond.

Then I continued by outlining why elites view the continuation of the ongoing policy as a necessary process. They see nuclear sharing primarily as a political tool to signal that they are responsible actors but also fulfilling their alliance commitments and an attempt to improve their own status within the alliance. While policy elites do view weapons as having a distinctive deterrent value, that was not seen as the primary reason for hosting. The views of the policy elites approximate the view that former US official Elaine Bunn called the 'wedding ring' theory of nuclear sharing.[110]

Last, I explained that while elites see that they are unwilling to make concessions that would appeal to the core demands of pro-disarmament voices, they end up offering symbolic adjustments. Participating in the TPNW MSP is the latest of those, but the

---

[107] Interview with a senior government official, January 2024
[108] Interview with a government official, January 2024; interview with a senior government official, January 2024
[109] None of the NATO countries attended the third MSP in March 2025.
[110] Bunn (2009)

governments of the host nations have made numerous such steps in the past. As the pressure of pro-disarmament civil society will increase, one could also reasonably expect that policy elites in the host nations would concede to other demands, such as contributing to environmental remediation funds or victim assistance funds. While the proponents will no doubt attempt to portray such steps as major wins and a support for the TPNW, it is more accurate to interpret them for what they are – small adjustments to avoid much bigger concessions.

Conclusion

One of my interviews brought me to a small, wood-panelled office in the middle of a Western European capital. My interviewee invited me to sit in a leather chair. As I took a sip of coffee from the porcelain cup with a golden rim, my eyes widened as I felt Vladimir Putin's cool gaze upon me. A famous photo of Putin, shot by the British-Greek photographer Platon, from the *Time Magazine*'s 2007 spread 'A Tsar Is Born', hung where normally a portrait of the head of state would be.[1] 'I wanted to put up the guy because of whom we are all here doing all these things for, to remind me every day why my work has a meaning', the respondent said. Replacing the head of state with Platon's photo was another sign of how the times, and the thinking about security, have shifted since the start of the Russian invasion of Ukraine.

It also spoke to the sense of responsibility that elites feel in their day-to-day execution of their tasks. For my interviewee, it was the Russian dictator, or, better to say, the defence against him, that was driving what needed to be done. Putin's chilling look reminded my interviewee daily to do everything possible to avoid having the dictator force his portrait onto the walls of offices like his in the Western European capitals. That was the job.

Yet writing this conclusion in April 2025, one more man would be on the mind of a European official dealing with nuclear deterrence: US President Donald Trump, who started his second term in office in January 2025. Within the first eight weeks of his presidency, Trump and his team criticised European allies harshly, questioned their democratic credentials, expressed repeated interest in annexing Greenland, appeared more than friendly towards Putin, and questioned the continuation of US support for Ukraine. This

---

[1] Platon (2007)

has understandably led to concern. Some even go so far as academic experts Mark Bell and Fabian Hoffmann, who wrote in an essay for *Foreign Affairs* that 'it has become increasingly clear to European leaders that remaining reliant on the United States to underwrite the continent's security would be a dangerous gamble'.[2]

I want to bring together the different arguments advanced in this book. I will first summarise the book's key findings. Then I will present the challenges that the Russian war in Ukraine, and Trump's return, have created for nuclear sharing and the challenges that lie ahead. Last, I will discuss the growing international backlash against nuclear sharing and how it is likely to evolve.

BOOK'S SUMMARY

As I argued in the theoretical Chapter 2, policymakers in democratic countries act under two forms of control – responsiveness and responsibility. Drawing on scholarship in the fields of public administration and public policy, I theorised that responsiveness is primarily related to pressures from below, whereas responsibility is primarily linked to perceived obligations to commitments made abroad, long-term policy-making, and the broader well-being of a country. Policy elites primarily lean towards decisions based on responsibility if commitments made abroad are at stake or if they feel that they understand the issue at hand better than the general public.

In Chapters 3–5, I outlined how public opinion, parties, civil society, and allies, as distinct sources of pressure, think about nuclear sharing and influence policy elites in the host nations.

First, I analysed public opinion. Scholarship has shown that the European publics have opposed nuclear sharing for a long time and have preferred disarmament. While small variations in timing and wording could explain some deviations, the trend was clear – across all host countries, whenever a survey was made, solid pluralities or even majorities were opposed. This changed, somewhat, after Russia's

---

[2] Bell and Hoffmann (2025)

invasion of Ukraine. The European publics became more supportive of nuclear sharing, and while they did not want to expand the sharing mission, its current form has attracted solid support. Hence, I mapped the support for nuclear sharing, use, and disarmament across the five host nations and explained which factors structure these attitudes. I demonstrated the relatively small differences across the host nations.

Second, I analysed the positions of political parties. I showed that the salience of nuclear sharing varied. The parties from the far left to the centre have been rather consistently opposed to it, with two prominent exceptions – the German Social Democrats and the German Greens, both of whom were torn due to intra-party debates, and so their positions were more moderate. However, even on the right, parties either chose to keep quiet about or were opposed to it. Surprisingly, however, the far-right and populist parties were not among those most strongly opposed. Looking at parliamentary behaviour, I showed major differences among the host nations. In Italy and Belgium, the parliamentary salience of sharing was low, and parliamentary behaviour did not follow any obvious pattern. By contrast, in Germany and the Netherlands, on most votes, the left-leaning parties voted primarily in favour of pro-disarmament motions, whereas the right-leaning ones voted primarily in opposition.

Third, looking at civil society, I discussed how the shift to a new narrative based on humanitarian disarmament favoured new actors, who have coalesced around ICAN. In addition, the emergence of these disarmament narratives and activists also created a favourable environment for the rise of a new academic community, keen to leverage its intellectual firepower to aid ICAN's ascension. Despite professing global ambitions and attempting to develop a global footprint, ICAN has remained a dominantly Western movement, with two-thirds of its partners based in Western countries. As I have also shown, on the local level, ICAN's attempts to rally locally for nuclear disarmament had unequal success in the host nations through its Cities Appeal campaign. In Italy, numerous small municipalities joined, but in the Netherlands, the success was much more limited. Drawing on illustrations from the two largest Dutch cities – Amsterdam and Rotterdam – I showed that the pro-disarmament motions were driven primarily by the broader left-wing logic rather than a specific concern for disarmament.

Fourth, I showed that the European allies of the host nations have for a long time paid very limited attention to nuclear sharing, but this has started to change more recently. NATO started to be explicit about nuclear sharing only after the rise of the humanitarian movement. However, after the TPNW, NATO has doubled down on its narrative about the usefulness of nuclear sharing for alliance coherence. Similar voices were heard from the US and other nuclear members of the alliance.

Last, I traced how policy elites in the host nations have interpreted these pressures. As I showed, they have primarily discussed nuclear sharing in the context of alliance responsibility and commitments. They have not especially seen the military value of these weapons but have regarded them as a sign of their own responsible statesmanship and living up to alliance commitments. Furthermore, it has allowed states who have given little to the alliance's conventional mission to claim credit and maintain that they contribute to its goals. However, policy elites were willing to make policy concessions, such as attending the TPNW MSP, particularly when these had few costs.

Taken together, my empirical work confirms that policy elites do indeed balance responsiveness and responsibility. Contrary to recent arguments, they do not ignore public demands – otherwise, these countries would never join events such as the MSPs. However, they do balance these demands with what they see as responsible policy-making. This does not mean that policy is undemocratic but rather that we need to use more detailed criteria for assessing democratic policy-making.

CHALLENGES AHEAD

Nuclear sharing, however, does not exist in a geopolitical vacuum. Because it was started and established as a response to a concrete geopolitical situation, the geopolitical shifts also influence its future. When I began writing this book, the most obvious challenge to the existing form of nuclear sharing seemed to be Russia's war of aggression against Ukraine. However, as I was completing the manuscript, a new challenge appeared – the second Trump term.

From the very beginning of the war, the Russian government has been using nuclear rhetoric against the West but also Ukraine. A simple chronology of Russian nuclear sabre-rattling would run hundreds of pages.[3] The goals are unclear – whether it was to discourage Western support to Ukrainians, prevent Western military intervention on the side of Ukraine to force Ukrainians into submission, or both.[4] The uncertainty therefore leads to competing assessments of whether the sabre-rattling has worked. Some argue that it did, because it persuaded the West not to intervene.[5] Others disagree, arguing that the Russians did not manage to achieve even more limited goals, such as forcing Ukraine to accept the Russian occupation of certain territories.[6]

What the invasion did achieve, however, is increasing the salience of nuclear weapons in Europe. Nuclear deterrence became more central to how European countries think about security. As I noted in Chapter 6, NATO has strengthened the language linked to nuclear deterrence and its importance for the alliance since the invasion.[7] Public perception of nuclear weapons has shifted, and public opinion has become more supportive of the arrangements. Civil society activism has quieted down a bit. The existing salience and growing awareness of the role of nuclear weapons in European security has reopened multiple paths for changes in the current arrangement.

Seen in 2025, the ongoing geopolitical realignment in the US has been a part of the reason the European NATO members yet again think much more about nuclear weapons. From the start of

---

[3] Horovitz and Arndt (2023)
[4] Horovitz and Arndt (2022)
[5] See, for instance, Gross Stein (2023)
[6] Arndt, et al. (2023)
[7] NATO (2023a, 2023b)

Trump's second term, European leaders have been concerned about the firmness of US commitment to defending European allies, including using nuclear weapons. To be clear, this is not purely due to Trump. The US has been shifting strategic attention to Asia for some time, spurred by the rise of China. Experts have for a long time been expecting that the US would reduce commitments to Europe and demand that those allies do more.[8] Even if Harris had won the election, this trend would have most likely continued. For a long time, European policymakers and experts alike considered the growing US focus on the Asia–Pacific and what that means for Europe. At the very best, some Europeans highlight the potential for cooperation and learning.[9] However, other experts are more concerned about what a two-contingency conflict would mean for European security.[10] As the US looks more towards the Asia–Pacific, European states are eagerly looking for precious signs of political commitment.

However, very early on, Trump took many steps that made European leaders concerned about the depth of US commitment to the defence of allied territory. Whether the speech of Vice President Vance at the Munich Security Conference questioning European values in February 2025,[11] the support of Trump's confidante (and financier) Elon Musk for the far right ahead of the 2025 German federal election,[12] or the attempts to strong-arm Ukraine to giving into an onerous ceasefire with Russia – all of these actions sent proverbial shivers down the leaders' spines. The dressing-down that Ukraine's war-battered President Volodymyr Zelensky received in the Oval Office gave European politicians pause.[13] Trump, who had called European countries 'delinquent' for their defence spending, refused to commit to defending them.[14] In a famous conversation

---

[8] Horovitz and Major (2025)
[9] Mattelaer (2021)
[10] See, for instance, the expert discussions in Majnemer and Repussard (2023).
[11] The White House (2025)
[12] France24 (2025)
[13] Khalid (2025)
[14] Wax (2024)

on the messaging app Signal, publicised in March 2025, senior US officials wrote that they 'hate bailing out' those 'pathetic' European allies.[15] Trump and his team repeatedly showed interest in taking over Canada and Denmark in the early months of the presidency. Polite experts talk of a 'crisis of confidence' in Europe.[16] Others talk of 'electroshock'.[17] On paper, of course, the US is still committed to NATO. But even if Europe – and the North Atlantic Alliance – survived the first Trump presidency successfully, there is no guarantee that NATO will survive the second one equally well.[18] At the June 2025 NATO Summit, the European allies caved in to the demand from the Trump administration to commit to spending 5 per cent of their GDP on defence and related expenses – for many, this exceeds even Cold War levels. While US administrations have been exasperated with what has been seen as anaemic defence spending in Europe for quite some time, this level of spending would mean doubling or even tripling the current expenditure for many countries.

Taken together, these centrifugal forces create a diverse set of scenarios.

One of them remains in the framework of the current arrangements but proposes to reshape them significantly. These proposals include expanding them to include new countries, such as Poland. As Polish experts Monika Sus and Łukasz Kulesa argued, the surprising fact is not that Polish leaders have shown interest in joining nuclear sharing but at what level of seniority these arguments were made.[19] The Polish desire is not new, but it strengthened after Russia's invasion of Ukraine. Poland is often mentioned as one of the most eager candidates.[20] First, it has traditionally connected its post-Cold War security to the alliance with the US, which by extension translates

---

[15] Goldberg (2025)
[16] Cameron (2025); Vaddi and Narang (2025)
[17] Maddox (2025)
[18] On NATO and Trump, see Schuette (2021)
[19] Sus and Kulesa (2023)
[20] Kacprzyk (2023)

into a desire to maintain and strengthen that alliance.[21] Second, it has invested in the JSF, which would make including it technically easier. Third, it is closer to the likely battlefield in a war between Russia and NATO and therefore has modest operational advantages. There are, however, major obstacles to such steps. On the one hand, NATO members are likely to oppose this as unnecessarily provoking Russia when the relations between West and Russia are already bad enough. In 2019, for instance, the Dutch government's Advisory Council for International Affairs advised that Russia would see stationing weapons in the east of the alliance as a provocation.[22] More seriously, however, it would violate the principle of 'Three Nos' agreed to by NATO and Russia and enshrined in the 1997 NATO–Russia Founding Act, which included no stationing of nuclear weapons in new member states. Doing so in Poland would tear through the act and be a sign of the final and total breakdown of relations, a step many member states are still unwilling to take.

However, the Trump administration's steps have revived a debate that has been reoccurring in Europe since the 1960s. Strengthening the European nuclear deterrent, also known as the 'Eurobomb', is an evergreen topic in European politics that reappeared following the Russian invasion of Ukraine and strengthened in the aftermath of Trump's re-election.[23] The debate about a Eurobomb comes up with quite some regularity, especially in Germany, where it sometimes also includes a debate about a German nuclear bomb.[24] In recent years, scholars and policymakers alike made a number of proposals for either a European or German bomb. Some German policymakers, by contrast, suggested 'Europeanising' the French nuclear deterrent.[25] In the period of uncertainty introduced by the Trump administration, experts returned to the questions of how to

---

[21] Lanoszka (2020)
[22] Advisory Council on International Affairs (2019)
[23] Onderco and Kühn (2025)
[24] Volpe and Kühn (2017); Kühn, et al. (2018); Meibauer and LaRoche (2024)
[25] For an overview, see Kühn (2024a).

reorganise nuclear deterrence in Europe. Proposals aimed at French or Franco-British deterrents were advanced.[26] However, French experts keep pointing out that French politics, strategy, and military practice put severe limits on what is seen as practically feasible.[27] However, all of these scenarios carry important political, military, and financial costs.[28] As mentioned, scholars have for a long time noted why such solutions are problematic. For starters, strategic and nuclear cooperation with France has been historically difficult, to put it very mildly.[29] The problem is not technical alone – as the French Admiral Pierre Vandier wrote in his recent book, 'France has the means to send [a] signal ... through ... stationing in allied countries of fighters from nuclear squadrons.'[30] However, the French readiness to take numerous necessary doctrinal and technical steps is very limited.[31] It is also unclear how the rest of Europe would react. Nevertheless, the debate's recurrence and that it seems to morph with every iteration emphasises its continuous appeal.

In the years to come, European countries will continue to oscillate between the two scenarios – some pulling towards US assurances, with others seeking European solutions. In April 2025, it seems premature to declare a winner. Will the status quo forces prevail? Or will the Trump-fuelled uncertainty coupled with the nearing end of the largest land war in Europe since World War II persuade European leaders to develop an alternative backup arrangement? It might be too early to say, but for European leaders (and scholars), these will be the major questions for years to come.

GROWING INTERNATIONAL BACKLASH

A separate type of a challenge is, however, associated with a growing international backlash against nuclear sharing. It can be seen

---

[26] Bell and Hoffmann (2025); Cameron (2025)
[27] See, for instance, Héloïse Fayet cited in *The Economist* (2025).
[28] See also Horovitz and Major (2023).
[29] Kunz and Kühn (2024)
[30] Vandier (2025, p.45)
[31] Wachs and Horovitz (2023)

in two ways. First, it is the continuous activity of an anti-nuclear civil society, including ICAN, against nuclear sharing. While, at the time of writing, ICAN activity in Europe has declined, which is likely explained by the shifting moods in Europe, the desire for nuclear abolition and disarmament might conceivably return. As the nuclear rhetoric in Europe increases, the pendulum of public opinion might swing back.[32] It is likely that ICAN's activities in Europe will continue to be supported, diplomatically, by some European TPNW members. Austria, in particular, has shown past interest in acting through European publics to put pressure on their governments when it comes to the TPNW.[33] For ICAN, the current period represents a challenge, but it has also used the situation to build relations in Central and Eastern Europe, regions where its foothold has been the weakest.[34] Whether this activism will be useful for the long-term future is unclear, however.

Second, criticism of nuclear sharing has also been increasing in diplomatic settings. Particularly following the NPT Review Conference in summer 2022, numerous countries started to criticise it as going against the spirit and letter of NPT. Historically, Russia was the largest critic, but after the deployment of tactical nuclear weapons to Belarus in 2024, that has quieted down. By contrast, China has now become a very vocal critic. Despite the argument to be made that the sharing arrangement does not contradict NPT as a law (as discussed in Chapter 1),[35] this does not mean that rhetorical pressure will not increase. The host countries have been very reluctant to answer and respond to such criticism. The first time a host country explicitly defended the arrangement was a German intervention at the 2023 NPT Preparatory Committee.[36] In the 2024 NPT Preparatory Committee meeting in Geneva, multiple NATO

---

[32] Horovitz and Onderco (2024)
[33] Ritchie and Kmentt (2021)
[34] See the description in Gibbons and Herzog (2024)
[35] Alberque (2017)
[36] Permanent Mission of the Federal Republic of Germany to the United Nations (2023)

countries explicitly defended nuclear sharing in their remarks and replies as being fully in line with their legal commitments.[37]

The international criticism of nuclear sharing will likely continue. It remains an open question whether China will continue to be on the forefront of this criticism, given its close relationship with Russia, and how sensitive European countries will be towards the criticism. The interest in nuclear disarmament among European allies is decreasing – none of the NATO allies attended the 2025 TPNW MSP, for instance. Given the tone of the debates in Europe, however, it is expected that European countries will continue to defend their reliance on nuclear deterrence, including nuclear sharing – so long as they become invested in the NPT and its review process.

CAN THE NUCLEAR FUTURE BE *MORE* RESPONSIVE?

It is unlikely that European countries will take large steps away from nuclear deterrence in the foreseeable future. If anything, the debates in Europe underscore that they will double down on some sort of nuclear deterrence. As they will (hopefully) remain democracies, a question remains whether the democratic quality of nuclear policymaking can be improved.

Seeing nuclear policy in general, and nuclear sharing in particular, through the prism of responsiveness versus responsibility helps us to both have a better grasp on how policymakers decide in democratic systems and understand the variation over time and space. Using this new dimension also adds to the scholarship on responsiveness and responsibility, since it not only expands scholarship into a new area but also allows us to better understand how commitments made abroad constrain or enable policy elites in changing existing policies.[38]

However, in the nuclear realm, many want to make nuclear sharing more responsive to the public mood. In the short term, the supporters of the current arrangement can point to a trend in the

[37] Reaching Critical Will (2024)
[38] See also van der Veer (2021)

European public opinion of emerging support for the NATO nuclear posture in Europe. As the Russian aggression against Ukraine rages on, Europeans are becoming slowly more supportive of the nuclear umbrella.[39] It is likely that the supporters of nuclear sharing, such as technocrats in various ministries, will appeal to this swing and argue that not dismantling these arrangements is the responsible choice. Elite and technocratic groups have, in other issue areas, used other types of crises to push or defend unpopular agendas.[40] Germany, for instance, has had virtually no pushback against the decision to invest an additional 100 billion euros into defence, including the purchase of new dual-capable F-35 fighter jets.[41] There was also little pushback against the March 2025 decision to change the constitution to enable higher defence spending. Given that the public appears, at least in the short term, to be supportive of this policy, it is likely that the dilemma between responsiveness and responsibility will not reappear.

Yet in the medium term, taking steps towards responsiveness is possible. The withdrawal of nuclear weapons from Europe, especially in the context of an arms control agreement between the US and Russia, does remain popular among the public, albeit highly unlikely at the time of writing. However, other options would go beyond Risse-Kappen's 'symbolic adjustments'.[42] One option would be to become more transparent about the current arrangements. The secrecy on the subject in Europe is much higher than secrecy in other policy areas. In the Netherlands, it is not even clear what the legal basis for the secrecy is.[43] And the Dutch situation is far from unique. This lack of a clear legal basis is separate from the discussion about why such secrecy is needed in the first place. In private conversations, US officials often point fingers at European

---

[39] Onderco et al. (2023); Onderco (2024)
[40] Kreuder-Sonnen (2019)
[41] Bunde (2022); Bunde and Onderco (2023)
[42] Risse-Kappen (1991, p. 502)
[43] Brixley-Williams (2020, p. 22)

governments unwilling to discuss and defend the existing arrangements before the domestic public. In public statements, European officials often cite legal arrangements with the US government, or NATO, that would prevent making even the weapons' location public. Yet there is little military reason for hiding which countries are hosts or at which airbases nuclear weapons are deployed, especially since that information has long been in the public domain.[44]

Similarly, European governments could become much more up front about why they think continuing nuclear sharing is important and under what conditions they would be willing to use the weapons.[45] They could discuss the rationale for maintaining nuclear deterrence in public, parliamentary settings. Thus far, this is severely lacking.[46] In many host nations, governments do not even go so far as to repeat the official alliance line that nuclear weapons 'preserve peace, prevent coercion and deter aggression'.[47] The doubts created by Trump's second administration has led policymakers to think about alternative nuclear arrangements, potentially opening doors for justifying why a nuclear umbrella is even needed.

They could be also much more up front in discussing the practice in multilateral settings. This would allow them to create a more honest relationship with the domestic public but also contribute to more honest conversations abroad. Justifying the need for nuclear weapons in Europe could also enable a better debate about how to progress towards nuclear disarmament, at least on the regional scale, without endangering the perceptions of security within the alliance.

However, understanding the dynamic between responsiveness and responsibility as the driving force behind the continuation of nuclear sharing puts demands on those advocating for their

---

[44] Kristensen and Korda (2022)
[45] Similar points were raised by the roundtable participants in a discussion held in The Hague in summer 2019, see Brixley-Williams (2020).
[46] Fuhrhop (2021)
[47] NATO (2023b)

withdrawal as well. In particular, it calls on them to start thinking seriously about a world where these weapons are withdrawn, what European security would look like in such a world, whether the cooperation of other partners is likely, and what it would look like if others do not cooperate.

Some proponents of withdrawal point to the opportunities for arms control agreements with Russia,[48] such as the withdrawal of all non-strategic nuclear weapons (hence, also those deployed by the US in Europe) from Europe or in general. While these have technical problems, those pale in contrast to the political issues.[49] After the war in Ukraine, where Russia's conventional forces have been shown to be relatively weak and ineffective, it is likely that Russia will see its nuclear deterrent even more as a key element of its security.[50]

Yet the majority of nuclear disarmament proponents have a hard time imagining what the world would look like if their wish were granted. Similarly, opponents of nuclear sharing have not engaged any arguments related to alliance commitments or alliance coherence. For instance, two members of the TPNW Scientific Advisory Group (including its co-chair) recently called for an end to nuclear sharing in Europe, without engaging any security-based counterarguments.[51] As I have explained, a successful argument must build on not only responsiveness but also responsibility in order to satisfy the needs of democratic policy-making.

Ultimately, the framework that includes both responsiveness and responsibility puts the onus on all participants. The future of nuclear sharing in Europe, a seemingly boring policy that is suddenly on the front page of many newspapers in Europe, invites us to think long and hard about the really important questions of European policy-making: our relationship with the US, European security

---

[48] Fuhrhop et al. (2020)
[49] Pomper et al. (2022)
[50] Wachs (2023). On the link between conventional inferiority and nuclear strategy in Russia, see Ven Bruusgaard (2020).
[51] Kütt et al. (2023)

cooperation, or the willingness of citizens to sacrifice things they hold dear for the defence of their country. In some ways, the readers of this book in 2026 are living through the most momentous times in European security in at least the last three decades, and nuclear weapons are at the centre of these debates. If our leaders get the key decisions wrong, for some Europeans, foreign leaders' photos will not appear only on the walls of cheeky officials' offices.

Bibliography

Achen, C. H., & Bartels, L. M. (2017). *Democracy for realists: Why elections do not produce responsive government* (2nd ed.). Princeton: Princeton University Press.

Acheson, R. (2021). *Banning the bomb, smashing the patriarchy*. London: Rowman & Littlefield.

Acheson, R. (2023). *Abolishing state violence: A world beyond bombs, borders, and cages*. Chicago: Haymarket Books.

Advisory Council on International Affairs. (2019). Nuclear weapons in a new geopolitical reality. An urgent need for new arms control initiatives. Retrieved from https://aiv-advice.nl/9w9

AfD. (2021). Deutschland – Aber normal. Programm der Alternative für Deutschland für die Wahl zum 20. Deutschen Bundestag. Retrieved from https://manifesto-project.wzb.eu/down/originals/2021-1/41953_2021.pdf

Akkerman, A., Mudde, C., & Zaslove, A. (2013). How populist are the people? Measuring populist attitudes in voters. *Comparative Political Studies, 47*(9), 1324–1353.

Alberque, W. (2017). *The NPT and the origins of NATO's nuclear sharing arrangements*. Paris: Institut français des relations internationales.

Aldrich, J. H., Gelpi, C., Feaver, P., Reifler, J., & Sharp, K. T. (2006). Foreign policy and the electoral connection. *Annual Review of Political Science, 9*(1), 477–502.

Almond, G. A. (1950). *The American people and foreign policy* (1st ed.). New York: Harcourt.

Alon-Barkat, S., & Gilad, S. (2016). Political control or legitimacy deficit? Bureaucracies' symbolic responses to bottom-up public pressures. *Policy & Politics, 44*(1), 41–58.

Anthony, I., & Janssen, J. (2010). The future of nuclear weapons in NATO. *Friedrich-Ebert-Stiftung. International Policy Analysis.* Retrieved from https://library.fes.de/pdf-files/id/ipa/07151.pdf

Arndt, A. C., Horovitz, L., Major, C., Schneider, J., & Wachs, L. (2021). Euro-Atlantic concerns regarding a US 'Sole Purpose' policy. *Stiftung Wissenschaft und Politik Working Paper nr 4.* Retrieved from www.swp-berlin.org/publications/products/arbeitspapiere/Working_Paper_European_SP_Perspectives.pdf

Arndt, A. C., Horovitz, L., & Onderco, M. (2023). Russia's failed nuclear coercion against Ukraine. *The Washington Quarterly, 46*(3), 167–184.

Aspinwall, M. (2007). Government preferences on European integration: An empirical test of five theories. *British Journal of Political Science, 37*(1), 89–114.

Astner, K., & Kütt, M. (2024). The treaty on the prohibition of nuclear weapons: Changing disarmament discourses in Germany? In U. Kühn (Ed.), *Germany and nuclear weapons in the 21st century: Atomic Zeitenwende?* (pp. 203–229). Abingdon: Routledge.

Auel, K., & Christiansen, T. (2015). After Lisbon: National parliaments in the European Union. *West European Politics, 38*(2), 261–281.

Auel, K., Eisele, O., & Kinski, L. (2018). What happens in Parliament stays in Parliament? Newspaper coverage of National Parliaments in EU affairs. *JCMS: Journal of Common Market Studies, 56*(3), 628–645.

Baehr, P. R. (1969). Kamerleden en regeringsdelegaties: Een oud probleem opnieuw bezien. *Acta Politica, 5*(1), 3–15.

Bailey, M. A. (2001). Quiet influence: The representation of diffuse interests on trade policy, 1983–94. *Legislative Studies Quarterly, 26*(1), 45–80.

Bardi, L., Bartolini, S., & Trechsel, A. H. (2014). Responsive and responsible? The role of parties in twenty-first century politics. *West European Politics, 37*(2), 235–252.

Baron, J., & Herzog, S. (2020). Public opinion on nuclear energy and nuclear weapons: The attitudinal nexus in the United States. *Energy Research & Social Science, 68*, 101567.

Baum, M. A., & Potter, P. B. K. (2015). *War and democratic constraint: How the public influences foreign policy*. Princeton, NJ: Princeton University Press.

Bayram, A. B. (2017). Due deference: Cosmopolitan social identity and the psychology of legal obligation in international politics. *International Organization, 71*(S1), S137–S163.

Becker, J., Jee, H., Budeanu, A., Love, M., & Benson, S. (2024). *European strategies in the shadow of Sino-American competition: A text-as-data approach*. United States Military Academy, West Point, 7 February. https://papers.ssrn.com/sol3/papers.cfm?abstract_id=4758032

Becker, J., & Malesky, E. (2017). The continent or the 'Grand Large'? Strategic culture and operational burden-sharing in NATO. *International Studies Quarterly, 61*(1), 163–180.

Bell, M. S., & Hoffmann, F. R. (2025). Europe's nuclear trilemma: The difficult and dangerous options for post-American deterrence. *Foreign Affairs*. Retrieved from www.foreignaffairs.com/europe/europes-nuclear-trilemma

Bender, B., McLeary, P., & Banco, E. (2022). U.S. speeds up plans to store upgraded nukes in Europe. *Politico*. Retrieved from www.politico.com/news/2022/10/26/u-s-plans-upgraded-nukes-europe-00063675

Bertsou, E., & Caramani, D. (2022). People haven't had enough of experts: Technocratic attitudes among citizens in nine European democracies. *American Journal of Political Science*, 66(1), 5–23.

Bertsou, E., & Pastorella, G. (2017). Technocratic attitudes: A citizens' perspective of expert decision-making. *West European Politics*, 40(2), 430–458.

Bickerton, C., & Accetti, C. I. (2017). Populism and technocracy. In C. R. Kaltwasser, P. Taggart, P. O. Espejo, & P. Ostiguy (Eds.), *The Oxford handbook of populism*. Oxford: Oxford University Press. Retrieved from www.oxfordhandbooks.com/view/10.1093/oxfordhb/9780198803560.001.0001/oxfordhb-9780198803560-e-24

Biddle, S. D., & Feaver, P. (1989). *Battlefield nuclear weapons: Issues and options*. Lanham, MD: University Press of America.

Bildt, C., & Sikorski, R. (2010). Next, the tactical nukes. *The New York Times*. Retrieved from www.nytimes.com/2010/02/02/opinion/02iht-edbildt.html

Bolton, M., & Minor, E. (2016). The discursive turn arrives in Turtle Bay: The international campaign to abolish nuclear weapons' operationalization of critical IR theories. *Global Policy*, 7(3), 385–395.

Boncourt, T., Debos, M., Delori, M., Pelopidas, B., & Wasinski, C. (2020). Que faire des interventions militaires dans le champ académique? Réflexions sur la nécessaire distinction entre expertise et savoir scientifique. *20 & 21. Revue d'histoire*, 145(1), 135–150.

Booth, K., & Wheeler, N. J. (2008). *The security dilemma: Fear, cooperation and trust in world politics*. Basingstoke & New York: Palgrave Macmillan.

Borger, J. (2010a). Barack Obama's hopes for a nuclear-free world fading fast. *The Guardian*. Retrieved from www.theguardian.com/world/2010/nov/16/barack-obama-nuclear-hopes-fading

Borger, J. (2010b). Five Nato states to urge removal of US nuclear arms in Europe. *The Guardian*. Retrieved from www.theguardian.com/world/2010/feb/22/nato-states-us-nuclear-arms-europe

Born, H., Gill, B., & Hänggi, H. (2011). *Governing the bomb: Civilian control and democratic accountability of nuclear weapons*. Oxford: Oxford University Press.

Borrie, J. (2014). Humanitarian reframing of nuclear weapons and the logic of a ban. *International Affairs*, 90(3), 625–646.

Börzel, T. A., & Zürn, M. (2021). Contestations of the liberal international order: From liberal multilateralism to postnational liberalism. *International Organization*, 75(2), 282–305.

Braun, B., & Düsterhöft, M. (2023). Noisy politics, quiet technocrats? Central banking in contentious times [Unpublished paper]. Retrieved from https://benjaminbraun.org/assets/Noisy_politics_quiet_technocrats.pdf

Brauß, H. (2020). Atomdebatte in der SPD: Rolf Mützenich hat Unrecht. *Frankfurter Allgemeine Zeitung*. Retrieved from www.faz.net/aktuell/politik/inland/atom-debatte-in-der-spd-rolf-muetzenich-hat-unrecht-16757761.html?printPagedArticle=true#pageIndex_2

Breen, L., & Eilstrup-Sangiovanni, M. (2024). Issue-adoption and campaign structure in transnational advocacy campaigns: A longitudinal network analysis. *European Journal of International Relations*, 30(2), 486–516.

Brinkel, B. F. M. (1982). Het IKV in woord en daad. *Christen Democratische Verkenningen*, 2(18), 60–71.

Brixley-Williams, S. (2020). Report: Differentiated nuclear responsibilities among non-nuclear possessor states – Perspectives from The Hague. *A report by The British American Security Information Council & The Institute for Conflict, Cooperation and Security*. Retrieved from https://basicint.org/report-differentiated-nuclear-responsibilities-among-non-nuclear-possessor-states-perspectives-from-the-hague/

Brixley-Williams, S., & Wheeler, N. J. (2020). Nuclear responsibilities: A new approach for thinking and talking about nuclear weapons. *A report by The British American Security Information Council & The Institute for Conflict, Cooperation and Security*. Retrieved from https://basicint.org/report-nuclear-responsibilities-a-new-approach-for-thinking-and-talking-about-nuclear-weapons/

Bronk, J. (2020). German decision to split tornado replacement is a poor one. *RUSI Defence Systems (Vol 22)*. Retrieved from https://rusi.org/explore-our-research/publications/rusi-defence-systems/german-decision-split-tornado-replacement-poor-one

Buddhability. (2022). How I found my purpose: Nuclear abolition edition. Retrieved from https://buddhability.org/podcast/how-i-found-my-purpose-nuclear-abolition-edition/

Budjeryn, M. (2022). *Inheriting the bomb: The collapse of the USSR and the nuclear disarmament of Ukraine*. Baltimore: Johns Hopkins University Press.

Bugos, S. (2019). Turkey shows nuclear weapons interest. *Arms Control Today*, 49(8), 24–25.

Buijs, P. (2018). The influence of NVMP's medical-humanitarian arguments on Dutch nuclear weapons politics: The Netherlands can make a difference in reaching a nuclear weapons-free world. *Medicine, Conflict and Survival*, 34(4), 313–323.

Bunde, T. (2022). Lessons (to be) learned? Germany's Zeitenwende and European security after the Russian invasion of Ukraine. *Contemporary Security Policy*, 43(3), 516–530.

Bunde, T. (2024). Nuclear Zeitenwende(n): Germany and NATO's nuclear posture. In U. Kühn (Ed.), *Germany and nuclear weapons in the 21st Century: Atomic Zeitenwende?* (pp. 87–111). Abingdon: Routledge.

Bunde, T., Hartmann, L., Stärk, F., Carr, R., Erber, C., Hammelehle, J., & Kabus, J. (2020). Zeitenwende, Wendezeiten: Sonderausgabe des Munich Security Report zur deutschen Außen- und Sicherheitspolitik. Retrieved from https://securityconference.org/assets/01_Bilder_Inhalte/03_Medien/02_Publikationen/MSC_Germany_Report_10-2020_De.pdf

Bunde, T., & Onderco, M. (2023). Permissive dissensus: The nuclear dimension of the German Zeitenwende. *The Nonproliferation Review*, 30(4–6), 221–240.

Bündnis 90/Die Grünen. (2002). Grün wirkt! – Unser Wahlprogramm 2002–2006. Retrieved from https://manifesto-project.wzb.eu/down/originals/2015-1/41113_2002.pdf

Bündnis 90/Die Grünen. (2005). Wahlprogramm 2005. Retrieved from https://manifesto-project.wzb.eu/down/originals/41113_2005.pdf

Bündnis 90/Die Grünen. (2013). Zeit für den grünen Wandel – teilhaben. einmischen. zukunft schaffen. *Bundestagswahlprogramm 2013 von BÜNDNIS 90 / DIE GRÜNEN*. Retrieved from https://manifesto-project.wzb.eu//down/originals/41113_2013.pdf

Bündnis 90/Die Grünen. (2017). Zukunft wird aus Mut gemacht. *Bundestagswahlprogramm 2017*. Retrieved from https://manifesto-project.wzb.eu//down/originals/2017-2/41113_2017.pdf

Bündnis 90/Die Grünen. (2021). Deutschland. Alles ist drin. Bundestagswahlprogramm 2021. Retrieved from https://manifesto-project.wzb.eu/down/originals/2021-1/41113_2021.pdf

Bündnis 90/Die Grünen. (2022). Beschluss (vorläufig). Wertegeleitet, multilateral, handlungsfähig: grüne Friedens- und Sicherheitspolitik in der Zeitenwende. *48. Ordentliche Bundesdelegiertenkonferenz*. Retrieved from: https://cms.gruene.de/uploads/documents/Beschluss_FS-12_Wertegeleitet_multilateral_handlungsf%C3%A4hig_gr%C3%BCne_Friedens-_und_Sicherheitspolitik_in_der_Zeitenwen.pdf

Bunn, M. E. (2009). Extended deterrence and assurance. Briefing to CSIS workshop, 3 June 2009. In C. A. Murdock & J. M. Yeats (Eds.), *Exploring the nuclear posture implications of extended deterrence and assurance: Workshop proceedings and key takeaways* (pp. 86–94). Washington, DC: Center for Strategic and International Studies.

Bunn, M. E. (2022). Extending nuclear deterrence and assuring US allies. In C. L. Glaser, A. Long, & B. Radzinsky (Eds.), *Managing US nuclear operations in the 21st century* (pp. 201–240). Washington, DC: Brookings Institution Press.

Busuioc, E. M., & Lodge, M. (2016). The reputational basis of public accountability. *Governance, 29*(2), 247–263.

Buteux, P. (1983). *The politics of nuclear consultation in NATO 1965–1980.* Cambridge, UK: Cambridge University Press.

Cameron, J. (2025). Eurodeterrent: A vision for an Anglo-French nuclear force. *War on the Rocks.* Retrieved from https://warontherocks.com/2025/03/eurodeterrent-a-vision-for-an-anglo-french-nuclear-force/

Caramani, D. (2020). Introduction: The technocratic challenge to democracy. In E. Bertsou & D. Caramani (Eds.), *The technocratic challenge to democracy* (pp. 1–26). London: Routledge.

Carpenter, D. (2010). *Reputation and power: Organizational image and pharmaceutical regulation at the FDA.* Princeton, NJ: Princeton University Press.

Carpenter, D., Chattopadhyay, J., Moffitt, S., & Nall, C. (2012). The complications of controlling agency time discretion: FDA review deadlines and postmarket drug safety. *American Journal of Political Science, 56*(1), 98–114.

Catanzaro, A., & Coticchia, F. (2018). *Al di là dell'Arcobaleno: i movimenti pacifisti italiani tra ideologie e contro-narrazioni strategiche.* Milano: Vita e pensiero.

Caughley, T., & Mukhatzhanova, G. (2017). Negotiation of a Nuclear Weapons Prohibition Treaty: Nuts and bolts of the Ban. *UNIDIR.* Retrieved from www.unidir.org/files/publications/pdfs/nuts-and-bolts-en-684.pdf

Cd&V. (2014). Het 3d plan van CD&V economische groei met sociale vooruitgang. Retrieved from https://manifesto-project.wzb.eu//down/originals/2019-1/21521_2014.pdf

Cd&V. (2019). Verkiezingsprogramma CD&V. Retrieved from https://manifesto-project.wzb.eu//down/originals/2020-1/21521_2019.pdf

CDU/CSU. (2013). Gemeinsam erfolgreich für Deutschland. Regierungsprogramm 2013–2017. Retrieved from https://manifesto-project.wzb.eu/down/originals/41521_2013.pdf

CDU/CSU. (2021). Das Programm für Stabilität und Erneuerung. Gemeinsam für ein modernes Deutschland. Retrieved from https://manifesto-project.wzb.eu/down/originals/2021-1/41521_2021.pdf

Center for Strategic and International Studies. (2024). Nuclear threats and the role of allies. *Project on Nuclear Issues.* Retrieved from www.youtube.com/watch?v=8jDqLj3JFw8

Centre Démocrate Humaniste. (2007). C'est l'heure h. Retrieved from https://manifesto-project.wzb.eu//down/originals/21522_2007.pdf

Centre Démocrate Humaniste. (2010). Un pacte pour sortir les Belges de crise. Retrieved from https://manifesto-project.wzb.eu//down/originals/21522_2010.pdf

Centre Démocrate Humaniste. (2014). Vivre mieux, c'est possible! Retrieved from https://manifesto-project.wzb.eu//down/originals/2022-1/21522_2014.pdf

Chiru, M., & Enyedi, Z. (2021). Who wants technocrats? A comparative study of citizen attitudes in nine young and consolidated democracies. *The British Journal of Politics and International Relations, 24*(1), 95–112.

Christen-Democratisch Appel. (2010). Slagvaardig en samen. Retrieved from https://manifesto-project.wzb.eu/down/originals/22521_2010.pdf

Christen-Democratisch Appel. (2021). Verkiezingsprogramma 2021–2025 Nu doorpakken. Retrieved from https://d14uo0i7wmc99w.cloudfront.net/CDA/2020/TK2021/CDA-verkiezingsprogramma%5B2021-2025%5D.pdf

ChristenUnie. (2010). Vooruitzien. Retrieved from https://manifesto-project.wzb.eu//down/originals/22526_2010.pdf

ChristenUnie. (2012). Voor de verandering. Retrieved from https://manifesto-project.wzb.eu//down/originals/2015-1/22526_2012.pdf

ChristenUnie. (2017). Hoopvol realistisch – Voorstellen voor een samenleving met toekomst. *Verkiezingsprogramma 2017–2021*. Retrieved from https://manifesto-project.wzb.eu//down/originals/2018-1/22526_2017.pdf

ChristenUnie. (2021). Kiezen voor wat echt telt. Retrieved from https://manifesto-project.wzb.eu//down/originals/2023-1/22526_2021.pdf

Clawson, R. A., & Oxley, Z. M. (2021). *Public opinion: Democratic ideals, democratic practice*. Thousand Oaks, CA: CQ Press.

CNAPD. (2019). Armes nucleaires – Pour qui votons-nous? Retrieved from www.cnapd.be/armes-nucleaires-elections-2019/

Coalition belge contre les armes nucléaires. (2020). Sondage YouGov: Plus de trois-quarts de la population belge demandent l'interdiction des armes nucléaires. Retrieved from https://nonukes.be/fr/sondage-yougov-plus-de-trois-quarts-de-la-population-belge-demandent-linterdiction-des-armes-nucleaires/

Colbourn, S. (2022). *Euromissiles: The nuclear weapons that nearly destroyed NATO*. Ithaca, NY: Cornell University Press.

Coticchia, F. (2016). A controversial warplane: Narratives, counternarratives, and the Italian debate on the F-35. *Alternatives: Global, Local, Political, 41*(4), 194–213.

Coticchia, F., & Vignoli, V. (2020a). Italian political parties and military operations: An empirical analysis on voting patterns. *Government and Opposition, 55*(3), 456–473.

Coticchia, F., & Vignoli, V. (2020b). Populist parties and foreign policy: The case of Italy's Five Star Movement. *The British Journal of Politics and International Relations, 22*(3), 523–541.

Craig, C., & Ruzicka, J. (2013). The nonproliferation complex. *Ethics & International Affairs*, 27(3), 329–348.

Creedon, M. R., Kyl, J. L., Billingslea, M. S., Duffy, G. C., Gordon-Hagerty, L. E., Gottemoeller, R. E., Heinrichs, R. L., Hyten, J. E., Kroenig, M. H., Miller, F. C., Scher, R. M., & Tomero, L. A. (2023). *America's strategic posture: The final report of the congressional commission on the strategic posture of the United States*. Washington, DC: House Armed Services Committee.

Crespy, A., Moreira Ramalho, T., & Schmidt, V. (2024). Beyond 'responsibility vs. responsiveness': Reconfigurations of EU economic governance in response to crises. *Journal of European Public Policy*, 31(4), 925–949.

Curtin, D. (2014). Challenging executive dominance in European Democracy. *The Modern Law Review*, 77(1), 1–32.

D66. (2010). We willen het anders. Retrieved from https://manifesto-project.wzb.eu//down/originals/22330_2010.pdf

D66. (2012). En nu vooruit. Retrieved from https://manifesto-project.wzb.eu//down/originals/2015-1/22330_2012.pdf

D66. (2016). D66 Verkiezingsprogramma 2017–2021. Retrieved from https://manifesto-project.wzb.eu//down/originals/2018-1/22330_2017.pdf

D66. (2021). Een nieuw begin laat iedereen vrij, maar niemand vallen. Retrieved from https://manifesto-project.wzb.eu//down/originals/2023-1/22330_2021.pdf

Daalder, I. (1993). Nuclear weapons in Europe: Why zero is better. *Arms Control Today*, 23(1), 15–18.

Dahl, R. A. (1985). *Controlling nuclear weapons: Democracy versus guardianship*. Syracuse, NY: Syracuse University Press.

Dahl, R. A. (2020). *On democracy [Veritas Paperback Edition]*. New Haven, CT: Yale University Press.

Dalaqua, R. H. (2013). 'Securing our survival (SOS)': Non-state actors and the campaign for a nuclear weapons convention through the prism of securitisation theory. *Brazilian Political Science Review*, 7(3), 90–117.

The Danish Defence Agreement 2005–2009 (Denmark). (2004).

Danish Diplomacy and Defense in Times of Change (Denmark). (2016).

Danish Security and Defence Towards 2035 (Denmark). (2022).

Davis, J. W., & Jasper, U. (2014). Non-strategic nuclear weapons as a 'Trojan horse': Explaining Germany's ambivalent attitude. *European Security*, 23(1), 15–30.

Day, B., & Waltzkin, H. (1985). The medical profession and nuclear war. *Journal of American Medical Association*, 254(5), 644.

De Kamer. (2022). Integraal Verslag (CRIV 55 COM 817). Retrieved from www.dekamer.be/doc/CCRI/pdf/55/ic817.pdf

de Maizière, T., Mitchell, A. W., Bew, J., Bossenmaier, G., Dalgaard-Nielsen, A., Dassù, M., Fotyga, A., Ildem, T., Védrine, H., & Verhagen, H. (2020). NATO 2030: United for a new era. Analysis and recommendations of the reflection group appointed by the NATO Secretary General. Retrieved from www.nato.int/nato_static_fl2014/assets/pdf/2020/12/pdf/201201-Reflection-Group-Final-Report-Uni.pdf

de Wilde, P., & Raunio, T. (2018). Redirecting national parliaments: Setting priorities for involvement in EU affairs. *Comparative European Politics, 16*(2), 310–329.

The Defence Concept (Poland). (2017).

The Defence Strategy of the Slovak Republic (Slovakia). (2005).

Defense in 2020 (Portugal). (2013).

Denk. (2017). DENKend aan Nederland. Retrieved from https://manifesto-project.wzb.eu//down/originals/2018-1/22321_2017.pdf

DENK. (2021). Verkiezingsprogramma DENK 2021–2025 DENK anders: Samen zijn wij Nederland. Denk voor de toekomst. Retrieved from www.bewegingdenk.nl/verkiezingsprogramma/

Department of Defense. (2010). *Nuclear posture review*. Washington, DC: Department of Defence.

Department of Defense. (2018). *Nuclear posture review*. Washington, DC: Office of the Secretary of Defense.

Department of Defense. (2022). *Nuclear posture review*. Washington, DC: Office of the Secretary of Defense.

Der Spiegel. (2005). Der Manager des Bösen. Retrieved from www.spiegel.de/politik/waffenabzug-a-860fec19-0002-0001-0000-000040266225?context=issue

Der Tagesspiegel. (2022). Zwei Drittel befürchten in Umfrage einen Dritten Weltkrieg. *Der Tagesspiegel Online*. Retrieved from www.tagesspiegel.de/politik/russlands-angriff-auf-die-ukraine-zwei-drittel-befuerchten-in-umfrage-einen-dritten-weltkrieg/28116150.html

Destradi, S., & Plagemann, J. (2019). Populism and International Relations: (Un)predictability, personalisation, and the reinforcement of existing trends in world politics. *Review of International Studies, 45*(5), 711–730.

Deutsch, K. W. (1966). Integration and arms control in the European political environment: A summary report. *The American Political Science Review, 60*(2), 354–365.

Deutscher Bundestag. (2023). Experten äußern sich besorgt zur globalen Abrüstungsarchitektur. Retrieved from www.bundestag.de/dokumente/textarchiv/2023/kw19-pa-ua-abruestung-946014

Deutscher Bundestag. (2021a). Abrüsten statt Aufrüsten – US-Atomwaffen aus Deutschland abziehen. *Dokumentations- und Informationssystem für*

Parlamentsmaterialien. Retrieved from https://dip.bundestag.de/vorgang/abr%C3%BCsten-statt-aufr%C3%BCsten-us-atomwaffen-aus-deutschland-abziehen/278243?f.deskriptor=Abr%C3%BCstung&rows=25&pos=9

Deutscher Bundestag. (2021b). Stenografischer Bericht. 207. Sitzung. Berlin, Freitag, den 29. Januar 2021. *Plenarprotokoll 19/207.* Retrieved from https://dipbt.bundestag.de/dip21/btp/19/19207.pdf

Die Linke. (2009). Konsequent sozial. Für Demokratie und Frieden. Retrieved from https://manifesto-project.wzb.eu/down/originals/41223_2009.pdf

Die Linke. (2013). 100 Prozent sozial. Retrieved from https://manifesto-project.wzb.eu/down/originals/41223_2013.pdf

Die Linke. (2017). Die Zukunft, für die wir kämpfen: Sozial. Gerecht. Frieden. Für Alle. Retrieved from https://manifesto-project.wzb.eu//down/originals/2017-2/41223_2017.pdf

Die Linke. (2021). Zeit zu handeln! Für soziale Sicherheit, Frieden und Klimagerechtigkeit. Retrieved from https://manifesto-project.wzb.eu//down/originals/2021-1/41223_2021.pdf

Dieterich, S., Hummel, H., & Marschall, S. (2010). Parliamentary war powers: A survey of 25 European parliaments. *Geneva Centre for the Democratic Control of Armed Forces. Occasional Paper No 21.* Retrieved from www.dcaf.ch/content/download/35827/526871/file/OP21_FINAL.pdf

Dieterich, S., Hummel, H., & Marschall, S. (2015). Bringing democracy back in: The democratic peace, parliamentary war powers and European participation in the 2003 Iraq War. *Cooperation and Conflict, 50*(1), 87–106.

Docherty, B. (2018). A 'light for all humanity': The treaty on the prohibition of nuclear weapons and the progress of humanitarian disarmament. *Global Change, Peace & Security, 30*(2), 163–186.

Don't Bank on the Bomb. (2023). Why Divest? A Focus on Governments. Retrieved from www.dontbankonthebomb.com/take-action-for-divestment/governments/

Driesen, D. M. (2020). The unitary executive theory in comparative context. *Hastings Law Journal, 72*(1), 1–54.

Eaves, E. (2021). Why is America getting a new $100 billion nuclear weapon? Retrieved from https://thebulletin.org/2021/02/why-is-america-getting-a-new-100-billion-nuclear-weapon/

Ecolo. (2010). Plateforme programmatique Ecolo. Retrieved from https://manifesto-project.wzb.eu//down/originals/21111_2010.pdf

Egeland, K. (2017a). How I learned to stop worrying and embrace diplomatic 'polarization'. *Peace Review, 29*(4), 482–488.

Egeland, K. (2017b). *The road to prohibition: Nuclear hierarchy and disarmament, 1968–2017.* Oxford, UK: University of Oxford.

Egeland, K. (2019). Nuclear abolition from Baruch to the ban. In C. M. Bailliet (Ed.), *Research handbook on international law and peace* (pp. 244–266). Cheltenham: Edward Elgar Publishing.

Egeland, K. (2020a). Spreading the burden: How NATO became a 'nuclear' alliance. *Diplomacy & Statecraft, 31*(1), 143–167.

Egeland, K. (2020b). Who stole disarmament? History and nostalgia in nuclear abolition discourse. *International Affairs, 96*(5), 1387–1403.

Egeland, K. (2021). Nuclear weapons and adversarial politics: Bursting the abolitionist 'Consensus'. *Journal for Peace and Nuclear Disarmament, 4*(1), 107–115.

Egeland, K., & Pelopidas, B. (2020). European nuclear weapons? Zombie debates and nuclear realities. *European Security, 30*(2), 237–258.

Egeland, K., & Pelopidas, B. (2025). No such thing as a free donation? Research funding and conflicts of interest in nuclear weapons policy analysis. *International Relations, 39*(1), 125–147. Retrieved from https://doi.org/10.1177/00471178221140000.

Erikson, R. S., MacKuen, M., & Stimson, J. A. (2002). *The macro polity*. New York: Cambridge University Press.

Eschle, C. (2021). Feminism and peace movements: Engendering anti-nuclear activism. In T. Väyrynen, É. Féron, S. Parashar, & C. Confortini (Eds.), *Routledge handbook of feminist peace research* (pp. 250–259). New York: Routledge.

Everts, P. (1984). The churches and attitudes on nuclear weapons: The case of the Netherlands. *Bulletin of Peace Proposals, 15*(3), 227–242.

Everts, P. (1985a). *Controversies at home: Domestic factors in the foreign policy of the Netherlands*. Dordrecht: Nijhoff.

Everts, P. (1985b). Public opinion on nuclear weapons, defense, and security: The case of the Netherlands. In G. Flynn & H. Rattinger (Eds.), *The public and Atlantic defense* (pp. 221–275). Totowa, NJ: Rowman & Allanheld.

Everts, P., & Isernia, P. (2015). *Public opinion, transatlantic relations and the use of force*. Basingstoke: Palgrave Macmillan.

Fearon, J. D. (1997). Signaling foreign policy interests. *Journal of Conflict Resolution, 41*(1), 68–90.

Fedina, K. (2024). How Finland approaches its new NATO role is a key decision for the New President. *RAND Corporation*. Retrieved from www.rand.org/pubs/commentary/2024/02/how-finland-approaches-its-new-nato-role-is-a-key-decision.html

Fetter, S., & Wolfsthal, J. (2018). No first use and credible deterrence. *Journal for Peace and Nuclear Disarmament, 1*(1), 102–114.

Finnemore, M., & Jurkovich, M. (2020). The politics of aspiration. *International Studies Quarterly, 64*(4), 759–769.

Flournoy, M., & Townsend, J. (2020). Striking at the Heart of the Trans-Atlantic Bargain. *Der Spiegel International*. Retrieved from www.spiegel.de/international/world/biden-advisers-on-nuclear-sharing-striking-at-the-heart-of-the-trans-atlantic-bargain-a-e6d96a48-68ef-49ab-8a0c-8a979abf2bb4

Fonck, D., Haesebrouck, T., & Reykers, Y. (2019). Parliamentary involvement, party ideology and majority-opposition bargaining: Belgian participation in multinational military operations. *Contemporary Security Policy*, 40(1), 85–100.

Foradori, P. (2012). Tactical nuclear weapons in Italy: Striking a balance between disarmament aspirations and alliance obligations. *The Nonproliferation Review*, 19(1), 13–29.

Foradori, P. (2014). Reluctant disarmer: Italy's ambiguous attitude toward NATO's nuclear weapons policy. *European Security*, 23(1), 31–44.

Fordham, B. O., & Flynn, M. (2023). Everything old is new again: The persistence of Republican opposition to multilateralism in American foreign policy. *Studies in American Political Development*, 37(1), 56–73.

Foyle, D. C. (1999). Linking public opinion and foreign policy. In *Counting the public in: Presidents, public opinion, and foreign policy*. New York: Columbia University Press.

Fraise, T. (2022). La question du secret nucléaire: technologie, secrets d'État et enjeux démocratiques. *Critique internationale*, 95(2), 172–181.

Fraise, T. (2023). Restricted democracies: Nuclear weapons programs, secrecy, and democracy in the United Kingdom, France, and Sweden (1939–1974) [unpublished PhD dissertation]. Paris: Sciences Po.

France24. (2025). Germany's far-right AfD basks in spotlight of Musk support. Retrieved from www.france24.com/en/live-news/20250216-germany-s-far-right-afd-basks-in-spotlight-of-musk-support

Franceschini, G. (2024). The Greens and nuclear weapons: Between disarmament aspirations and pragmatism. In U. Kühn (Ed.), *Germany and nuclear weapons in the 21st century: Nuclear Zeitenwende?* (pp. 182–202). Abingdon: Routledge.

Frankland, E. G. (1999). The Green Party's transformation: The 'New Politics' party grows up. In P. H. Merk (Ed.), *The federal Republic of Germany at Fifty* (pp. 147–159). New York: New York University Press.

Freedman, L., & Michaels, J. H. (2019). *The evolution of nuclear strategy* (4th ed.). London: Palgrave Macmillan.

Freie Demokratische Partei. (2009). Die Mitte stärken. Deutschlandprogramm 2009. Retrieved from https://manifesto-project.wzb.eu/down/originals/41420_2009.pdf

Freie Demokratische Partei. (2013). Damit Deutschland stark bleibt. *Bürgerprogramm 2013*. Retrieved from https://manifesto-project.wzb.eu//down/originals/41420_2013.pdf

Freie Demokratische Partei. (2017). Schauen wir nicht länger zu – Das Wahlprogramm der Freien Demokraten zur Bundestagswahl 2017. Retrieved from https://manifesto-project.wzb.eu/down/originals/2017-2/41420_2017.pdf

Freie Demokratische Partei. (2021). Nie gab es mehr zu tun – Das Wahlprogramm der Freien Demokraten. Retrieved from https://manifesto-project.wzb.eu/down/originals/2021-1/41420_2021.pdf

Frühling, S., & O'Neil, A. (2017). Nuclear weapons, the United States and alliances in Europe and Asia: Toward an institutional perspective. *Contemporary Security Policy, 38*(1), 4–25.

Fuhrhop, P. (2021). The German debate: The Bundestag and nuclear deterrence. In A. Morgan & A. Péczeli (Eds.), *Europe's evolving deterrence discourse* (pp. 27–38). Livermore, CA: Lawrence Livermore National Laboratory.

Fuhrhop, P., Kühn, U., & Meier, O. (2020). Creating an opportunity to withdraw U.S. nuclear weapons from Europe. *Arms Control Today*. Retrieved from www.armscontrol.org/act/2020-10/features/creating-opportunity-withdraw-us-nuclear-weapons-europe#endnote05

Fuhrmann, M., & Sechser, T. S. (2014a). Nuclear strategy, nonproliferation, and the causes of Foreign nuclear deployments. *The Journal of Conflict Resolution, 58*(3), 455–480.

Fuhrmann, M., & Sechser, T. S. (2014b). Signaling alliance commitments: Hand-tying and Sunk Costs in extended nuclear deterrence. *American Journal of Political Science, 58*(4), 919–935.

Fursdon, E. (1980). *The European defence community: A history*. London & Basingstoke: Macmillan Press.

Futter, A., & Samuel, O. (2024). Accommodating Nutopia: The nuclear ban treaty and the developmental interests of Global South countries. *Review of International Studies, 50*(5), 799–820.

Garamone, J. (2019). U.S. begins process of 'Unwinding' Turkey from F-35 Program, DOD Officials Say *US Department of Defense*. Retrieved from www.defense.gov/News/News-Stories/Article/Article/1908351/us-begins-process-of-unwinding-turkey-from-f-35-program-dod-officials-say/

Gavin, F. J. (2012). *Nuclear statecraft: History and strategy in America's atomic age*. Ithaca, NY: Cornell University Press.

Gavin, F. J. (2015). Strategies of inhibition: US grand strategy, the nuclear revolution, and nonproliferation. *International Security, 40*(1), 9–46.

Geis, A., & Wagner, W. (2008). From democratic peace to democratic distinctiveness: A critique of democratic exceptionalism in peace and conflict studies. *Comparative Research in Law & Political Economy. Research Paper No. 39/2008*. Retrieved from https://digitalcommons.osgoode.yorku.ca/clpe/208

Gemeente Amsterdam. (2020). *Bestuurlijke reactie op het initiatiefvoorstel van Raadslid Roosma (GroenLinks) getiteld 'Ban de Bom' (29 September 2020)*.

Gemeente Amsterdam / Gemeenteraad. (2019). *Instemmen met het initiatiefvoorstel 'Ban de Bom. Zeg ja tegen het VN kernwapenverdrag en zeg nee tegen belastingontwijkende wapenproducenten' van de leden Roosma (GroenLinks), Bakker (SP), Simons (BIJ1), Mbarki (PvdA), Van Lammeren (PvdD) en Kılıç (DENK) en kennisnemen van de bestuurlijke reactie. (Initiatiefvoorstel)*.

Gemeente Amsterdam / Gemeenteraad. (2021). *Instemmen met het gewijzigde initiatiefvoorstel 'Ban de Bom. Zeg ja tegen het VN-kernwapenverdrag en zeg nee tegen belastingontwijkende wapenproducenten' van de leden Roosma, N.T. Bakker, Mbarki, Van Lammeren en Kik en het voormalig lid Simons en kennisnemen van de bestuurlijke reactie op het oorspronkelijke voorstel. VN2021-000324 (Initiatiefvoorstel)*.

Gemeente Rotterdam / College van Burgemeester en Wethouders. (2020). Afdoeningsvoorstel van motie 'Ondertekening ICAN Cities Appeal' (8 December 2020). Retrieved from https://gemeenteraad.rotterdam.nl/Reports/Document/b12d9685-50b8-4e57-a00d-38cdb666c1ca?documentId=bf566c16-21e4-4fef-8577-43a3ccf8fbd5

Gemeente van Rotterdam. (2020). Gemeenteraad donderdag 1 oktober 2020 (Agenda). Retrieved from https://gemeenteraad.rotterdam.nl/Agenda/Index/5a1fa524-ef35-4a3c-8b69-986256f92ab4

Gerzhoy, G. (2015). Alliance coercion and nuclear restraint: How the United States thwarted West Germany's nuclear ambitions. *International Security, 39*(4), 91–129.

Gheorghe, E. (2022). Balance of power redux: Nuclear alliances and the logic of extended deterrence. *The Chinese Journal of International Politics, 15*(1), 87–109.

Gibbons, R. D. (2017). The nuclear Ban Treaty: How did we get here, what does it mean for the United States? *War on the Rocks*. Retrieved from https://warontherocks.com/2017/07/the-nuclear-ban-treaty-how-did-we-get-here-what-does-it-mean-for-the-united-states/

Gibbons, R. D. (2018). The humanitarian turn in nuclear disarmament and the treaty on the prohibition of nuclear weapons. *The Nonproliferation Review, 25*(1–2), 11–36.

Gibbons, R. D. (2022). *The Hegemon's tool kit*. Ithaca, NY: Cornell University Press.

Gibbons, R. D., & Herzog, S. (2023). Nuclear disarmament and Russia's War on Ukraine: The ascendance and uncertain future of the treaty on the prohibition of nuclear weapons. In R. D. Gibbons, S. Herzog, W. Wan, & D. Horschig (Eds.), *The altered nuclear order in the wake of the Russia-Ukraine War* (pp. 1–36). Cambridge, MA: American Academy of Arts & Sciences.

Gibbons, R. D., & Herzog, S. (2024). Treaty design and norm entrepreneurs: Nuclear disarmament advocates adapt to the Russia–Ukraine War [working paper].

Goldberg, J. (2025). The trump administration accidentally texted me its war plans. *The Atlantic*. Retrieved from www.theatlantic.com/politics/archive/2025/03/trump-administration-accidentally-texted-me-its-war-plans/682151/

Götz, N. (2005). On the origins of 'Parliamentary Diplomacy'. *Cooperation and Conflict, 40*(3), 263–279.

Götz, N. (2011). *Deliberative diplomacy: The Nordic approach to global governance and societal representation at the United Nations*. Dordrecht: Republic of Letters Publishing.

Government of Norway. (2009). Non-paper on including tactical nuclear weapons in Europe in a broader nuclear disarmament and arms control process (with Government of Poland). Retrieved from www.regjeringen.no/globalassets/upload/ud/vedlegg/sikkerhetspol/nonpaper_nuclear.pdf

Government Office of the Slovak Republic. (2016). Biela kniha o obrane Slovenskej republiky (submission for a cabinet meeting). Retrieved from www.rokovanie.sk/Rokovanie.aspx/NezaradenyMaterialDetail?idMaterial=25762

Gravelle, T. B., Reifler, J., & Scotto, T. J. (2017). The structure of foreign policy attitudes in transatlantic perspective: Comparing the United States, United Kingdom, France and Germany. *European Journal of Political Research, 56*(4), 757–776.

Gravelle, T. B., Reifler, J., & Scotto, T. J. (2020). Personality traits and foreign policy attitudes: A cross-national exploratory study. *Personality and Individual Differences, 153*, 109607.

Gravelle, T. B., Reifler, J., & Scotto, T. J. (2021). The structure of foreign policy attitudes among middle power publics: A transpacific replication. *Australian Journal of International Affairs, 75*(2), 217–236.

Greenpeace. (2019). Greenpeace-Umfrage zum Ende des INF-Vertrags: Große Mehrheit will keine Atomwaffen in Deutschland. Retrieved from www.greenpeace.de/sites/default/files/publications/umfrage_ende_inf-vertrag.pdf

Greenpeace. (2020). Greenpeace-Umfrage zu Atomwaffen und Atomwaffenverbotsvertrag. Retrieved from www.greenpeace.de/publikationen/umfrage_atomwaffenverbotsvertrag__0.pdf

Greenpeace. (2021). Greenpeace-Umfrage: Große Mehrheit will Deutschlands Beitritt zum Atomwaffenverbotsvertrag. Retrieved from https://greenwire.greenpeace.de/group/themengruppe-frieden/inhalt/greenpeace-umfrage-grosse-mehrheit-will-deutschlands-beitritt-zum

Groen. (2010). Programma Federale Verkiezingen 2010. Retrieved from https://manifesto-project.wzb.eu//down/originals/21112_2010.pdf

Groen. (2014). Samen beter doen. Retrieved from https://manifesto-project.wzb.eu//down/originals/2019-1/21112_2014.pdf

Groen. (2019). Menselijker Eerlijker Gezonder. Retrieved from https://manifesto-project.wzb.eu//down/originals/2020-1/21112_2019.pdf

GroenLinks. (2010). Klaar voor de toekomst. Retrieved from https://manifesto-project.wzb.eu/down/originals/22110_2010.pdf

GroenLinks. (2012). Groene kansen voor Nederland. Retrieved from https://manifesto-project.wzb.eu//down/originals/2015-1/22110_2012.pdf

GroenLinks. (2017). Tijd voor verandering. *Verkiezingsprogramma GroenLinks 2017–2021*. Retrieved from https://manifesto-project.wzb.eu//down/originals/2018-1/22110_2017.pdf

GroenLinks. (2021). Verkiezingsprogramma GroenLinks 2021. Retrieved from https://groenlinks.nl/sites/groenlinks/files/2021-02/Verkiezingsprogramma%20GroenLinks%202021_2.pdf

GroenLinks Amsterdam. (2021). Amsterdam sluit zich aan bij wereldwijd verband van steden tegen kernwapens. Retrieved from https://amsterdam.groenlinks.nl/nieuws/amsterdam-sluit-zich-aan-bij-wereldwijd-verband-van-steden-tegen-kernwapens

GroenLinks Rotterdam. (n.d.). Stephan Leewis. Retrieved from https://rotterdam.groenlinks.nl/stephan-leewis

Gross Stein, J. (2023). Escalation management in Ukraine: 'Learning by Doing' in response to the 'Threat that Leaves Something to Chance'. *Texas National Security Review*, 6(3), 29–50.

Haftendorn, H. (1996). *NATO and the nuclear revolution: A crisis of credibility, 1966–1967*. Oxford, UK: Oxford University Press.

Halás, M. (2023). A manifesto for the Czech Membership in NATO's Nuclear Sharing Club. *Institute of International Relations Prague*. Retrieved from www.iir.cz/en/a-manifesto-for-the-czech-membership-in-nato-s-nuclear-sharing-club-1

Hammer, M. (2020). The collapse of global arms control. *TIME*. Retrieved from https://time.com/6334258/putin-nuclear-arms-control/

Haworth, A. R., Sagan, S. D., & Valentino, B. A. (2019). What do Americans really think about conflict with nuclear North Korea? The answer is both reassuring and disturbing. *Bulletin of the Atomic Scientists*, 75(4), 179–186.

Henke, M., & Maher, R. (2021). The populist challenge to European defense. *Journal of European Public Policy*, 28(3), 389–406.

Henley, J. (2023). Rural populist party emerges as big winner in Dutch elections. *The Guardian*. Retrieved from www.theguardian.com/world/2023/mar/16/rural-populist-party-farmer-citizen-movement-big-winner-dutch-elections

Herzog, S., & Sukin, L. (2023). Nightmares behind the South Korean President's alarming comments. *Carnegie Endowment for International Peace*. Retrieved from https://carnegieendowment.org/2023/01/25/dueling-nuclear-nightmares-behind-south-korean-president-s-alarming-comments-pub-88879

Heuser, B. (1995). The development of NATO's nuclear strategy. *Contemporary European History*, 4(1), 37–66.

Heuser, B., & Stoddart, K. (2017). Difficult Europeans: NATO and tactical/non-strategic nuclear weapons in the Cold War. *Diplomacy & Statecraft*, 28(3), 454–476.

Heyne, L., & Lobo, M. C. (2021). Technocratic attitudes and voting behaviour ten years after the Eurozone crisis: Evidence from the 2019 EP elections. *Electoral Studies*, 70, 102288.

Hofmann, S. C. (2013). *European security in NATO's shadow: Party ideologies and institution building*. Cambridge, UK: Cambridge University Press.

Hofmann, S. C., & Martill, B. (2021). The party scene: New directions for political party research in foreign policy analysis. *International Affairs*, 97(2), 305–322.

Holsti, O. R. (1992). Public opinion and Foreign policy: Challenges to the Almond-Lippmann consensus. *International Studies Quarterly*, 36(4), 439–466.

Hooghe, L., & Marks, G. (2009). A postfunctionalist theory of European integration: From permissive consensus to constraining dissensus. *British Journal of Political Science*, 39(1), 1–23.

Horn, A., Kevins, A., Jensen, C., & Kersbergen, K. V. (2017). Peeping at the corpus – What is really going on behind the equality and welfare items of the Manifesto project? *Journal of European Social Policy*, 27(5), 403–416.

Horovitz, L. (2014). Why do they want American Nukes? Central and Eastern European positions regarding US nonstrategic nuclear weapons. *European Security*, 23(1), 73–89.

Horovitz, L., & Arndt, A. (2022). Russia's catch-all nuclear rhetoric in its war against Ukraine. *SWP Comment No 60*. Retrieved from www.swp-berlin.org/publications/products/comments/2022C60_Russia_NuclearRhetoric.pdf

Horovitz, L., & Arndt, A. (2023). One year of nuclear rhetoric and escalation management in Russia's war against Ukraine: An updated chronology. *SWP Research Division International Security Working Paper Nr. 1/2023*. Retrieved from www.swp-berlin.org/publikation/one-year-of-nuclear-rhetoric-and-escalation-management-in-russias-war-against-ukraine-an-updated-chronology

Horovitz, L., & Major, C. (2023). Der gefährliche Traum von der deutschen Atombombe. *Der Spiegel*. Retrieved from www.spiegel.de/politik/deutschland/aufruestung-der-gefaehrliche-traum-von-der-deutschen-atombombe-gastbeitrag-a-a2cbeefb-22f7-4e88-8880-69915d9a56cf

Horovitz, L., & Major, C. (2025). Europäische Sicherheit unter Trump II: Viel Druck, doch womöglich wenig Wandel. In L. von Daniels & S. Mair (Eds.), *Trumps Rückkehr und Europas außenpolitische Herausforderungen* (pp. 19–23). Berlin: Stiftung Wissenschaft und Politik.

Horovitz, L., & Onderco, M. (2024). How Germans learned to stop worrying and love the bomb, then probably start worrying again. *The War on the Rocks*. Retrieved from https://warontherocks.com/2023/10/how-germans-learned-to-stop-worrying-and-love-the-bomb-then-probably-start-worrying-again/

Hug, S. (2010). Selection effects in roll call votes. *British Journal of Political Science, 40*(1), 225–235.

Hummel, H. (2024). Contested nuclear sharing in Belgium: Domestic political dynamic for the nuclear weapons ban. *Journal for Peace and Nuclear Disarmament, 7*(2), 468–493.

Hunt, J. R. (2022). *The nuclear club: How America and the world policed the atom from Hiroshima to Vietnam*. Stanford, CA: Stanford University Press.

Hurwitz, J., & Peffley, M. (1987). How are foreign policy attitudes structured? A hierarchical model. *American Political Science Review, 81*(4), 1099–1120.

ICAN. (2017). Deutsche wollen andere Atomwaffenpolitik der Regierung. Retrieved from www.icanw.de/wp-content/uploads/2018/07/YouGov-Umfrage_Atomwaffen_2018.pdf

ICAN. (2018a). One year on: European attitudes toward the Treaty on the Prohibition of Nuclear Weapons. Retrieved from https://d3n8a8pro7vhmx.cloudfront.net/ican/pages/714/attachments/original/1575571450/YouGov_ICAN_EUNATOTPNW2018.pdf?1575571450

ICAN. (2018b). Umfrage: Deutsche wollen Abzug der Atomwaffen. Retrieved from www.icanw.de/wp-content/uploads/2018/07/YouGov-Umfrage_Atomwaffen_2018.pdf

ICAN. (2019a). Polls: Public opinion in EU host states firmly opposes nuclear weapons. Retrieved from www.icanw.org/polls_public_opinion_in_eu_host_states_firmly_opposes_nuclear_weapons

ICAN. (2019b). Umfrage: Deutsche gegen neue Atombomber. Retrieved from www.icanw.de/wp-content/uploads/2019/04/2019-04_YouGov-Ergebnisse_de.pdf

ICAN. (2020). ICAN Cities Appeal. Retrieved from https://cities.icanw.org/list_of_cities

ICAN. (2021). NATO public opinion on nuclear weapons. Retrieved from https://d3n8a8pro7vhmx.cloudfront.net/ican/pages/234/attachments/original/1611134933/ICAN_YouGov_Poll_2020.pdf

Infratest-Dimap. (2022). US-Atombomben in Deutschland: 52 Prozent für Verbleib, 39 Prozent für Abzug. Retrieved from www.infratest-dimap.de/umfragen-analysen/bundesweit/umfragen/aktuell/us-atombomben-in-deutschland-52-prozent-fuer-verbleib-39-prozent-fuer-abzug/

Interview with Beatrice Fihn. (2022). *Nuclear Proliferation International History Project*. Retrieved from https://digitalarchive.wilsoncenter.org/document/interview-beatrice-fihn

Interview with Daniel Högsta. (2022). *Nuclear Proliferation International History Project*. Retrieved from https://digitalarchive.wilsoncenter.org/document/interview-daniel-hogsta

Interview with Francesco Vignarca. (2023). *Nuclear Proliferation International History Project*. Retrieved from https://digitalarchive.wilsoncenter.org/document/interview-francesco-vignarca

Interview with Hirotsugu Terasaki. (2023). *Nuclear Proliferation International History Project*. Retrieved from https://digitalarchive.wilsoncenter.org/document/interview-hirotsugu-terasaki

Interview with Melissa Parke. (2024). *Nuclear Proliferation International History Project*. Retrieved from https://digitalarchive.wilsoncenter.org/document/interview-melissa-parke

Interview with Oliver Meier. (2022). *Nuclear Proliferation International History Project*. Retrieved from https://digitalarchive.wilsoncenter.org/document/interview-oliver-meier

Interview with Ray Acheson. (2023). *Nuclear Proliferation International History Project*. Retrieved from https://digitalarchive.wilsoncenter.org/document/interview-ray-acheson

Interview with Sico van der Meer. (2022). *Nuclear Proliferation International History Project*. Retrieved from https://digitalarchive.wilsoncenter.org/document/interview-sico-van-der-meer

Interview with Susi Snyder. (2022). *Nuclear Proliferation International History Project*. Retrieved from https://digitalarchive.wilsoncenter.org/document/interview-susi-snyder

Interview with Xanthe Hall. (2023). *Nuclear Proliferation International History Project*. Retrieved from https://digitalarchive.wilsoncenter.org/document/interview-xanthe-hall

IPPNW. (2016). Meinungen zu Atomwaffen. Retrieved from www.ippnw.de/commonFiles/pdfs/Atomwaffen/forsaumfrage_Atomwaffen_2016.pdf

Italia Europa Insieme. (2018). Insieme è meglio. Retrieved from https://manifesto-project.wzb.eu//down/originals/2019-1/32022_2018.pdf

Jakobi, A. (2025). Engaging in and with complexity: Local actors, Mayors for Peace and the global nuclear order. *Cambridge Review of International Affairs*, 38(3), 319–341.

Jervis, R. (1976). *Perception and misperception in international politics.* Princeton, NJ: Princeton University Press.

Jolly, S., Bakker, R., Hooghe, L., Marks, G., Polk, J., Rovny, J., Steenbergen, M., & Vachudova, M. A. (2022). Chapel Hill expert survey trend file, 1999–2019. *Electoral Studies*, 75, 102420.

Jonter, T. (2016). *The key to nuclear restraint: The Swedish plans to acquire nuclear weapons during the Cold War.* London: Palgrave.

Kaarbo, J. (2015). A foreign policy analysis perspective on the domestic politics turn in IR theory. *International Studies Review*, 17(2), 189–216.

Kaarbo, J., & Lantis, J. S. (2003). The 'greening' of German foreign policy in the Iraq case: Conditions of junior party influence in governing coalitions. *Acta Politica*, 38(3), 201–230.

Kabinetsreactie op AIV-adviesrapport 'Kernwapens in een nieuwe geopolitieke werkelijkheid' [Brief van de ministers van buitenlandse zaken en van defensie]. (2019). Retrieved from www.tweedekamer.nl/downloads/document?id=fb2b0d 74-bbb3-4039-9fae-d5bbe764c341&title=Kabinetsreactie%20op%20AIV-adviesrapport%20%22Kernwapens%20in%20een%20nieuwe%20geopoli tieke%20werkelijkheid%22.pdf

Kacprzyk, A. (2023). NATO nuclear adaptation: Rationales for expanding the force posture in Europe. *Polish Institute of International Affairs*. Retrieved from www.pism.pl/webroot/upload/files/Raport/PISM%20Report%20NATO%20 Nuclear%20Adaptation.pdf

Kamp, K.-H., & Remkes, R. C. N. (2011). Options for NATO nuclear sharing arrangements. In S. Andreasen & I. Williams (Eds.), *Reducing nuclear risks in Europe: A framework for action* (pp. 76–95). Washington, DC: Nuclear Threat Initiative.

Kaplan, F. M. (2020). *The bomb: Presidents, generals, and the secret history of nuclear war.* New York: Simon & Schuster.

Karlas, J. (2011). Parliamentary control of EU affairs in Central and Eastern Europe: Explaining the variation. *Journal of European Public Policy*, 18(2), 258–273.

Kassenova, T. (2022). *Atomic Steppe: How Kazakhstan gave up the bomb.* Stanford, CA: Stanford University Press.

Keidan, C. (2017). Interview: Adessium Foundation. *Alliance Magazine*. Retrieved from www.alliancemagazine.org/interview/interview-adessium-foundation/

Kelleher, C. M. (1975). *Germany and the politics of nuclear weapons.* New York: Columbia University Press.

Keman, H. (1986). Welfare and warfare. Critical options and conscious choice in public policy. In R. Wildenmann (Ed.), *Managing mixed economies* (pp. 97–141). Berlin: Walter de Gruyter.

Kertzer, J. D. (2013). Making sense of isolationism: Foreign policy mood as a multilevel phenomenon. *The Journal of Politics, 75*(1), 225–240.

Kesgin, B., & Kaarbo, J. (2010). When and how parliaments influence foreign policy: The case of Turkey's Iraq decision. *International Studies Perspectives, 11*(1), 19–36.

Key Jr., V. O. (1961). *Public opinion and American democracy*. New York: Alfred A. Knopf.

Khalessi, D. (2015). Strategic ambiguity: Nuclear sharing and the secret strategy for drafting articles I and II of the nonproliferation treaty. *The Nonproliferation Review, 22*(3–4), 421–439.

Khalid, A. (2025). Zelenskyy's visit to the White House ends abruptly after Oval Office spat. *NPR*. Retrieved from www.npr.org/2025/02/28/nx-s1-5312076/zelenskyys-visit-to-the-white-house-ends-abruptly-after-oval-office-spat

Kibaroğlu, M. (2005). Isn't it time to say farewell to Nukes in Turkey? *European Security, 14*(4), 443–457.

Kingdom of the Netherlands. (2017). Explanation of vote of the Netherlands on text of Nuclear Ban Treaty. Retrieved from www.permanentrepresentations.nl/latest/news/2017/07/07/explanation-of-vote-of-ambassador-lise-gregoire-on-the-draft-text-of-the-nuclear-ban-treaty

Kingdon, J. W. (2014). *Agendas, alternatives, and public policies*. Harlow: Pearson.

Kmentt, A. (2021). *The treaty prohibiting nuclear weapons: How it was achieved and why it matters*. London: Routledge.

Knopf, J. W. (1998). *Domestic society and international cooperation: The impact of protest on US arms control policy*. Cambridge, UK: Cambridge University Press.

Knorr, K. (1959). The strained alliance. In K. Knorr (Ed.), *NATO and American security* (pp. 3–10). Princeton, NJ: Princeton University Press.

Koch, L. L., & Wells, M. (2021). Still Taboo? Citizens' attitudes toward the use of nuclear weapons. *Journal of Global Security Studies, 6*(3), ogaa024.

Koch, S. J. (2012). *The presidential nuclear initiatives of 1991–1992*. Washington, DC: National Defense University Press.

Krause, K. (2014). Transnational civil society activism and international security politics: From landmines to global zero. *Global Policy, 5*(2), 229–234.

Krepon, M. (2021). *Winning and losing the nuclear peace: The rise, demise, and revival of arms control*. Stanford, CA: Stanford University Press.

Kreps, S. (2010). Elite consensus as a determinant of alliance cohesion: Why public opinion hardly matters for NATO-led operations in Afghanistan. *Foreign Policy Analysis, 6*(3), 191–215.

Kreuder-Sonnen, C. (2019). *Emergency powers of international organizations: Between normalization and containment.* Oxford: Oxford University Press.

Krieger, D., & Ikeda, D. (2002). *Choose hope.* Santa Monica: Middleway Press.

Kristensen, H. M. (1995). The 520 Forgotten Bombs: How U.S. and British nuclear weapons in Europe undermine the Non-Proliferation Treaty. *Greenpeace International.* Retrieved from http://mkiftbv.nukestrat.com/pubs/520bombs.pdf

Kristensen, H. M. (2015). Nuclear weapons in NATO's deterrence posture: Status quo or change? In S. Von Hlatky & A. Wenger (Eds.), *The future of extended deterrence* (pp. 135–152). Washington, DC: Georgetown University Press.

Kristensen, H. M., & Korda, M. (2022). United States nuclear weapons, 2022. *Bulletin of the Atomic Scientists, 78*(3), 162–184.

Kristensen, H. M., & Korda, M. (2023a). United States nuclear weapons, 2023. *Bulletin of the Atomic Scientists, 79*(1), 28–52.

Kristensen, H. M., & Korda, M. (2023b). World nuclear forces. In Stockholm International Peace Research Institute (Ed.), *SIPRI yearbook 2023: Armaments, disarmament and international security* (pp. 247–336). Oxford: Oxford University Press.

Kristensen, H. M., Korda, M., Johns, E., & Knight, M. (2023). Nuclear weapons sharing, 2023. *Bulletin of the Atomic Scientists, 79*(6), 393–406.

Kuhn, F. (2023). Making nuclear sharing credible again: What the F-35A means for NATO. *War on the Rocks.* Retrieved from https://warontherocks.com/2023/09/making-nuclear-sharing-credible-again-what-the-f-35a-means-for-nato/

Kühn, U. (2024a). Germany debates nuclear weapons, again. But now it's different. *Bulletin of the Atomic Scientists.* Retrieved from https://thebulletin.org/2024/03/germany-debates-nuclear-weapons-again-but-now-its-different/#post-heading

Kühn, U. (Ed.) (2024b). *Germany and nuclear weapons in the 21st century: Nuclear Zeitenwende?* Abingdon: Routledge.

Kühn, U., Volpe, T., & Thompson, B. (2018, 15 August). Tracking the German Nuclear Debate. Retrieved from https://carnegieendowment.org/2018/08/15/tracking-german-nuclear-debate-pub-72884

Kunz, B., & Kühn, U. (2024). German musings about a Franco-German or German Bomb. In U. Kühn (Ed.), *Germany and nuclear weapons in the 21st century: Nuclear Zeitenwende?* (pp. 112–135). Abingdon: Routledge.

Kurosaki, A. (2020). Public opinion, party politics and alliance: The influence of domestic politics on Japan's reliance on the U. S. nuclear umbrella, 1964–8. *The International History Review, 42*(4), 774–793.

Kütt, M., Podvig, P., & Mian, Z. (2023). Bombs away: Confronting the deployment of nuclear weapons in non-nuclear weapon countries. *Bulletin of the*

Atomic Scientists. Retrieved from https://thebulletin.org/2023/07/bombs-away-confronting-the-deployment-of-nuclear-weapons-in-non-nuclear-weapon-countries/#post-heading

Laffan, B. (2014). Testing times: The growing primacy of responsibility in the euro area. *West European Politics, 37*(2), 270–287.

Lambert, A. J., Scherer, L. D., Schott, J. P., Olson, K. R., Andrews, R. K., O'Brien, T. C., & Zisser, A. R. (2010). Rally effects, threat, and attitude change: An integrative approach to understanding the role of emotion. *Journal of Personality and Social Psychology, 98*(6), 886.

Lambert, A. J., Schott, J. P., & Scherer, L. (2011). Threat, politics, and attitudes: Toward a greater understanding of rally-'round-the-flag effects. *Current Directions in Psychological Science, 20*(6), 343–348.

Lanoszka, A. (2020). Poland in a time of geopolitical flux. *Contemporary Politics, 26*(4), 458–474.

Lantis, J. S. (2009). Strategic culture and tailored deterrence: Bridging the gap between theory and practice. *Contemporary Security Policy, 30*(3), 467–485.

Larsen, J. A. (2015). US extended deterrence and Europe: Time to consider alternative structures? In S. Von Hlatky & A. Wenger (Eds.), *The future of extended deterrence* (pp. 41–70). Washington, DC: Georgetown University Press.

Larson, D. W., Paul, T. V., & Wohlforth, W. C. (2014). Status and world order. In T. V. Paul, D. Welch Larson, & W. C. Wohlforth (Eds.), *Status in world politics* (pp. 3–30). Cambridge, UK: Cambridge University Press.

Lederer, E. M. (2020). US urges countries to withdraw from UN nuke ban treaty. *Associated Press News*. Retrieved from https://apnews.com/article/nuclear-weapons-disarmament-latin-america-united-nations-gun-politics-4f109626a1cdd6db10560550aa1bb491

Lehmann, P., Franzmann, S., Burst, T., Lewandowski, J., Matthieß, T., Regel, S., Riethmüller, F., & Zehnter, L. (2023a). *Manifesto Corpus. Version: 2023-1.* Berlin: Wissenschaftszentrum Berlin für Sozialforschung.

Lehmann, P., Franzmann, S., Burst, T., Regel, S., Riethmüller, F., Volkens, A., Weßels, B., & Zehnter, L. (2023b). *The Manifesto Data Collection. Manifesto Project (MRG/CMP/MARPOR). Version 2023a*: Wissenschaftszentrum Berlin für Sozialforschung (WZB) / Göttinger Institut für Demokratieforschung (IfDem).

Leonard, C. (2023). Lockheed Martin's $1.7 trillion F-35 fighter jet is 10 years late and 80% over budget—And it could be one of the Pentagon's biggest success stories. *Fortune.* Retrieved from https://fortune.com/longform/lockheed-martin-f-35-fighter-jet/

Lévêque, C. M., Castello, S., & Carbonell, A. (2017). Origins and evolutions of the Adessium Foundation: From the inspiration of a family to an impactful foundation. *Fondazione Lang Italia.* Retrieved from https://en.fondazionelan gitalia.it/2017/11/29/origins-and-evolutions-of-the-adessium-foundation-from-the-inspiration-of-a-family-to-an-impactful-foundation/

Lewis, P. M. (2009). *A New approach to nuclear disarmament: Learning from International Humanitarian Law Success (ICNND Paper No. 13).* Canberra: International Commission on Nuclear Non-Proliferation and Disarmament.

Liberi e Uguali. (2018). Programma Liberi e Uguali. Retrieved from https://manifesto-project.wzb.eu//down/originals/2019-1/32031_2018.pdf

Lieber, K. A., & Press, D. G. (2020). *The myth of the nuclear revolution: Power politics in the atomic age.* Ithaca, NY: Cornell University Press.

Lijphart, A. (1999). *Patterns of democracy: Government forms and performance in thirty-six countries.* New Haven: Yale University Press.

Lin-Greenberg, E. (2021). Soldiers, pollsters, and international crises: Public opinion and the military's advice on the use of force. *Foreign Policy Analysis, 17*(3), orab009.

Lord, C. (2011). The political theory and practice of parliamentary participation in the Common Security and Defence Policy. *Journal of European Public Policy, 18*(8), 1133–1150.

Lunn, S. (2018). NATO nuclear sharing: Consultation. In S. Andreasen, I. Williams, B. Rose, H. M. Kristensen, S. Lunn, E. J. Moniz, & S. Nunn (Eds.), *Building a safe, secure, and credible NATO nuclear posture* (pp. 41–46). Washington, DC: Nuclear Threat Initiative.

Lutsch, A. (2016). Merely 'Docile self-deception'? German experiences with nuclear consultation in NATO. *Journal of Strategic Studies, 39*(4), 535–558.

Lutsch, A. (2019). *Westbindung oder Gleichgewicht? Die nukleare Sicherheitspolitik der Bundesrepublik Deutschland zwischen Atomwaffensperrvertrag und NATO-Doppelbeschluss.* Oldenbourg: de Gruyter.

Lutsch, A. (2020). The zero option and NATO's dual-track decision: Rethinking the paradox. *Journal of Strategic Studies, 43*(6–7), 957–989.

Maddox, B. (2025). Trump's 'electroshock' on Ukraine ends the debate: Europe cannot rely on the US for its security. *Chatham House.* Retrieved from www.chathamhouse.org/2025/02/trumps-electroshock-ukraine-ends-debate-europe-cannot-rely-us-its-security

Mair, P. (2009). Representative versus responsible government. *MPIfG Working Paper 09/8.* Retrieved from https://pure.mpg.de/rest/items/item_1232487/component/file_1232485/content

Mair, P. (2013). Smaghi vs. the parties: Representative government and institutional constraints. In A. Schäfer & W. Streeck (Eds.), *Politics in the age of austerity* (pp. 143–168). Cambridge: Polity.

Majnemer, J., & Repussard, E.-N. (2023). *NATO'S new 'Deterrence Baseline' and the future of extended nuclear deterrence*. Steyning: Wilton Park.

Maor, M., & Sulitzeanu-Kenan, R. (2016). Responsive change: Agency output response to reputational threats. *Journal of Public Administration Research and Theory, 26*(1), 31–44.

Mattelaer, A. (2021). Nuclear sharing and NATO as a 'nuclear alliance'. In S. Frühling & A. O'Neil (Eds.), *Alliances, nuclear weapons and escalation: Managing deterrence in the 21st century* (pp. 123–131). Canberra: ANU Press.

Mattelaer, A. (2024). A nuclear alliance. In J. A. Olsen (Ed.), *Routledge handbook of NATO* (pp. 93–105). Abingdon: Routledge.

Mehr Fortschritt wagen: Bündnis für Freiheit, Gerechtigkeit und Nachhaltigkeit. Koalitionsvertrag zwischen SPD, Bündnis 90/Die Grünen und FDP. (2021). Retrieved from www.bundesregierung.de/resource/blob/974430/1990812/93bd8d9b17717c351633635f9d7fba09/2021-12-10-koav2021-data.pdf?download=1

Meibauer, G., & LaRoche, C. D. (2024). German Atomwaffen and the superweapon trap. *The War on the Rocks*. Retrieved from https://warontherocks.com/2024/05/german-atomwaffen-and-the-superweapon-trap/

Meier, O., & Vieluf, M. (2021). Upsetting the nuclear order: How the rise of nationalist populism increases nuclear dangers. *The Nonproliferation Review, 28*(1–3), 13–35.

Meijer, H., & Wyss, M. (Eds.). (2018). *The handbook of European defence policies & armed forces*. Oxford: Oxford University Press.

Mekata, M. (2018). How transnational civil society realized the Ban Treaty: An interview with Beatrice Fihn. *Journal for Peace and Nuclear Disarmament, 1*(1), 79–92.

Melissen, J. (1994). Nuclearizing NATO, 1957–1959: The 'Anglo-Saxons', nuclear sharing and the fourth country problem. *Review of International Studies, 20*(3), 253–275.

Mello, P. A. (2012). Parliamentary peace or partisan politics? Democracies' participation in the Iraq War. *Journal of International Relations and Development, 15*(3), 420–453.

Mian, Z. (2009). Beyond the security debate: The moral and legal dimensions of abolition. In G. Perkovich & J. M. Acton (Eds.), *Abolishing nuclear weapons: A debate* (pp. 295–305). Washington, DC: Carnegie Endowment for International Peace.

Michaels, J. H. (2022). 'No annihilation without representation': NATO nuclear use decision-making during the Cold War. *Journal of Strategic Studies, 46*(5), 1010–1036.

Miles, S. (2020). *Engaging the evil empire: Washington, Moscow, and the beginning of the end of the Cold War*. Ithaca, NY: Cornell University Press.

Ministerie van Buitenlandse Zaken. (2012). *Tactische diplomatie voor een Strategisch Concept: De Nederlandse inzet voor het NAVO Strategisch Concept 2010*. Den Haag: Ministerie van Buitenlandse Zaken.

Ministerie van Buitenlandse Zaken. (2022). Kamerbrief uitvoering motie aanwezigheid bij vergadering het Verdrag verbod kernwapens. Retrieved from www.rijksoverheid.nl/documenten/kamerstukken/2022/08/16/kamerbrief-inzake-uitvoering-motie-21501-02-nr-2497-over-regeringsaanwezigheid-bij-de-vergadering-van-het-verdrag-inzake-het-verbod-op-kernwapens

Ministry of Defence of the Czech Republic. (2015). Security strategy of the Czech Republic. Retrieved from www.army.cz/images/id_8001_9000/8503/Security_Strategy_2015.pdf

Ministry of Foreign Affairs of the Czech Republic. (2023). Security strategy of the Czech Republic. Retrieved from https://mzv.gov.cz/file/5161068/Security_Strategy_of_the_Czech_Republic_2023.pdf

Morcinek, M. (2018). Inspekteur der Luftwaffe muss gehen: Über einen Kampfjet gestolpert? *ntv*. Retrieved from www.n-tv.de/politik/Inspekteur-der-Luftwaffe-muss-gehen-article20340680.html

Moschella, M. (2024). *Unexpected revolutionaries: How central banks made and unmade economic orthodoxy*. Ithaca, NY: Cornell University Press.

Möser, R. (2019). 'The major prize': Apartheid South Africa's accession to the Treaty on the Non-Proliferation of Nuclear Weapons, 1988–91. *The Nonproliferation Review, 26*(5–6), 559–573.

Mudde, C. (2004). The populist Zeitgeist. *Government and Opposition, 39*(4), 541–563.

Müller, H., & Risse-Kappen, T. (1987). Origins of estrangement: The peace movement and the changed image of America in West Germany. *International Security, 12*(1), 52–88.

National Defence Concept (Latvia). (2016).

National Security Concept (Estonia). (2017).

National Security Concept (Latvia). (2002).

National Security Strategy (Hungary). (2004).

National Security Strategy (Hungary). (2020).

National Security Strategy (Poland). (2020).

NATO. (2010). Active Engagement, Modern Defence. NATO 2010 Strategic Concept. Retrieved from www.nato.int/nato_static_fl2014/assets/pdf/pdf_publications/20120214_strategic-concept-2010-eng.pdf

NATO. (2012). Deterrence and defence posture review. Retrieved from www.nato.int/cps/en/natohq/official_texts_87597.htm

NATO. (2014). Wales Summit Declaration Issued by the Heads of State and Government participating in the meeting of the North Atlantic Council in

Wales. Retrieved from www.nato.int/cps/en/natolive/official_texts_112964.htm?selectedLocale=en

NATO. (2016). Warsaw Summit Communiqué Issued by the Heads of State and Government participating in the meeting of the North Atlantic Council in Warsaw 8–9 July 2016. Retrieved from www.nato.int/cps/en/natolive/official_texts_133169.htm?selectedLocale=en

NATO. (2017). North Atlantic Council Statement on the Treaty on the Prohibition of Nuclear Weapons. Retrieved from www.nato.int/cps/en/natohq/news_146954.htm

NATO. (2018). Brussels Summit Declaration Issued by the Heads of State and Government participating in the meeting of the North Atlantic Council in Brussels 11–12 July 2018. Retrieved from www.nato.int/cps/en/natolive/official_texts_156624.htm?selectedLocale=en

NATO. (2019). London Declaration Issued by the Heads of State and Government participating in the meeting of the North Atlantic Council in London 3–4 December 2019. Retrieved from www.nato.int/cps/en/natolive/official_texts_171584.htm?selectedLocale=en

NATO. (2020a). NATO's nuclear deterrence policy and forces. Retrieved from www.nato.int/cps/en/natohq/topics_50068.htm

NATO. (2020b). North Atlantic Council Statement as the Treaty on the Prohibition of Nuclear Weapons Enters into Force. Retrieved from www.nato.int/cps/en/natohq/news_180087.htm

NATO. (2021). Brussels Summit Communiqué. Retrieved from www.nato.int/cps/en/natohq/news_185000.htm

NATO. (2022). NATO 2022 Strategic Concept. Retrieved from www.nato.int/nato_static_fl2014/assets/pdf/2022/6/pdf/290622-strategic-concept.pdf

NATO. (2023a). NATO's nuclear deterrence policy and forces. Retrieved from www.nato.int/cps/en/natohq/topics_50068.htm

NATO. (2023b). Vilnius Summit Communiqué. Issued by NATO Heads of State and Government participating in the meeting of the North Atlantic Council in Vilnius 11 July 2023. Retrieved from www.nato.int/cps/en/natohq/official_texts_217320.htm

NATO. (2025). Secretary General's Annual Report 2024. Retrieved from www.nato.int/nato_static_fl2014/assets/pdf/2025/4/pdf/sgar24-en.pdf#page=1

Nieuw-Vlaamse Alliantie. (2019). Voor Vlaanderen. Voor Vooruitgang. Retrieved from https://manifesto-project.wzb.eu//down/originals/2020-1/21916_2019.pdf

Nobel Prize Outreach. (2025). International campaign to abolish nuclear weapons *NobelPrize.Org*. Retrieved from www.nobelprize.org/prizes/peace/2017/ican/facts/

Noël, A., & Thérien, J.-P. (2023). Left and right: The significance of a global distinction. In J. L. Maynard & M. L. Haas (Eds.), *The Routledge handbook of ideology and international relations* (pp. 249–266). Abingdon: Routledge.

Nolan, J. E. (1989). *Guardians of the arsenal: The politics of nuclear strategy*. New York: Basic Books.

Norman, D. J. (2019). Transnational civil society and informal public spheres in the nuclear non-proliferation regime. *European Journal of International Relations, 25*(2), 486–510.

Norris, R. S., Arkin, W. M., & Burr, W. (1999). Where they were. *Bulletin of the Atomic Scientists, 55*(6), 26–35.

Norris, R. S., & Kristensen, H. M. (2004). US nuclear weapons in Europe, 1954–2004. *Bulletin of the Atomic Scientists, 60*(6), 76–77.

Nouripour, O. (2021). Multilateral für die EU als Friedensmacht, für Klimaschutz und Demokratie. *Zeitschrift für Außen- und Sicherheitspolitik, 14*(2), 165–175.

Nuti, L. (2010). Negotiating with the enemy and having problems with the allies: The impact of the non-proliferation treaty on transatlantic relations. In J. M. Hanhimäki, G.-H. Soutou, & B. Germond (Eds.), *The Routledge handbook of transatlantic security* (pp. 89–102). London: Routledge.

Nuti, L. (2016). Extended deterrence and national ambitions: Italy's nuclear policy, 1955–1962. *Journal of Strategic Studies, 39*(4), 559–579.

Nuti, L. (2017). Italy as a hedging state? The problematic ratification of the non-proliferation treaty. In E. Bini & I. Londero (Eds.), *Nuclear Italy. An international history of Italian Nuclear Policies during the Cold War* (pp. 119–139). Trieste: Edizioni Università di Trieste.

Nuti, L. (2021). NATO's role in nuclear non-proliferation and arms control: A (critical) history. *Instituto Affari Internazionali*. Retrieved from www.iai.it/en/pubblicazioni/natos-role-nuclear-non-proliferation-and-arms-control-critical-history

NVMP Artsen voor Vrede. (2019). Urgent Appeal for a nuclear weapon free world: Connecting the medical-humanitarian and political perspectives. *Final report of the NVMP-congres 'Urgent Appeal for a nuclear weapon free world' 26-11-2019 at The Hague Peace Palace*. Retrieved from www.nvmp.org/wp-content/uploads/2020/01/EINDRAPPORT261119.pdf

Nystuen, G., Egeland, K., & Hugo, T. G. (2018). The TPNW: Setting the record straight. *Norwegian Academy of International Law*. Retrieved from http://intlaw.no/wp-content/uploads/2018/10/TPNW-Setting-the-record-straight-Oct-2018-WEB-1.pdf

Obranná stratégia SR 2021. (2021). Retrieved from www.mosr.sk/data/files/4286_obranna-strategia-sr-2021.pdf

Oktay, S. (2022). *Governing abroad: Coalition politics and foreign policy in Europe*. Ann Arbor: University of Michigan Press.

Onderco, M. (2017). Why nuclear weapon ban treaty is unlikely to fulfil its promise. *Global Affairs, 3*(4-5), 391–404.

Onderco, M. (2018). Parliamentarians in government delegations: An old question still not answered. *Cooperation and Conflict, 53*(3), 411–428.

Onderco, M. (2019). Partisan views of Russia: Analyzing European party electoral manifestos since 1991. *Contemporary Security Policy, 40*(4), 526–547.

Onderco, M. (2020). The programme for promoting nuclear non-proliferation and the NPT extension. *The International History Review, 42*(4), 851–868.

Onderco, M. (2021). The Dutch debate: Activism vs. pragmatism. In A. Morgan & A. Péczeli (Eds.), *Europe's evolving deterrence discourse* (pp. 39–50). Livermore, CA: Lawrence Livermore National Laboratory.

Onderco, M. (2024). German public opinion on nuclear weapons: Before and after the Russia's invasion of Ukraine. In U. Kühn (Ed.), *Germany and nuclear weapons in the 21st century: Nuclear Zeitenwende?* (pp. 136–154). Abingdon: Routledge.

Onderco, M., Etienne, T. W., & Smetana, M. (2022). Ideology and the red button: How ideology shapes nuclear weapons' use preferences in Europe. *Foreign Policy Analysis, 18*(4), orac022.

Onderco, M., & Joosen, R. (2022). Nuclear weapons in the Tweede Kamer: Analysis of nuclear motions in the Dutch House of Representatives in times of contestation. *Global Studies Quarterly, 2*(3), ksac028.

Onderco, M., & Kühn, U. (2025). Organizing nuclear policies in Europe: Of bricoleur plurality, architect absence, and spoiler disruption. *International Politics*, 1–12. https://doi.org/10.1057/s41311-024-00640-2

Onderco, M., & Smetana, M. (2021). German views on US nuclear weapons in Europe: Public and elite perspectives. *European Security, 30*(4), 630–648.

Onderco, M., Smetana, M., & Etienne, T. W. (2023). Hawks in the making? European public views on nuclear weapons post-Ukraine. *Global Policy, 14*(2), 305–317.

Onderco, M., & Vignoli, V. (2022). The supporters of the ban treaty are not a monolith. Don't treat them as such. *European Leadership Network*. Retrieved from www.europeanleadershipnetwork.org/commentary/the-supporters-of-the-ban-treaty-are-not-a-monolith-dont-treat-them-as-such/

Oppenheimer, A. G. (2010). *Conflicts of solidarity: Nuclear weapons, liberation movements, and the politics of peace in the Federal Republic of Germany, 1945–1975*. Chicago: The University of Chicago. Retrieved from www.proquest.com/dissertations-theses/conflicts-solidarity-nuclear-weapons-liberation/docview/756452922/se-2?accountid=170813

Orient, J. M. (1988). International physicians for the prevention of nuclear war: Messiahs of the nuclear age? *The Lancet, 332*(8621), 1185–1186.

Ostermann, F., & Stahl, B. (2022). Theorizing populist radical-right foreign policy: Ideology and party positioning in France and Germany. *Foreign Policy Analysis, 18*(3), orac006.

Owen, J. M. (2004). Democratic peace research: Whence and whither? *International Politics, 41*(4), 605–617.

Page, B. I., & Shapiro, R. Y. (1992). *The rational public: Fifty years of trends in Americans' policy preferences*. Chicago: University of Chicago Press.

Parke, M. (2025). *Opening Remarks at ICAN Campaigner Forum*. Presented at the ICAN Campaigner Forum, Riverside Church, New York.

Partij van de Arbeid. (2010). Iedereen telt mee: De kracht van Nederland. Retrieved from https://manifesto-project.wzb.eu/down/originals/22320_2010.pdf

Partij van de Arbeid. (2012). Nederland – Sterker & Socialer. *Verkiezingsprogramma Tweede Kamerverkiezingen 2012*. Retrieved from https://manifesto-project.wzb.eu//down/originals/2015-1/22320_2012.pdf

Partij van de Arbeid. (2014). Onze toekomst is sociaal. Retrieved from https://manifesto-project.wzb.eu//down/originals/2019-1/21230_2014.pdf

Partij van de Arbeid. (2017). Een verbonden samenleving. *Verkiezingsprogramma 2017*. Retrieved from https://manifesto-project.wzb.eu//down/originals/2018-1/22320_2017.pdf

Partij van de Arbeid. (2021). Verkiezingsprogramma PvdA 2021–2025: Ons plan voor een eerlijker en fatsoenlijker Nederland. Retrieved from www.pvda.nl/wp-content/uploads/2021/02/PvdA-verkiezingsprogramma-2021-2025-Ons-plan-voor-een-eerlijker-en-fatsoenlijker-Nederland.pdf

Partij voor de Dieren. (2017). Hou vast aan je idealen. Retrieved from https://manifesto-project.wzb.eu//down/originals/2018-1/22951_2017.pdf

Partij voor de Dieren. (2021). Verkiezingsprogramma Partij voor de Dieren Tweede Kamerverkiezingen Plan B: Idealisme is het nieuwe realisme. Retrieved from www.partijvoordedieren.nl/uploads/algemeen/Verkiezingsprogramma-Partij-voor-de-Dieren-Tweede-Kamerverkiezingen-2021.pdf

Partij voor de Vrijheid. (2010). De agenda van hoop en optimisme. Retrieved from https://manifesto-project.wzb.eu//down/originals/22722_2010.pdf

Patton, T., Philippe, S., & Mian, Z. (2019). Fit for purpose: An evolutionary strategy for the implementation and verification of the treaty on the prohibition of nuclear weapons. *Journal for Peace and Nuclear Disarmament, 2*(2), 387–409.

PAX No Nukes. (2016). Verbied kernwapens in Nederland. Voorstel aan de Tweede Kamer. Burgerinitiatief Teken tegen kernwapens [bijlage bij kamerstuk 34419 nr 1]. Retrieved from https://zoek.officielebekendmakingen.nl/blg-688950

PAX No Nukes. (2018). Largest Dutch pension fund ABP to divest from nuclear weapons. Retrieved from https://nonukes.nl/largest-dutch-pension-fund-abp-divest-nuclear-weapons/

Péczeli, A. (2013). *Central European Perspectives on NATO's Nuclear Policy*. Paper presented at the Project on Nuclear Issues Fall Conference, Washington, DC.

Pelopidas, B. (2017). The unbearable lightness of luck: Three sources of overconfidence in the manageability of nuclear crises. *European Journal of International Security*, 2(2), 240–262.

Pelopidas, B. (2021). *Repenser les choix nucléaires*. Paris: Presses de Sciences Po.

Pelopidas, B., & Verschuren, S. C. J. (2023). Writing IR after COVID-19: Reassessing political possibilities, good faith, and policy-relevant scholarship on climate change mitigation and nuclear disarmament. *Global Studies Quarterly*, 3(1), ksad006.

Pereira, M. M., & Öhberg, P. (2023). The expertise paradox: How policy expertise can hinder responsiveness. *British Journal of Political Science*, 54(2), 474–491.

Perier, M. (2019, 15 October). Peace, democracy and nuclear weapons. Interview with Kjølv Egeland. Retrieved from www.sciencespo.fr/ceri/en/content/peace-democracy-and-nuclear-weapons-interview-kjolv-egeland

Permanent Mission of the Federal Republic of Germany to the United Nations. (2023). General Statement by the Federal Republic of Germany during the Preparatory Committee for the 2026 Review Conference of the Parties to the Treaty on the Non-Proliferation of Nuclear Weapons (NPT). Retrieved from https://reachingcriticalwill.org/images/documents/Disarmament-fora/npt/prepcom23/statements/31July_Germany.pdf

Pesu, M., & Juntunen, T. (2023). Finland in a nuclear alliance: Recalibrating the dual-track mindset on deterrence and arms control. *FIIA Briefing Paper 375*. Retrieved from www.fiia.fi/en/publication/finland-in-a-nuclear-alliance

Peters, D., Wagner, W., & Deitelhoff, N. (2010). *The parliamentary control of European security policy*. Oslo: ARENA.

Peters, R. (2023). NATO's nuclear posture needs updating. *The Heritage Foundation*. Retrieved from www.heritage.org/defense/report/natos-nuclear-posture-needs-updating

Petrova, M. H. (2018). Weapons prohibitions through immanent critique: NGOs as emancipatory and (de)securitising actors in security governance. *Review of International Studies*, 44(4), 619–653.

Philippe, S., & Statius, T. (2021). *Toxique: Enquête sur les essais nucléaires français en Polynésie*. Paris: Presses universitaires de France.

Pifer, S. (2015). US-Russia relations in the Obama Era: From reset to refreeze? In Institute for Peace Research and Security Policy at the University of Hamburg (Ed.), *OSCE Yearbook 2014* (pp. 111–124). Baden-Baden: Nomos.

Pilat, J. F. (2016). A reversal of fortunes? Extended deterrence and assurance in Europe and East Asia. *Journal of Strategic Studies, 39*(4), 580–591.

Platon. (2007, 31 December). A Tsar is Born [A Photograph for TIME Magazine]. *TIME*, 46–47.

Pomper, M. A., Alberque, W., Brown, J., Marshall L., Moon, W. M., & Sokov, N. (2022). Everything Counts: Building a Control Regime for Nonstrategic Nuclear Warheads in Europe. *CNS Occasional Paper 55.* Retrieved from https://nonproliferation.org/op55-everything-counts-building-a-control-regime-for-nonstrategic-nuclear-warheads-in-europe/

Portela, C. (2014). The rise and fall of Spain's 'nuclear exceptionalism'. *European Security, 23*(1), 90–105.

Potter, W. C. (2017). Disarmament diplomacy and the Nuclear Ban Treaty. *Survival, 59*(4), 75–108.

PRESIDENT'S VISIT, Paris, May 31-June 2, 1961. Memorandum of Conversation. (1961). *Foreign Relations of the United States, 1961–1963, Volume XIV, Berlin Crisis, 1961–1962.* Retrieved from https://history.state.gov/historicaldocuments/frus1961-63v14/d30

Press, D. G., Sagan, S. D., & Valentino, B. A. (2013). Atomic aversion: Experimental evidence on taboos, traditions, and the non-use of nuclear weapons. *American Political Science Review, 107*(1), 188–206.

Price, R. (1998). Reversing the gun sights: Transnational civil society targets land mines. *International Organization, 52*(3), 613–644.

PS. (2014). Plus fortes ensemble – Pour un avenir plus juste. Retrieved from https://manifesto-project.wzb.eu//down/originals/2022-1/21322_2014.pdf

Putnam, R. D. (1993). What makes democracy work? *National Civic Review, 22*(2), 101–107.

Rapnouil, M. L., Varma, T., & Witney, N. (2018). Eyes Tight Shut: European attitudes towards nuclear deterrence. *European Council on Foreign Relations.* Retrieved from https://ecfr.eu/special/eyes_tight_shut_european_attitudes_towards_nuclear_deterrence/

Rathbun, B. C. (2004). *Partisan interventions: European party politics and peace enforcement in the Balkans.* Ithaca: Cornell University Press.

Rathbun, B. C. (2012). *Trust in international cooperation: International security institutions, domestic politics, and American multilateralism.* Cambridge, UK & New York: Cambridge University Press.

Rathbun, B. C. (2013). Steeped in international affairs?: The foreign policy views of the tea party. *Foreign Policy Analysis, 9*(1), 21–37.

Rauh, C. (2016). *A responsive technocracy? EU politicisation and the consumer policies of the European Commission.* Colchester, UK: ECPR Press.

Raunio, T., & Wagner, W. (2017). Towards parliamentarisation of foreign and security policy? *West European Politics*, *40*(1), 1–19.

Reaching Critical Will. (2024). NPT News in Review, Vol. 19, No. 2. Retrieved from https://reachingcriticalwill.org/images/documents/Disarmament-fora/npt/NIR2024/NIR19.2.pdf

Rendall, M. (2007). Nuclear weapons and intergenerational exploitation. *Security Studies*, *16*(4), 525–554.

Rendall, M. (2022). Nuclear war as a predictable surprise. *Global Policy*, *13*(5), 782–791.

Risse-Kappen, T. (1983). Déjà Vu: Deployment of nuclear weapons in West Germany historical controversies. *Bulletin of Peace Proposals*, *14*(4), 327–336.

Risse-Kappen, T. (1988). *The zero option: INF, West Germany, and arms control.* Boulder: Westview Press.

Risse-Kappen, T. (1991). Public opinion, domestic structure, and foreign policy in liberal democracies. *World Politics*, *43*(4), 479–512.

Ritchie, N. (2013). Valuing and devaluing nuclear weapons. *Contemporary Security Policy*, *34*(1), 146–173.

Ritchie, N. (2014). Waiting for Kant: Devaluing and delegitimizing nuclear weapons. *International Affairs*, *90*(3), 601–623.

Ritchie, N. (2016). *Pathways to nuclear disarmament: Delegitimizing nuclear violence.* Paper presented at the United Nations General Assembly Open-ended Working Group on 'Taking forward multilateral nuclear disarmament negotiations' (11 May 2016), Palais de Nations, Geneva.

Ritchie, N., & Kmentt, A. (2021). Universalising the TPNW: Challenges and opportunities. *Journal for Peace and Nuclear Disarmament*, *4*(1), 70–93.

Ritchie, N., & Kupriyanov, M. (2023). Understanding the humanitarian consequences and risks of nuclear weapons. *Federal Ministry of European and International Affairs (Republic of Austria) & University of York.* Retrieved from www.bmeia.gv.at/fileadmin/user_upload/Zentrale/Aussenpolitik/Abruestung/Understanding_the_Humanitarian_Consequences_and_Risks_of_Nuclear_Weapons.pdf

Robinson, T. (2019). Interview with Susi Snyder, Don't Bank on the Bomb. *Pressenza International Press Agency.* Retrieved from www.pressenza.com/2019/07/interview-with-susi-snyder-dont-bank-on-the-bomb/

Rudolf, P. (2020). Deutschland, die Nato und die nukleare Abschreckung *SWP-Studie 2020/S.* Retrieved from www.swp-berlin.org/10.18449/2020S11/

Ruff, T. (2018). Negotiating the UN treaty on the prohibition of nuclear weapons and the role of ICAN. *Global Change, Peace & Security*, *30*(2), 233–241.

Russett, B., & Oneal, J. R. (2001). *Triangulating peace: Democracy, interdependence, and international organizations.* New York: W. W. Norton.

Rynning, S. (2024). *NATO: From cold war to Ukraine, a history of the world's most powerful alliance*. London: Yale University Press.
Sagan, S. D. (2009). Shared responsibilities for nuclear disarmament. *Daedalus*, 138(4), 157–168.
Sagan, S. D., & Valentino, B. A. (2017). Revisiting Hiroshima in Iran: What Americans really think about using nuclear weapons and killing noncombatants. *International Security*, 42(1), 41–79.
Sagan, S. D., & Valentino, B. A. (2018). Not just a war theory: American public opinion on ethics in combat. *International Studies Quarterly*, 62(3), 548–561.
Saldžiūnas, V. (2020). JAV branduoliniai ginklai Europoje vėl skelia žiežirbas: kaip tai atsilieps Lietuvai [US nuclear weapons are sparking again in Europe: How this will affect Lithuania]. *DELFI Žinios*. Retrieved from www.delfi.lt/news/daily/lithuania/jav-branduoliniai-ginklai-europoje-vel-skelia-ziezirbas-kaip-tai-atsilieps-lietuvai.d?id=84352581
Sasikumar, K. (2007). India's emergence as a 'responsible' nuclear power. *International Journal*, 62(4), 825–844.
Sauer, T. (2014). Ceci n'est pas une…American nuclear weapon in Belgium. *European Security*, 23(1), 58–72.
Saunders, E. N. (2014). Good democratic leadership in foreign affairs: An elite-centered approach. In J. Kane & H. Patapan (Eds.), *Good democratic leadership: On prudence and judgment in modern democracies*. Oxford: Oxford University Press. Retrieved from https://doi.org/10.1093/acprof:oso/9780199683840.003.0010
Saunders, E. N. (2019). The domestic politics of nuclear choices: A review essay. *International Security*, 44(2), 146–184.
Saunders, E. N. (2024). *The insiders' game: How elites make war and peace*. Princeton, NJ: Princeton University Press.
Savage, C. (2007). *Takeover: The return of the imperial presidency and the subversion of American democracy*. New York: Little, Brown and Company.
Sayle, T. A. (2019). *Enduring alliance*. Ithaca, NY: Cornell University Press.
Sayle, T. A. (2020). A nuclear education: The origins of NATO's Nuclear Planning Group. *Journal of Strategic Studies*, 43(6–7), 920–956.
Scarry, E. (2014). *Thermonuclear monarchy: Choosing between democracy and doom*. New York: W. W. Norton.
Schapper, A., & Dee, M. (2024). Super-networks shaping international agreements: Comparing the climate change and nuclear weapons arenas. *International Studies Quarterly*, 68(1), sqad105.
Schelling, T. C. (1960). *The strategy of conflict*. Cambridge, MA: Harvard University Press.

Schelling, T. C. (1966). *Arms and influence*. New Haven, CT: Yale University Press.

Schindler, F. (2022). Der Atomwaffen-Plan der AfD-Jugend. Retrieved from www.welt.de/politik/deutschland/plus241641601/AfD-Der-Atomwaffen-Plan-der-Jungen-Alternative.html

Schneider, J. (2016). *Amerikanische Allianzen und nukleare Nichtverbreitung: Die Beendigung von Kernwaffenaktivitäten bei Verbündeten der USA*. Baden-Baden: Nomos.

Schuette, L. A. (2021). Why NATO survived Trump: The neglected role of Secretary-General Stoltenberg. *International Affairs*, 97(6), 1863–1881.

Schulte, P. (2015). NATO's protracted debate over nuclear weapons. In S. Von Hlatky & A. Wenger (Eds.), *The future of extended deterrence* (pp. 107–134). Washington, DC: Georgetown University Press.

Schultz, K. A. (1998). Domestic opposition and signaling in international crises. *American Political Science Review*, 92(4), 829–844.

Schwartz, D. (1983). *NATO's nuclear dilemmas*. Washington, DC: The Brookings Institution.

Science and Security Board. (2024). A moment of historic danger: It is still 90 seconds to midnight. *Bulletin of the Atomic Scientists*. Retrieved from https://thebulletin.org/doomsday-clock/current-time/

Sechser, T. S. (2016). Sharing the bomb: How foreign nuclear deployments shape nonproliferation and deterrence. *The Nonproliferation Review*, 23(3–4), 443–458.

Security Environment Review (Belgium). (2019).

Security Strategy of the Czech Republic 2011 (Czechia). (2011).

Shirobokova, E. (2018). The Netherlands and the prohibition of nuclear weapons. *The Nonproliferation Review*, 25(1–2), 37–49.

Sinistra Ecologia Libertà. (2013). Benvenuta Sinistra. Retrieved from https://manifesto-project.wzb.eu//down/originals/32230_2013.pdf

Smetana, M., & Onderco, M. (2022). Elite-public gaps in attitudes to nuclear weapons: New evidence from a survey of German citizens and parliamentarians. *International Studies Quarterly*, 66(2), sqac017.

Smetana, M., Onderco, M., & Etienne, T. (2021). Do Germany and the Netherlands want to say goodbye to US nuclear weapons? *Bulletin of the Atomic Scientists*, 77(4), 215–221.

Smetana, M., & Wunderlich, C. (2021). Forum: Nonuse of nuclear weapons in world politics: Toward the third generation of 'Nuclear Taboo' research. *International Studies Review*, 23(3), 1072–1099.

Snyder, G. H. (1984). The security dilemma in alliance politics. *World Politics*, 36(4), 461–495.

Snyder, S. (2024). About. Retrieved from https://susisnyder.com/about/
Socialistische Partij. (2010). Een beter Nederland voor minder geld. Retrieved from https://manifesto-project.wzb.eu/down/originals/22220_2010.pdf
Socialistische Partij. (2012). Nieuw vertrouwen. *Verkiezingsprogramma SP 2013–2017*. Retrieved from https://manifesto-project.wzb.eu//down/originals/2015-1/22220_2012.pdf
Socialistische Partij. (2017). Programma voor een sociaal Nederland. Retrieved from https://manifesto-project.wzb.eu//down/originals/2018-1/22220_2017.pdf
Socialistische Partij. (2021). Stel een daad: Verkiezingsprogramma van de SP voor de Tweede Kamerverkiezingen van 17 maart 2021. Retrieved from www.sp.nl/sites/default/files/verkiezingsprogramma_2021-2025.pdf
Somerville, A., Kearns, I., & Chalmers, M. (2012). *Poland, NATO and non-strategic nuclear weapons in Europe*. London: Royal United Services Institute.
Sonne, W. (2018). *Leben mit der Bombe: Atomwaffen in Deutschland*. Wiesbaden: Springer.
Sorg, A., & Wucherpfennig, J. (2023). Do foreign military deployments provide assurance? Unpacking the micro-mechanisms of burden sharing in alliances. *International Studies Quarterly, 68*(3), sqae107.
Sorg, T. A. (2023). A theory of U.S. nuclear weapon deployments (unpublished paper).
Sozialdemokratische Partei. (2021). Aus Respekt vor deiner Zukunft. *Das Zukunftsprogramm der SPD*. Retrieved from www.spd.de/fileadmin/Dokumente/Beschluesse/Programm/SPD-Zukunftsprogramm.pdf
Sozialdemokratische Partei Deutschland. (2013). Das wir entscheidet. *Das Regierungsprogramm 2013–2017*. Retrieved from https://manifesto-project.wzb.eu//down/originals/41320_2013.pdf
sp.a. (2014). Verkiezingen 2014 – Programma sp.a. Retrieved from https://manifesto-project.wzb.eu/down/originals/2019-1/21321_2014.pdf
sp.a. (2019). Zekerheid voor iedereen. Retrieved from https://manifesto-project.wzb.eu//down/originals/2020-1/21321_2019.pdf
Spanish Security Strategy – Everyone's Responsibility (Spain). (2011).
SPD. (2009). Sozial und Demokratisch. Anpacken. Für Deutschland. Das Regierungsprogramm der SPD. Retrieved from https://manifesto-project.wzb.eu/down/originals/41320_2009.pdf
SPD. (2017). Es ist Zeit für mehr Gerechtigkeit: Zukunft sichern, Europa stärken. Retrieved from https://manifesto-project.wzb.eu/down/originals/2017-2/41320_2017.pdf
Spektor, M. (2023). The upside of western hypocrisy. *Foreign Affairs*. Retrieved from www.foreignaffairs.com/united-states/upside-western-hypocrisy-global-south-america

Sprenger, S. (2020). Germany's Defence Ministry is under the gun to name a Tornado replacement. *Defense News*. Retrieved from www.defensenews.com/global/europe/2020/04/20/germanys-defence-ministry-is-under-the-gun-to-name-a-tornado-replacement

Sprenger, S. (2022). Germany to buy F-35 warplanes for nuclear deterrence. *Defense News*. Retrieved from www.defensenews.com/global/europe/2022/03/14/germany-to-buy-f-35-warplanes-for-nuclear-deterrence/

The State Defence Concept (Latvia). (2012).

Stavridis, S., & Jančić, D. (Eds.). (2017). *Parliamentary diplomacy in European and global governance*. Leiden: Brill.

Stoeckel, F., Mérola, V., Thompson, J., Lyons, B., & Reifler, J. (2023). Public perceptions and misperceptions of political authority in the European Union. *European Union Politics, 25*(1), 42–62.

The Strategic Vision for Defence (Belgium). (2016).

Suchy, P., & Thayer, B. A. (2014). Weapons as political symbolism: The role of US tactical nuclear weapons in Europe. *European Security, 23*(4), 509–528.

Sukin, L., & Lanoszka, A. (2022). Poll: Russia's nuclear saber-rattling is rattling neighbors' nerves. *Bulletin of the Atomic Scientists*. Retrieved from https://thebulletin.org/2022/04/poll-russias-nuclear-saber-rattling-is-rattling-neighbors-nerves/

Sus, M., & Kulesa, Ł. (2023). Breaking the silence: Explaining the dynamics behind Poland's desire to join NATO nuclear sharing in light of Russian aggression against Ukraine. *The Nonproliferation Review, 30*(4–6), 241–263.

Sus, M., & Kulesa, Ł. (2024). Tempting but (still) unrealistic? Explaining the dynamics behind Poland's will to join NATO nuclear sharing in light of Russian aggression against Ukraine [Working Paper].

Tallberg, J., & Zürn, M. (2019). The legitimacy and legitimation of international organizations: Introduction and framework. *The Review of International Organizations, 14*(4), 581–606.

Tannenwald, N. (2002). *The nuclear taboo the United States and the non-use of nuclear weapons since 1945*. Cambridge, UK: Cambridge University Press.

ter Veer, B. (1988). The struggle against the deployment of cruise missiles the learning process of the Dutch Peace Movement. *Bulletin of Peace Proposals, 19*(2), 213–222.

Tertrais, B. (2017). 'On The Brink'—Really? Revisiting nuclear close calls since 1945. *The Washington Quarterly, 40*(2), 51–66.

The Economist. (2025, 12 March). Europe thinks the unthinkable on a nuclear bomb. Retrieved from www.economist.com/international/2025/03/12/europe-thinks-the-unthinkable-on-a-nuclear-bomb

The Lancet. (1991). IPPNW-resting on its Nobel laurels? *The Lancet, 338*(8759), 90.

The Simons Foundation. (2007). Global public opinion on nuclear weapons. Retrieved from www.thesimonsfoundation.ca/sites/default/files/2007%20 Poll%20on%20Global%20Public%20Opinion%20on%20Attitudes%20 Towards%20Nuclear%20Weapons_0.pdf

The White House. (2025). Remarks by Vice President Vance at the Munich Security Conference. Retrieved from www.whitehouse.gov/remarks/2025/02/remarks-by-vice-president-vance-at-the-munich-security-conference/

Thomeczek, J. P. (2025). Moderate in power, populist in opposition? Die Linke's populist communication in the German states. *Journal of Political Ideologies*, *30*(1), 155–174.

Trachtenberg, M. (1999). *A constructed peace: The making of the European Settlement, 1945–1963*. Princeton, NJ: Princeton University Press.

Tweede Kamer der Staten-Generaal. (2015). Nucleaire ontwapening en non-proliferatie. Motie van het lid Sjoerdsma [33.783, nr 19]. Retrieved from https://zoek.officielebekendmakingen.nl/kst-33783-19.html

Tweede Kamer der Staten-Generaal. (2016a). Burgerinitiatief Teken tegen kernwapens. Brief van de minister van buitenlandse zaken [34419, nr 2]. Retrieved from https://zoek.officielebekendmakingen.nl/kst-34419-2.html

Tweede Kamer der Staten-Generaal. (2016b). Motie van de leden Sjoerdsma en Servaes over een impuls aan wereldwijde nucleaire ontwapening. Retrieved from www.tweedekamer.nl/kamerstukken/detail?id=2016Z08726&did=2016D18014

Tweede Kamer der Staten-Generaal. (2016c). Motie van de leden Sjoerdsma en Van Bommel over inzage in de bilaterale verdragen tussen de VS en Nederland. Retrieved from www.tweedekamer.nl/kamerstukken/detail?id=2016Z08725&did=2016D18012

Tweede Kamer der Staten-Generaal. (2016d). Motie van het lid Servaes c.s. over doeltreffende maatregelen om te komen tot een kernwapenvrije wereld. Retrieved from www.tweedekamer.nl/kamerstukken/detail?id=2016Z08727&did=2016D18016

Tweede Kamer der Staten-Generaal. (2016e). Motie van het lid Voordewind over het gefaseerd afstoten van de Nederlandse kernwapentaak. Retrieved from www.tweedekamer.nl/kamerstukken/detail?id=2016Z08729&did=2016D18018

Tweede Kamer der Staten-Generaal. (2019). Hoorzitting / rondetafelgesprek: Kabinetsreactie op AIV-advies inzake kernwapens. Retrieved from www.tweedekamer.nl/debat_en_vergadering/commissievergaderingen/details?id=2019A02694

Tweede Kamer der Staten-Generaal. (2022). Motie van de leden Jasper Van Dijk en Sjoerdsma (21 501-02). Retrieved from https://zoek.officielebekendmakingen.nl/kst-21501-02-2497.html

Tweede Kamer der Staten-Generaal. (2024a). Burgerinitiatief. Retrieved from www.tweedekamer.nl/kamerleden_en_commissies/commissies/verz/burgerinitiatieven

Tweede Kamer der Staten-Generaal. (2024b). De spanning in Europa m.b.t. kernwapens (hoorzitting). *Commissie: Buitenlandse Zaken*. Retrieved from www.tweedekamer.nl/debat_en_vergadering/commissievergaderingen/details?id=2024A00250

Udum, Ş. (2020). Issues in Turkish-U.S. relations: A politico-psychological analysis through problematic cases. In O. Örmeci & H. Işıksal (Eds.), *Historical examinations and current issues in Turkish-American relations* (pp. 221–243). Berlin: Peter Lang.

United Nations. (2022). Draft Vienna Declaration of the 1st Meeting of States Parties of the Treaty on the Prohibition of Nuclear Weapons 'Our Commitment to a World Free of Nuclear Weapons'. *TPNW/MSP/2022/CRP.8*. Retrieved from https://reachingcriticalwill.org/images/documents/Disarmament-fora/nuclear-weapon-ban/1msp/documents/draft-declaration.pdf

Vaddi, P., & Narang, V. (2025). Building a Euro deterrent: Easier said than done. *Strategic Simplicity*. Retrieved from https://strategicsimplicity.substack.com/p/building-a-euro-deterrent-easier

Valášek, T. (2011). Central Europe and NATO's nuclear deterrent. In M. Chalmers & A. Somerville (Eds.), *If the bombs go: European perspectives on NATO's nuclear debate* (pp. 21–28). London: The Royal United Services Institute for Defence and Security Studies.

van der Harst, J. (1997). Kernwapens? Geen bezwaar. *Transaktie, 26*(4), 295–517.

van der Veer, R. A. (2020). Technocratic responsiveness. In E. Bertsou & D. Caramani (Eds.), *The technocratic challenge to democracy* (pp. 75–90). London: Routledge.

van der Veer, R. A. (2021). Audience heterogeneity, costly signaling, and threat prioritization: Bureaucratic reputation-building in the EU. *Journal of Public Administration Research and Theory, 31*(1), 21–37.

van der Veer, R. A., & Meibauer, G. (2023). Populism, technocracy and the (de)legitimation of international organizations (working paper).

van der Zeijden, W. (2014). A Dutch revolt? The salience of the nonstrategic nuclear weapons issue in Dutch politics. *European Security, 23*(1), 45–57.

van Dijk, R. (2012). 'A mass psychosis': The Netherlands and NATO's dual-track decision, 1978–1979. *Cold War History, 12*(3), 381–405.

van Dijk, R., & Schaaper, J. (2015). The Inter-Church Peace Council and the nuclear arms race. *NPIHP Research Updates*. Retrieved from www.wilsoncenter.org/publication/the-IKV-and-the-nuclear-arms-race

Vandier, P. (2025). *Deterrence in the third nuclear age*. Cham: Palgrave Macmillan.
Ven Bruusgaard, K. (2020). Russian nuclear strategy and conventional inferiority. *Journal of Strategic Studies, 44*(1), 3–35.
Vignarca, F. (2023). *Disarmo Nucleare. È ora di mettere al bando le armi nucleari. Prima che sia troppo tardi*. Milano: Altra Economia.
Vignoli, V. (2020). Where are the doves? Explaining party support for military operations abroad in Italy. *West European Politics, 43*(7), 1455–1479.
Vlaamsvredesinstituut. (2014). Opinies over kernwapens op Belgisch grondgebied. Retrieved from https://vlaamsvredesinstituut.eu/wp-content/uploads/2019/03/factsheet_opiniepeiling_kernwapens.pdf
Volkspartij voor Vrijheid en Democratie. (2017). Zeker Nederland. *VVD Verkiezingsprogramma 2017–2021*. Retrieved from https://manifesto-project.wzb.eu//down/originals/2018-1/22420_2017.pdf
Volkspartij voor Vrijheid en Democratie. (2021). Verkiezingsprogramma 2021–2025 Samen aan de slag: Nieuwe keuzes voor een nieuwe tijd. Retrieved from www.vvd.nl/content/uploads/2021/02/VP-VVD-2021-2025-def.pdf
Volpe, T., & Kühn, U. (2017). Germany's nuclear education: Why a few elites are testing a taboo. *The Washington Quarterly, 40*(3), 7–27.
von Hlatky, S., & Lambert-Deslandes, É. (2024). The Ukraine war and nuclear sharing in NATO. *International Affairs, 100*(2), 509–530.
von Hlatky, S., & Wenger, A. (Eds.). (2015). *The future of extended deterrence: The United States, NATO, and beyond*. Washington, DC: Georgetown University Press.
Wachs, L. (2023). Russian nuclear roulette? Elites and public debates on nuclear weapons in Moscow after Ukraine. *The Nonproliferation Review, 30*(4–6), 173–196.
Wachs, L., & Horovitz, L. (2023). Frankreichs Atomwaffen und Europa: Optionen für eine besser abgestimmte Abschreckungspolitik. *SWP-Aktuell 2023/A 07*. Retrieved from www.swp-berlin.org/publikation/frankreichs-atomwaffen-und-europa
Wagner, W. (2020). *The democratic politics of military interventions: Political parties, contestation, and decisions to use force abroad*. Oxford, UK: Oxford University Press.
Wagner, W., Herranz-Surrallés, A., Kaarbo, J., & Ostermann, F. (2018). Party politics at the water's edge: Contestation of military operations in Europe. *European Political Science Review, 10*(4), 537–563.
Wagner, W., Peters, D., & Glahn, C. (2010). *Parliamentary war powers around the world, 1989–2004. A new dataset [Occasional Paper No. 22]*. Geneva: Geneva Centre for the Democratic Control of Armed Forces.

Wax, E. (2024). Trump vowed he'd 'never' help Europe if it's attacked, top EU official says. *Politico*. Retrieved from www.politico.eu/article/donald-trump-vow-never-help-europe-attack-thierry-breton/

Weisglas, F., & de Boer, G. (2007). Parliamentary diplomacy. *The Hague Journal of Diplomacy, 2*(1), 93–99.

Wellerstein, A. (2021). *Restricted data: The history of nuclear secrecy in the United States*. Chicago, IL: University of Chicago Press.

Welty, E. (2020). Religious advocacy and activism for the treaty on the prohibition of nuclear weapons. In M. B. Bolton, S. Njeri, & T. Benjamin-Britton (Eds.), *Global activism and humanitarian disarmament* (pp. 103–138). Cham: Springer International Publishing.

Wenzelburger, G., & Böller, F. (2020). Bomb or build? How party ideologies affect the balance of foreign aid and defence spending. *The British Journal of Politics and International Relations, 22*(1), 3–23.

White Book on National Security of the Republic of Poland (Poland). (2013). Warsaw: The National Security Bureau.

White Paper (Greece). (2014).

White Paper on German Security Policy and the Future of the Bundeswehr (Germany). (2016).

Wittkopf, E. R. (1981). The structure of foreign policy attitudes: An alternate view. *Social Science Quarterly, 62*(1), 108.

Wittner, L. S. (2003). *Toward nuclear abolition: A history of the world nuclear disarmament movement, 1971 to the present*. Stanford, CA: Stanford University Press.

Wood, M. (2021). Europe's new technocracy: Boundaries of public participation in EU institutions. *JCMS: Journal of Common Market Studies, 59*(2), 459–473.

Woolf, A. F. (2021). Nonstrategic Nuclear Weapons. Retrieved from https://fas.org/sgp/crs/nuke/RL32572.pdf

Working Worldwide for the Security of the Netherlands – An Integrated International Security Strategy 2018–2022 (Netherlands). (2018).

Yost, D. S. (2011). The US debate on NATO nuclear deterrence. *International Affairs, 87*(6), 1401–1438.

Yost, D. S., & Glad, T. C. (1982). West German party politics and theater nuclear modernization since 1977. *Armed Forces & Society, 8*(4), 525–560.

Zaller, J. (1992). *The nature and origins of mass opinion*. Cambridge, UK: Cambridge University Press.

Zhelyazkova, A., Bølstad, J., & Meijers, M. J. (2019). Understanding responsiveness in European Union politics: Introducing the debate. *Journal of European Public Policy, 26*(11), 1715–1723.

Index

Achen, Christopher, 36, 39
Acheson, Ray, 110
Acronym Institute, 113
activism against nuclear weapons, 2, 14, 46, 127–128, 171
   academic connections of, 108–111
   by ICAN, 101–108
      in host nations, 119–127
      young-old distinction in, 111–117
   in Netherlands, 1, 101, 114–117
   after Russian invasion of Ukraine, 173
Adessium Foundation (Netherlands), 114
AfD (Alternative for Germany, political party), 94
alliance. *See* NATO
Amsterdam, Cities Appeal supported by, 125–126
arms control
   global, 1
   negotiations, 22
Arndt, Anna Clara, 28
audiences
   domestic, 11
      in nuclear sharing policies, 44–46
   external, technocratic responsiveness to, 14, 47
   and policy elites, 10
Austria and TPNW, 178
avoidance, as coping strategy of policy elites, 148

B61 warheads, 24
Balieberaad (nuclear disarmament meeting, Amsterdam, 2016), 115, 116
Bartels, Larry, 36, 39
Batistelli, Fabrizio, 149
Becker, Jordan, 130
Belgium
   anti-nuclear weapons activism in, 123, 125
   participation in MSPs of ICAN by, 164
   policy elites in, nuclear sharing justifications by, 154
   political parties in, nuclear weapons views of, 80, 87, 92, 95
   public opinion in, on nuclear weapons, 50, 56–59, 65
Bell, Mark, 170
Bertsou, D., 63
Biden, Joe, 131
Bij1 (political party, Netherlands), 83
Bildt, Carl, 134
Breen, Laura, 103
Brixley-Williams, S., 37
Brosio, Manlio, 158
Buijs, Peter, 115, 117
Bulletin of the Atomic Scientists (journal), 107
Bunn, Elaine, 29, 167

Calovini, Giangiacomo, 155
Caramani, Daniele, 63
CDA (Christian democratic political party, Netherlands), 93–94
CDU/CSU coalition (Christian democratic political parties, Germany), 92
central banks, public pressure on, 35
Centre Démocrate Humaniste (political party, Belgium), 92
CHES (Chapel Hill Expert Survey), 77, 97, 124
China, criticism on nuclear sharing by, 178, 179
Christian Democratic and Flemish Party (political party, Belgium), 92
Christian democratic parties, nuclear weapons views of, 92–94
CI (cooperative internationalism), 61, 64
Cities Appeal campaign (ICAN), 14, 122–127, 171
Citizens Initiatives (Netherlands), 120–122
civil society
   anti-nuclear activism of, 14, 46, 127–128, 171
   academic connections, 108–111

225

civil society (cont.)
    in Netherlands, 101
    on nuclear sharing, 178
    Green Party participation in, 84
    transnational, 46
Cold War
    end of, and nuclear deterrence, 1, 23
    foreign policies in, 39
    NATO's containment strategy in, 27
Comparative Manifesto Project (CMP), 77, 78
comparative studies, of politics, 77
consultations between US and Western Europe, 20–22
credibility, of nuclear deterrence strategies, 27, 29
Crespy, Amandine, 36
CU (Christian Union, political party, Netherlands), 93–94
Czech Republic, nuclear deterrence views of, 135–136

D66 (Democrats 66, political party, Netherlands), 91
Daalder, Ivo, 130, 143
Daalder Group (NATO), 24
Dahl, Robert, 33
DCA countries. See host nations (of nuclear sharing)
DDPR (Deterrence and Defence Posture Review, NATO), 143, 144
Dee, Megan, 106
democracies
    control by policy elites in, 5, 170
    foreign policy/nuclear sharing control in, 13, 33, 34–35, 72–74
    public trust in, 62
democratic peace concept, 35
DENK (political party, Netherlands), 89
Denmark
    nuclear deterrence views of, 136, 137
    security policies of, 129
depoliticisation of policies
    in democracies, 35
    nuclear sharing policies, 62
Die Linke (political party, Germany)
    nuclear weapons views of, 83–84
    political strategies of, 96
Doctors for Peace (Dutch Society for Medical Polemology, NVMP), 101, 115, 116
dual track strategy (NATO), 22

Eblenkamp, Florian, 112
ECFR (European Council on Foreign Relations), study on nuclear deterrence, 132–133
Ecolo (political party, Belgium), 80
Egeland, Kjølv, 109–110
Eilstrup-Sangiovanni, Mette, 103
elections
    foreign policy issues in, 39
    nuclear weapons issues in, 78
elites. See policy elites/policymakers
Estonia, nuclear deterrence views of, 136
ethics, of research interviews, 12
EU, and technocratic responsiveness, 43
Eurobomb project, 176
Euromissile crisis, 22
Europe. See Western Europe
European Defence Community, 17
European Security (journal), 7
executive dominance, in foreign and security policies, 33
Eyes Tight Shut (ECFR report), 132–133

Faber, Mient-Jan, 115
FDP (Free Democratic Party, political party, Germany), 90
Fetter, Steven, 28
fighter jets, Western European renewal of, 25, 89, 119, 161–163
Fihn, Beatrice, 110, 112
Fındıklı (Turkey), Cities Appeal supported by, 123
Finland, nuclear deterrence views of, 133
Five Star Movement (political party, Italy), 81
Flournoy, Michele, 132
foreign policy
    attitudes, measuring of, 63–64
    democratic control of, 33, 34–35, 72–74, 75
    electoral salience of, 39
    knowledge of, 60
    public opinion on, 39, 61
    and Russia's invasion of Ukraine, 67
Foyle, Douglas, 35, 36
France
    nuclear disarmament policies of, 24
    nuclear weapons cooperation with, 133, 177
Franceschini, Giorgio, 84
Free and Equal (political party, Italy), 81
Freeze Movement, 113

INDEX 227

Fuhrmann, Matthew, 6
Führop, Pia, 151

Gaulle, Charles de, 27
gender patterns, in public opinion on
    nuclear weapons surveys, 57, 58
Genot, Zoé, 1
Germany. *See also* West Germany
    anti-nuclear weapons activism in, 119,
        123, 128
    Eurobomb debates in, 176
    fighter jet purchase debate in, 25, 94
    ICAN affiliate in, 113
    nuclear deterrence debates in, 150
    parliamentary activities in, 96
    policy elites in
        nuclear sharing justifications by,
            153, 154, 157, 158, 159
        symbolic adjustments by, 161–163
    political parties in
        nuclear weapons views of, 72–73,
            83, 88, 90, 92, 95, 156
        and TPNW, 165–167
    public opinion in
        on nuclear deterrence, 56–57
        on nuclear sharing, 31, 49–51
        on nuclear weapons, 57–59, 65
Gheorghe, Eliza, 18, 19
Gibbons, Rebecca Davis, 104, 105, 128
global justice, 61
governments
    public trust in, 51–53
    transparency on nuclear policies by,
        180–182
grafting, 105
Gravelle, Thomas, 61
green political parties, nuclear weapons
    views of, 80–87
Greenpeace, 114
Greens (Bündnis 90/Die Grünen, political
    party, Germany), 84–87,
    165–166, 171
Groen! (green political party, Belgium), 80
GroenLinks (GL) (green political party,
    Netherlands), 81

Hall, Xanthe, 112, 113, 114
Helfand, Ira, 113
Herzog, Stephen, 128
historical studies, on nuclear deterrence/
    nuclear sharing, 6

history, of nuclear sharing, 13
Hlatky, Stéfanie von, 6, 7, 27
Hoffmann, Fabian, 170
Högsta, Daniel, 110, 112
Horovitz, Liviu, 28
host nations (of nuclear sharing), 17
    allies of, 14
    civil society of, 14
    dual-capable aircrafts hosted by, 141
    ICAN's activism in, 119–127, 128
    and NPT criticism, 178
    nuclear deterrence debates/policies in,
        38, 148–152
        impact on US nuclear policy of, 41
        scholarship on, 111
    policy elites in
        nuclear sharing justifications by,
            152–167
        responsiveness of, 40
        symbolic adjustments by, 161, 168
    political parties' views on nuclear
        weapons/nuclear sharing in
        manifestos, 78–95
        parliamentary activities, 95–99,
            100, 171
    public opinion on nuclear weapons/
        nuclear sharing in, 70–71, 170
        explanations of, 60–69
        mapping of, 51–59
    security policies of, 146
Hug, Simon, 96
Hugo, Torbjørn Graff, 109
Humanistic Democratic Centre Party
    (political party, Belgium), 92
humanitarian consequences of nuclear
    weapons, 105–106, 109

ICAN (International Campaign to
    Abolish Nuclear Weapons)
    activism of, 171
        academic connections, 110
        decline of, 178
        in host nations, 119–127, 128
        and TPNW, 101–108
        Western focus in, 117–119
        young-old distinction, 111–117
    influence of, 14, 46, 106
    NGO partners of, 117, 118
    Nobel Peace Prize won by, 164
    research funding by, 109
Ikeda, Daisaku, 108

INF Treaty (Intermediate Nuclear Forces
    Treaty, 1987), 23
intermediate-range missiles, ban on, 23
international relations, public opinion
    studies in, 60
internationalism, 61
interviews, 12
IPPNW (International Physicians for
    Prevention of Nuclear War),
    47, 104
  German branch, 113
  Netherlands branch, 115
ISG (international steering group), 113
isolationism, 61, 66
Italy
  anti-nuclear weapons activism in, by
    ICAN, 119, 123, 125, 171
  JSF purchase debate in, 25, 119, 148
  policy elites in, nuclear sharing
    justifications by, 158
  political parties in, nuclear weapons
    views of, 81
  public opinion in
    on nuclear deterrence, 56–57
    on nuclear non-proliferation, 50
    on nuclear weapons, 50, 51, 57–59,
      148–150
Italy Europe Together (left-wing political
    party, Italy), 81

Jervis, Robert, 75
Johnson, Rebecca, 113
JSFs (Joint Strike Fighter), Western European
    purchase of, 25, 89, 119
justice, global, 61

Kaarbo, Juliet, 100
Kemp, Karl-Heinz, 28
Keul, Katja, 72–73
Key, V. O., 34
Kibaroğlu, Mustafa, 100, 155, 158, 159
Klooker, Reynold, 101, 102
Kmentt, Alexander, 111
knowledge
  of foreign policy, 60
  of nuclear weapons, 53–55
Kohl, Helmut, 38
Krause, Keith, 107
Kristensen, Hans, 20, 28
Kulesa, Łukasz, 175
Kütt, Moritz, 111

Lambert-Deslandes, Émile, 27
land mines, nuclear weapons likened to, 105
Larsen, Jeffrey, 23
Latvia, nuclear strategies of, 135–136
Leewis, Stephan, 127
Left Ecology Freedom (left-wing party,
    Italy), 81
left–right axis in politics, 75
left-wing political parties
  nuclear weapons views of, 80–90, 98,
    124–127, 171
  worldviews of, 75–76
Lewis, Patricia, 108
liberal parties, nuclear weapons views of,
    90–92
Lieber, Kier, 27
London Summit Statement (NATO,
    2019), 143
Lunn, Simon, 22

Mair, Peter, 4, 13, 35, 36, 37
Manifesto Corpus, 78
Marrone, Alessandro, 149, 150, 153
Mattelaer, Alexander, 27
MC 58 document (NATO), 19
McNamara, Robert, 21
Meer, Sico van der, 116, 121
Meier, Oliver, 112, 113, 163
Merkel, Angela, 93
methodologies of research, 11–12
MI (militant internationalism), nuclear
    sharing views of, 61, 64
Mian, Zia, 108
Michaels, Jeffrey, 20
Miles, Simon, 38
military goals of nuclear sharing, 26–29
Müllner, Karl, 161
municipal politics, support for anti-nuclear
    weapons activism in, 124–127

NAC (North Atlantic Council, NATO),
    138, 143
NAIL (Norwegian Academy of International
    Law), 109
Narang, Vipin, 1
nationalist parties, nuclear weapons views
    of, 94–95
NATO
  Cold War strategy of, 27
  Daalder Group, 24
  decision-making in, 138

dual track strategy of, 22
member states commitments and
    responsibilities of, 38, 141
    for nuclear sharing, 38, 141, 147,
        153–156, 172
member states status in, as nuclear
    sharing justification, 156–159
member states views on nuclear
    sharing/nuclear deterrence,
    129–130, 132–138, 144
    scholarship on, 132–133
    United States, 130–132
nuclear strategies of, 3, 19, 21, 133,
    138–144
    impact of Russia's invasion of
        Ukraine on, 139–143, 144–145,
        172–177
    NPG (Nuclear Planning Group),
        21, 138
withdrawal from, debates on, 82–83
NATO–Russia Founding Act (1997), 176
Netherlands
    anti-nuclear weapons activism in,
        114–117
        by ICAN, 119, 120–122, 124,
            125–127, 171
    JSF purchase debate in, 25
    nuclear policy in, 24, 150
        and parliamentary activities, 96, 151
    participation in TPNW by, 163, 164–165
    policy elites in, nuclear sharing
        justifications by, 153, 154,
        157, 159
    political parties in, nuclear weapons
        views of, 81–83, 89, 91–92, 93,
        94, 95, 98
    public opinion in
        on nuclear deterrence, 56–57
        on nuclear weapons, 57–59
NGOs (nongovernmental organisations)
    influence on nuclear sharing
        policies of, 46
    partner organizations of ICAN, 117, 118
Nobel Peace Prize for ICAN, 164
Noël, Alain, 75
Non-Proliferation and Disarmament
    Initiative, 40
nonproliferation of nuclear weapons.
    See also NPT (Nonproliferation
    Treaty)
    political parties' views on, 93

public opinion on, 50, 68
US support for, 30
Norpocalypse, 106
Norway, nuclear disarmament activism
    support by, 105
NPG (Nuclear Planning Group, NATO),
    21, 138
NPRs (Nuclear Posture Reviews,
    government reports,
    United States), 130–132
NPT (Nonproliferation Treaty)
    criticism on nuclear sharing by
        signatories of, 178
    and NATO nuclear strategies, 142
    negotiations for, 20
nuclear attacks. *See* nuclear strikes
nuclear deterrence
    debates on, 148–152
    NATO strategies on, 2–3, 6, 17–19,
        133, 141
        after Russian invasion of Ukraine,
            173, 176
        after Cold War, 1
    member states views of, 132–138
    nuclear sharing as part of, 26–29,
        159–160
    public opinion on, 56
nuclear disarmament. *See also* withdrawal
    of nuclear weapons
    civil society activism for, 127–128, 171
        academic connections, 108–111
        by ICAN, 101, 111–128
    debates, 23–25, 115
    decreasing interest in, 179
    policies
        debates on, 25
        of host nations, 40
        public trust in, 51–53
    political parties' views on
        in Germany, 93
        in Netherlands, 89, 92
    public opinion on
        in Germany, 50
    responses by policy elites, 147–152,
        160, 167
    by Ukraine, Kazakhstan and
        South Africa, 42
nuclear missions of NATO, obligations to
    contribute to, 38
nuclear sharing, 2–3, 16
    European political parties on, 14

nuclear sharing (cont.)
  future of, 15, 182
    expansion, 68, 175
  goals of
    and alternatives, 41–42
    military, 26–29
    political, 29–30
  history of, 13
    emergence, 6, 17–26
    possible ending, 23–26
  host nations. *See* host nations
    (of nuclear sharing)
  justifications for, by policy elites and
    governments, 38, 152–160, 167
  NATO member states views on,
    129–130, 144
    scholarship on, 132–133
    United States, 130–132
  NATO strategies on, 3, 138–144, 172–177
    after Russia's invasion of Ukraine,
    144–145
  opposition to, 3–4, 177–179
    activism against, 14, 46, 101
    research on, 7, 11
    undemocraticness criticism, 13, 31
  policies
    depoliticisation of, 62
    elite control of, 4, 146, 172
    and public pressure, 31–32, 147–152
    responsibility of policymakers,
    37–43
    responsiveness of policymakers,
    38–43, 44–47, 179–183
    symbolic adjustments by
    policymakers, 160–167
    technocratic dominance in, 33,
    43, 62
    transnational civil society
    influence on, 46
nuclear strikes
  Russian threats of, 173
  technical capabilities for launching of,
  28–29
nuclear umbrella
  of NATO, 21
  of US, in Asia, 42
nuclear weapons. *See also* nonproliferation
    of nuclear weapons; nuclear
    disarmament
  carriers of, 25
  knowledge of, 53–55

modernisation of, 25
NATO strategies on, 3, 133
  impact of Russia's invasion of
    Ukraine on, 172–177
  opposition to, anti-NATO
    characterization of, 147
  political parties' views on, 14, 99–100
    manifestos, 78–95
    parliamentary activities, 74, 95–99
    scholarship on, 74, 77–78
  public opinion on, 13, 39
    explanations of, 60–69
    mapping of, 48–59
  testing of, 42
  in Western Europe, 17, 19
    after Cold War, 23
    US owned, 1, 18, 20
nuclear weapons convention, 104–105
NVA (New Flemish Alliance, political
    party, Belgium), 95
Nystuen, Gro, 109

Obama, Barack, 3, 23, 130
obligations of NATO member states.
    See NATO, member
    states commitments and
    responsibilities of
online activism, 108

pacifism
  in Italy, 119
  of radical left, 82
Parke, Melissa, 107, 111
parliaments
  European
    debates on nuclear weapons, 74
    foreign policy involvement of, 72–74
  in host nations, nuclear weapons/
    nuclear sharing issues in, 95–99,
    100, 171
Party for the Animals (PvdD, animal
    rights political party,
    Netherlands), 82
PAX/IKV Pax Christi (peace movement,
    Netherlands), 114–115, 116,
    120–122, 128
peace, democratic, 35
Pearson, Lester, 20
Pelopidas, Benoît, 109, 110, 111
Pike, Emma, 108
Platon, 169

Poland
  nuclear deterrence views of, 133–135
  nuclear sharing possibly extended to, 175
policy elites/policymakers. *See also* technocratic elites/technocrats
  control by, 10
  in democracies, 5, 170
  of nuclear sharing/nuclear deterrence policies, 4, 146, 172
  sources of, 4
  and public pressure for nuclear disarmament, 147–152, 167
  responsibility of, 172
  responsiveness of, 15, 44–47, 179–183
  justifications for nuclear sharing of, 152–160, 167
  symbolic adjustments in nuclear sharing policies by, 160–167
political goals of nuclear sharing, 29–30
political parties
  foreign policy views of, 75–77
  nuclear weapons/nuclear sharing views of, 14, 99–100, 171
  manifestos, 78–95
  parliamentary activities, 95–99, 100
  scholarship on, 74, 77–78
politicians
  lobby activities of ICAN directed to, 119
  nuclear sharing views of, 72–73
politics
  comparative studies of, 77
  democratic, policies shielded from, 34, 35, 72–74
  in host nations, on nuclear weapons/nuclear sharing, 95–99, 100, 171
  in Turkey, military and foreign affairs debates in, 100
  left-right axis in, 75
  municipal, and anti-nuclear weapons activism, 124–127
populism, 39
  nuclear weapons/nuclear sharing views of, 63, 66, 94–95
Potter, Bill, 104
Prague Castle speech (Obama, 2009), 3
Presidential Nuclear Initiatives, 23
Press, Daryl, 27
Price, Richard, 105
public opinion
  and foreign policy-making, 34–35, 39
  on nuclear weapons/nuclear sharing, 13, 31, 39, 48–53, 70–71, 170
  explanations of, 60–69
  mapping of, 48–59
  responsiveness of policymakers/technocrats to, 31–32, 147–152, 160, 180
Putin, Vladimir, 169
PvdA (Social Democratic Party, Netherlands), 89
PVV (Party for Freedom, Netherlands), 94

radical left political parties, nuclear weapons views of, 80–87
radical right political parties, nuclear weapons views of, 94–95
Rathbun, Brian, 75
Remkes, Robertus, 28
responsibility
  of governments, in nuclear weapons sphere, 37, 38, 152
  of NATO member states. *See* NATO, member states commitments and responsibilities of
  of policymakers, 147
    as democratic control mechanism, 4, 36–37, 170
    in nuclear sharing policies, 37–38, 172
responsiveness of policymakers
  as democratic control mechanism, 4, 5, 15, 170
  in nuclear sharing policies, 38–43, 44–47, 172
  technocratic, 43–45
  theory of, 13, 34–37, 147
Rete Pace e Disarmo (ICAN affiliate in Italy), 119
right-wing political parties
  nuclear weapons views of, 90–95, 98, 171
  worldviews of, 76–77
risks, nuclear, 107
Risse-Kappen, Thomas, 41, 147, 160
Ritchie, Nick, 108, 110, 111
Roberts, Brad, 155, 156, 160
Roosma, Femke, 126
Rotterdam, Cities Appeal supported by, 126
Russia. *See also* Soviet Union
  invasion of Ukraine by, 25
  impact on nuclear weapons/nuclear sharing strategies of, 67–69, 172–177

Russia *See also* Soviet Union (cont.)
    impact on Western European nuclear disarmament activism of, 128
    NATO's nuclear strategy after, 139–143, 144–145
    violations of and withdrawals from arms control treaties by, 2

Sayle, Timothy, 21
Schapper, Andrea, 106
Schelling, Thomas, 29
Schmid, Nils, 88, 154, 157
Schulte, Paul, 29
Sechser, Tom, 6
secrecy, on nuclear policies, 148–149, 180
Securing Our Survival (report, IPPNW), 104
Security and Defence Towards 2035 (report, government of Denmark), 129
security policy
    of Denmark, 129
    of Europe
        reliance on United States of, 170
        after Russian invasion of Ukraine, 173
    of host nations, 146
    technocratic control of, 33, 44
    and worldviews of political parties, 75
Sikorski, Radosław, 134
Slovakia, nuclear deterrence views of, 137
Snyder, Susi, 112, 114–116, 117
social democratic parties, nuclear weapons views of, 87–90
Socialist Party (political party, Belgium), 87
Socialist Party (SP, political party, Netherlands), 82–83
Soviet Union. *See also* Russia
    arms strategies of, 22
Sp.a (political party, Belgium), 87
SPD (Social Democratic Party, Germany), 88–89, 171
SS-20 missiles (Soviet Union), 22
status in international politics justification for nuclear sharing, 156–159
Stenger, Ralf, 88, 89
Støre, Jonas Gahr, 134
Strategic Concept (NATO, 2010), 143
Struyk, Miriam, 114
surveys of public opinion
    on nuclear deterrence and nuclear sharing, 48–59
    on nuclear weapons, 13

Sus, Monika, 175
symbolic adjustments, 147
    in nuclear sharing policies, 160–167

tax avoidance, by weapons producers, 126
technical capabilities, to launch nuclear strikes, 28–29
technocracies, 44
    public opinion on, 62–63, 66–67
technocratic elites/technocrats. *See also* policy elites/policymakers
    control of nuclear sharing by, 41, 43
    responsiveness of, 14, 43–45, 47, 180
    for nuclear policies, 31–32
    theory of, 13
technocratic policy-making, dominance in nuclear policies of, 33, 62
Terasaki, Hirotsuku, 113, 118
Thérien, Jean-Philippe, 75
Time Magazine, 1
Tornado aircrafts, German debate over replacement of, 161–163
TPNW (Treaty on the Prohibition of Nuclear Weapons), 3, 26
    civil society activism for, 101
    by ICAN, 101–108
    Czech views of, 136
    database of writings on, 110
    European members of, 178
    MSP (Meeting of States Parties) of, 140
    participation of host nations in, 164–167
    NATO's rejection of, 143
    and nuclear sharing policies, symbolic adjustments by policy elites in response to, 163–167
    public opinion on, 50
    Scientific Advisory Group of, 108
    US views of, 132
The TPNW: Setting the Record Straight (report, NAIL), 110
Trachtenberg, Marc, 17, 26
transparency, about nuclear policies, 180–182
Trump, Donald, 131, 169, 174–175
trust, public
    in governments, on nuclear disarmament, 51–53
    in representative democracy, 62
Turkey
    coup attempt in, 1
    ICAN activism in, 123

JSF purchase debate in, 25
nuclear deterrence debates in, 150
policy elites in, nuclear sharing
　justifications by, 155, 157, 158
politics in, military and foreign affairs
　debates in, 100
public opinion in
　on nuclear deterrence, 56–57
　on nuclear weapons, 57–59, 65

Udum, Şebnem, 100, 159
Ukraine, Russia's invasion of, 25
　impact on nuclear weapons/nuclear
　　sharing strategies of, 67–69,
　　139–143, 144–145, 172–177
　impact on Western European nuclear
　　disarmament activism of, 128
Ülgen, Sinan, 150, 157, 158
United Kingdom, nuclear weapons of, 133
United States
　commitments to European security of,
　　173–177
　nonproliferation supported by, 30
　nuclear sharing strategy of, 19, 130–132
　nuclear weapons of
　　in Western Europe, 1, 18, 20
　　procedures for use of, 20–22
　　relations of host nations with, 41,
　　　158–159
　use of force, political views on, 76, 77

Vandier, Pierre, 177
Veer, Reinout van der, 44
Velzen, Krista van, 116
Vignarca, Francesco, 119, 123
Vignoli, Valerio, 166
Vilnius Summit Statement (NATO, 2023),
　139–142
Volkel airbase (Netherlands), anti-nuclear
　activism at, 1
voting behaviour, of political parties, 97–99

Wagner, Wolfgang, 76
Wales Summit Declaration (NATO, 2014),
　143, 144
Warsaw Communiqué (NATO, 2016), 144
weapons producers, tax avoidance by, 126

Wenger, Andreas, 6
West, ICAN's focus on, 117–119
West Germany. *See also* Germany
　nuclearisation of, prevention of, 21
Western Europe
　ICAN's activities in, 118, 178
　nuclear carriers of, renewal of, 25
　nuclear deterrence by, 2–3, 18
　nuclear weapons in, 17, 19
　　after Cold War, 23
　　consultations with US on use of,
　　　20–22
　　public opinion on, 13
　　US owned, 1, 20
　security policy of
　　after Russian invasion of Ukraine,
　　　173–177
　　reliance on US, 170
Westerwelle, Guido, 23, 91
Wheeler, Nicholas, 37
WILPF (Women's International League for
　Peace and Freedom), 114
withdrawal from public pressure, by policy
　elites, 148
withdrawal of nuclear weapons. *See also*
　nuclear disarmament
　political parties' views on, 80–87
　public opinion on, 180
　　in host nations, 58–59, 64–66
　　by US from Western Europe, 23, 130
　worldviews by proponents of, 181–182
Wittkopf, E. R., 61
Wolfsthal, Jon, 28
Woolf, Amy, 28
Workers' Party (PVDA, political party,
　Belgium), 80
worldviews
　of political parties, 75–77
　of proponents of nuclear withdrawal,
　　181–182

youth
　German, 38
　nuclear disarmament activism by, 112,
　　116–117

Zelensky, Volodymyr, 174

For EU product safety concerns, contact us at Calle de José Abascal, 56–1°,
28003 Madrid, Spain or eugpsr@cambridge.org.

www.ingramcontent.com/pod-product-compliance
Ingram Content Group UK Ltd.
Pitfield, Milton Keynes, MK11 3LW, UK
UKHW020436070226
467784UK00021B/435